ANIMAL RIGHTS LAW

Second Edition

by
Margaret C. Jasper

Oceana's Legal Almanac Series:
Law for the Layperson

2002
Oceana Publications, Inc.
Dobbs Ferry, New York

Library of Congress Control Number: 2002101366

ISBN: 0-379-11363-5

Oceana's Legal Almanac Series: Law for the Layperson
ISSN 1075-7376

To My Husband Chris

Your love and support
are my motivation and inspiration

-and-

In memory of my son, Jimmy

Table of Contents

ABOUT THE AUTHOR

MARGARET C. JASPER is an attorney engaged in the general practice of law in South Salem, New York, concentrating in the areas of personal injury and entertainment law. Ms. Jasper holds a Juris Doctor degree from Pace University School of Law, White Plains, New York, is a member of the New York and Connecticut bars, and is certified to practice before the United States District Courts for the Southern and Eastern Districts of New York, the United States Court of Appeals for the Second Circuit, and the United States Supreme Court.

Ms. Jasper has been appointed to the panel of arbitrators of the American Arbitration Association and the law guardian panel for the Family Court of the State of New York, is a member of the Association of Trial Lawyers of America, and is a New York State licensed real estate broker and member of the Westchester County Board of Realtors, operating as Jasper Real Estate, in South Salem, New York. Margaret Jasper maintains a website at http://members.aol.com/JasperLaw.

Ms. Jasper is the author and general editor of the following legal almanacs: Juvenile Justice and Children's Law; Marriage and Divorce; Estate Planning; The Law of Contracts; The Law of Dispute Resolution; Law for the Small Business Owner; The Law of Personal Injury; Real Estate Law for the Homeowner and Broker; Everyday Legal Forms; Dictionary of Selected Legal Terms; The Law of Medical Malpractice; The Law of Product Liability; The Law of No-Fault Insurance; The Law of Immigration; The Law of Libel and Slander; The Law of Buying and Selling; Elder Law; The Right to Die; AIDS Law; The Law of Obscenity and Pornography; The Law of Child Custody; The Law of Debt Collection; Consumer Rights Law; Bankruptcy Law for the Individual Debtor; Victim's Rights Law; Animal Rights Law; Workers' Compensation Law; Employee Rights in the Workplace; Probate Law; Environmental Law; Labor Law; The Americans with Disabilities Act; The Law of Capital Punishment; Education Law; The Law of Violence Against Women; Landlord-Tenant Law; Insurance Law; Religion and the Law; Commercial Law; Motor Vehicle Law; Social Security Law; The Law of Drunk Driving; The Law of Speech and the First Amendment;

Employment Discrimination Under Title VII; Hospital Liability Law; Home Mortgage Law Primer; Copyright Law; Patent Law; Trademark Law; Special Education Law; The Law of Attachment and Garnishment; Banks and their Customers; and Credit Cards and the Law.

INTRODUCTION

"The greatness of a nation and its moral progress can be judged by the way its animals are treated."—Mahatma Gandhi

Most human beings will agree that cruelty to animals is wrong, and many have decided that it is their responsibility to take an active role in protecting animals. This almanac sets forth the history of the animal rights movement and the positions taken by various proponents of this movement. The underlying principle held by animal rights supporters is that "human animals" must demonstrate compassion and concern for the pain and suffering of "nonhuman animals." Yet, the topic of animal rights creates much debate, even among its supporters.

The most extreme animal rights activist groups take the position that there is no justification to harming any living animal, and that all exploitation of animals must be ended. To this end, they support vegetarianism, and denounce animal experimentation and the wearing of animal skins and fur. They view civil disobedience as a moral imperative. In the media, they have been portrayed as quasi-terrorists who try to impose their views on the public by any means necessary.

At the other end of the spectrum, there are animal rights proponents with a more moderate view, who acknowledge the suffering of animals, and attempt to reduce that suffering by fighting for the "humane" treatment of animals. These groups generally do not propose outright elimination of the use and exploitation of animals for legitimate purposes.

This almanac presents a general discussion of animal rights law, and the various organizations that support such legal rights. The evolution of animal rights legislation, such as anti-cruelty statutes, the Federal Animal Welfare Act, and the Endangered Species Act are examined. The legal rights afforded animals in particular situations are also explored, including laboratory animals, livestock, marine mammals, domesticated animals, and endangered animal species. This almanac also discusses the rights of individuals to house companion animals, the rights of students to abstain from animal experimentation in the classroom, and the rights of hunters to engage in their sport without harassment.

The Appendix provides the text of applicable statutes, a directory of animal rights organizations, and other pertinent information and data. The

Glossary contains definitions of many of the terms used throughout the almanac.

CHAPTER 1:
THE ANIMAL RIGHTS MOVEMENT

AN OVERVIEW

A discussion on animal "rights" inevitably invites inquiry into the source of those rights. Are animals automatically entitled to certain rights, as co-tenants of this planet, which humans are obligated to recognize and respect? Are animal rights merely a gratuitous gesture by humans motivated by a sense of moral responsibility?

Many animal rights supporters believe that human and nonhuman animals are codependent, and that our continued existence is very much dependent upon our efforts to respect our environment and preserve plant and animal species.

The bottom line for all animal rights supporters is the importance of compassion and concern for the pain and suffering of nonhumans. Today, more and more people are expressing concern for the animal species. Vegetarianism is common, and many people have given up red meat and dairy products.

Publicity concerning the horrific treatment of animals in scientific experimentation has led to a significant public outcry for more humane treatment of laboratory animals. Many citizens were alarmed when the torturous treatment of livestock was brought to light. Many zoos have changed their environment to permit animals to roam freely in a recreation of their natural habitat, rather than live encaged.

LEGISLATIVE EFFORTS

As further set forth in this almanac, legislation has been enacted which seeks to eliminate or reduce the suffering of animals, e.g. the Animal Welfare Act and the Humane Slaughter Act.

However, critics of these laws argue that additional protection must be afforded animals which goes further than merely calling for "humane" treatment. They argue that laws which are designed to reduce animal suffering and death, to be effective, must have at least the following three features:

1. The laws must prohibit animal exploitation and not merely ban "unnecessary" suffering or promote "humane" treatment.

2. The laws must explicitly recognize that animals have interests which cannot be sacrificed or traded away for mere consequential reasons, i.e., the efficient use and exploitation of the animal.

3. Recognition that animals are entitled to respect and recognition of their rights and interests because they are creatures with inherent value which exceeds any property rights or interests humans may claim.

ANIMAL RIGHTS ORGANIZATIONS

The movement to recognize that animals are entitled to certain basic legal rights has been embraced by a number of organizations. These groups are known generally as "animal rights" organizations, although their positions on many issues concerning animal rights differs greatly.

Although proponents of animal rights have the same basic objective—i.e., to protect living creatures from unnecessary pain and suffering,—there is a broad spectrum of opinions among various groups concerning the means to achieve this objective, and whether there is any limit to the rights which should be extended animals.

Therefore, within the overall definition of animal rights organizations, there exist differences among the various movements. The three major distinctions fall under the labels of (1) animal welfare; (2) strict animal rights; and (3) animal liberation.

Animal Welfare

Although the Animal Welfare movement does, in fact, support rights for animals—e.g. that animals have the "right" not to be mistreated—it basically encompasses mainstream organizations with moderate views, such as the Society for the Prevention of Cruelty to Animals, and the Humane Society.

The Animal Welfare movement acknowledges the suffering of nonhumans and attempts to reduce that suffering through "humane" treatment, but its objective is not to eliminate the use and exploitation of animals. For example, an animal welfare proponent is not necessarily a vegetarian, and may see nothing wrong with eating meat. However, the animal welfare proponent would be concerned over whether the slaughter of livestock is undertaken in a humane manner.

Animal welfarists, unlike strict animal rights supporters, believe that if there is justification, then certain animal rights may be sacrificed. For example, an animal welfarist would likely support a law regulating the number of chickens allowed to be transported in a single crate because it would effectively reduce animal suffering due to overcrowding. Although transporting more chickens in one shipment may be more economical, such a regulation recognizes that animals are entitled to considerate treatment which must not be ignored merely because it would further a human interest.

Nevertheless, a strict animal rights activist would argue that such a law does not go far enough because it does not deny that an animal is human property, and merely substitutes one form of exploitation with another, i.e. the slaughter and consumption of the animal.

Strict Animal Rights

As set forth above, in its strictest interpretation, animal rights activists hold the most extreme views concerning the rights to be afforded animals. They argue that animal welfare groups do not go far enough in that they continue to promote the exploitation of animals, albeit in a more "humane" manner.

The strict animal rights movement explicitly rejects all exploitation of animals for any purpose whatsoever. Their fundamental principle is that non-human animals deserve to live natural lives which are free from harm, abuse, and exploitation perpetrated by humans.

A strict animal rights proponent would most likely be a vegetarian who (1) avoids wearing leather or fur; (2) refuses to purchase products that involve testing on animals or which may harm animals, such as pesticides; (3) protests hunting; and (4) boycotts companies that exploit animals.

The strict animal rights proponent is not merely concerned with the humanity of animal treatment, but argues that animals, like humans, have the right to be free from human cruelty and exploitation. They refer to the practice of withholding such rights to animals based on their species membership as "specieism," and seek to abolish the status of animals as human property.

Animal rights activists try to extend these rights beyond our human species to include other animals, who are also capable of feeling pain, fear, hunger, and thirst. The more extreme element considers forceful or unlawful action a moral imperative in the protection of animals. Actions taken by animal rights activists range from non-threatening legal behavior to unlawful activities, and may include:

> 1. Sit-ins at companies involved in animal exploitation, and the sabotage and destruction of associated property.

2. Harassment and boycott of companies and/or persons involved in animal exploitation activities; and

3. Infiltration of companies involved in animal exploitation activities.

Some people believe animal rights activists are advocates of violence when it supports their cause. Animal rights proponents counter that their struggle is one of peace, as evidenced by their attempt to reduce animal suffering and death. They argue that this negative portrayal is actually an organized attempt on the part of those who profit from animal exploitation, to scare the public into rejecting the animal rights struggle in favor of the more moderate animal welfare perspective.

Animal Liberation

Animal "liberation" is a term used by certain animal rights activists who prefer to compare the movement to gain animal rights to a liberation movement, such as the women's liberation movement. The use of the term "liberation" avoids the commonly encountered resistance among some people who are reluctant to acknowledge that animals are entitled to so-called "rights."

The acknowledged difference between the Animal Liberation movement and the strict Animal Rights movement concerns animal experimentation. Whereas the strict animal rights proponent seeks to end all animal experimentation, the animal liberationists acknowledge that there may be some cases when such experimentation is morally defensible.

A national directory of animal rights organizations is set forth at Appendix 1.

PEOPLE FOR THE ETHICAL TREATMENT OF ANIMALS (PETA)

Perhaps one of the most well known animal rights organizations is People for the Ethical Treatment of Animals (PETA). PETA is an international non-profit organization based in Norfolk, Virginia, and the largest animal rights organization in the world. It was founded in 1980 and is dedicated to establishing and protecting the rights of all animals. PETA's position is that animals should not be eaten, worn, nor used for experimentation or entertainment.

PETA works through public education, cruelty investigations, research, animal rescue, legislation, special events, celebrity involvement, and direct action. Among other things, PETA focuses its efforts on ending animal abuse in factory farms, laboratories, the fur trade, and the entertainment industry.

For example, PETA has been responsible for the closure of the largest horse slaughterhouse in the United States. PETA also uncovered abuse in animal experimentation, leading to the precedent-setting Silver Spring monkeys case, which resulted in the first arrest and conviction of an animal experimenter in the United States on charges of cruelty to animals.

PETA was also successful in virtually eradicating animal testing by the cosmetics industry. Through the use of video surveillance and investigations, PETA has uncovered many instances of animal cruelty and has been responsible for the prosecution of many entities under the Animal Welfare Act. As part of its public education and publicity campaign, PETA has also engaged many top recording artists, entertainers, and models in its campaign against furriers, and has successfully crippled this once lucrative industry. They have also educated the student population about their right to seek alternatives to engaging in animal experimentation in the classroom.

Most recently, PETA has successfully led a campaign against Burger King, which forced the company to formulate new guidelines concerning its facilities and suppliers. For example, Burger King has agreed to (i) conduct unannounced inspections of its slaughterhouses and take action against those facilities that fail the inspections; (ii) establish animal-handling verification guidelines for all cattle, swine, and poultry slaughterhouses; (iii) give laying hens 75 square inches of cage space, require that the birds be able to stand fully upright, and require two water-drinkers per cage; (iv) stop purchasing from suppliers who "force-molt"—i.e., starve chickens in order to force them to lay more eggs; (v) develop auditing procedures for the handling of broiler chickens; (vi) institute humane-handling procedures for chickens at the slaughterhouse; and (vii) purchase pork from farms that do not confine sows to stalls.

CHAPTER 2:
ANIMAL ANTI-CRUELTY LEGISLATION

HISTORICAL BACKGROUND

The first animal anti-cruelty law in the United States dates back to 1641, when the Puritans of the Massachusetts Bay Colony enacted their first legal code, known as "The Body of Liberties." The Code was comprised of one hundred "liberties." The ninety-second liberty forbid cruelty to animals under penalty of prosecution.

Although cruelty to animals was also punishable under the common law, there were no statutory provisions preventing animal cruelty—other than these early Puritan laws—until the New York State Legislature enacted its first animal anti-cruelty statute in 1828.

By 1921, all jurisdictions had some type of animal anti-cruelty statute on the books. Punishments varied under these laws, but generally included a monetary fine and/or a term of imprisonment. Most statutes defined cruelty to include the following:

1. The unnecessary or cruel torture, mutilation, beating or killing of an animal;

2. The deprivation of necessary sustenance, e.g. food and water, to an impounded animal;

3. The use of an animal for fighting or baiting;

4. The carrying of an animal in or upon any vehicle in a cruel or inhuman manner;

5. The use of dogs for pulling carts, carriages, trucks or other vehicles, for business purposes, without license to do so.

6. Abandonment of a maimed, sick, infirmed or disabled animal.

Nevertheless, most early laws specifically exempted animal experimentation from its cruelty laws provided the experiments were conducted properly under the auspices of a scientific organization, such as a medical college or university.

MODERN DAY LEGISLATION

Modern day animal anti-cruelty statutes exist in all fifty states, as well as the United States territories. Most jurisdictions provide that any non-human living creature is protected under the statute. Some statutes limit protection to domestic animals, captive animals, and/or warm-blooded animals.

Excerpts from state anti-cruelty statutes are set forth at Appendix 2.

Protected Rights

These statutes generally prohibit cruel treatment as defined in the earlier statutes; and acknowledge that animals have certain rights, as further discussed below. Nevertheless, prosecutions under such laws are rare and the penalties are relatively minor, thus, lessening the deterrence factor. Animal rights activists are therefore concerned with strengthening the animal protection laws.

The Right to Nourishment and Adequate Living Conditions

Most states prohibit the deprivation of necessary sustenance and/or the failure to provide an adequate supply of food, water and shelter to a confined animal. Some states require that confined animals receive adequate exercise, ventilation, light, space and clean living conditions.

The Right to Protection from Abandonment

Most states prohibit an owner or responsible person from abandoning an animal without providing adequately for its care. A minority of states provide that the abandonment must be willful, cruel or intentional to be a violation, or that the abandonment was of a domestic animal, or a dying or disabled animal.

The Right to Protection from Poisoning

Most animal anti-cruelty statutes specifically prohibit the poisoning of an animal to inflict injury or death. Again, depending on the jurisdiction, this protection may be limited to certain categories of animals, e.g. domestic animals, livestock, dogs, etc.

The Right to Humane Transportation

Most animal anti-cruelty statutes specifically require that the transport of animals be humanely undertaken. For example, many statutes specify that animals must have room to both stand and recline during transportation; must be provided adequate food and water; and must not have their feet or legs tied together during transport.

Standard of Proof

Many jurisdictions qualify the manner in which the offense takes place in order to be deemed a violation, such as "willfully," maliciously," intentionally," negligently," or cruelly." Each qualifier carries with it a different standard of proof which must be met in order to find the offender liable. Some jurisdictions hold offenders strictly liable for an act of animal cruelty without regard to the offender's mental state.

Exemption for Scientific Experimentation

Many modern day anti-cruelty statutes exempt animals used for scientific experimentation from their protection, although most laws maintain that such treatment must be carried out in a "humane" manner. Nevertheless, "painful" treatment is not generally prohibited provided it is "necessary" to the experiment.

DOMESTIC ANIMALS

Dogs and cats are by far the most popular household pets, yet they have a long history of exploitation and persecution. This is in large part due to their use in laboratory experimentation, as further discussed in this almanac. In addition, overbreeding these animals for sale as pets is a continuing problem which has led to restrictions on commercial breeding in many jurisdictions.

Some states have enacted laws which prohibit the sale of puppies under a certain age, or until weaned. In addition, the federal Animal Welfare Act specifically authorized the Secretary of Agriculture to set a minimum sale age for puppies, which was subsequently set at 8 weeks of age, also provided the animal is weaned.

Overpopulation has led to the enactment of mandatory sterilization laws in a number of states. To this end, many states and animal welfare groups also provide low-cost spaying or neutering clinics for cat and dog owners. Some states charge higher licensing fees for animals which are not rendered incapable of reproduction.

As set forth above, the animal anti-cruelty legislation is generally applicable to domestic pets. Abandonment and poisoning are criminal acts in almost all jurisdictions. Many states have sought to strengthen their animal theft laws, particularly because so many pet thefts occur for the purpose of resale to laboratories for experimentation purposes.

CHAPTER 3:
MARINE MAMMALS

IN GENERAL

Prior to 1972, and the passage of the Marine Mammal Protection Act, there were virtually no restrictions on the killing of marine mammals. Large populations of these creatures, including whales and dolphins, were completely wiped out, and some species of marine mammals were even rendered extinct by the unregulated slaughter for commercial gain. For example, sea otters were virtually extinct due to aggressive fur trading and, as further discussed below, the blue whale population was reduced to approximately twenty in number by the year 1965, due to extensive commercial whaling.

THE MARINE MAMMAL PROTECTION ACT OF 1972

Recognizing the importance of protecting these beautiful and intelligent ocean creatures, the Marine Mammal Protection Act was passed following lengthy hearings. The Act set forth a moratorium on the "taking"—i.e., hunting, capturing, killing, etc.—of a marine mammal. The moratorium may be waived only when, and if, the marine mammal population reaches its ideal population goal. In that event, a permit may be granted. There are strict monetary fines and/or imprisonment for violations of the moratorium.

The Act confers jurisdiction on the Secretary of Commerce over whales, dolphins, sea lions and seals, and the Secretary of the Interior over polar bears, manatees, sea otters and walrus. The Act further authorizes the Secretary of Treasury to pay a bounty to any individual who gives information leading to the conviction of anyone who violates the Act.

COMMERCIAL WHALING

The largest creature known to live on the earth—the blue whale—was rendered commercially extinct. In fact, by 1965, only 20 blue whales were known to still exist. Their population was routinely being wiped out by hunters who caused the animal to die a slow torturous death by use of an enormous explosive harpoon.

It was not until these animals were near extinction that the International Whaling Commission (IWC)—consisting of thirty-six member nations—finally made attempts to protect the remaining animals, a movement spearheaded by the United States government.

In 1971, all of the great whales were placed on the U.S. Endangered Species List. Because the number of whales dwindled, and the smaller whales hardly made whaling a commercially viable business, most countries abandoned commercial whaling. Nevertheless, a proposed 10-year moratorium on whaling was defeated by the IWC. Up until the mid-1970's, Japan and Russia continued to conduct the largest whaling operations in the world.

The aggressive campaign by legislators and animal welfare and environmental groups to end whaling has been called the most successful protective effort on behalf of endangered animals. In 1982, a moratorium on commercial whaling was finally approved by the IWC. Japan attempted to defy the moratorium until legal action was taken against it to enforce the IWC moratorium. Japan lost its case at the U.S. Supreme Court level, and eventually ceased commercial whaling.

Nevertheless, throughout the late 1980's, several countries—including Japan, Norway, and Iceland—granted themselves permits to continue whale killing under the pretext of scientific research, although the whale meat subsequently found its way into the stream of commerce.

THE TUNA INDUSTRY

In the early 1970's, the public was horrified to learn that hundreds of thousands of dolphins were killed by tuna fishermen in a single year. The dolphins were killed or seriously injured in the giant seines used to capture the tuna.

Despite passage of the Marine Mammal Protection Act in 1972, tuna fishermen were given a 2-year exemption which allowed them to continue this incidental killing of dolphin. In the meantime, they were supposed to develop equipment which would significantly reduce and ultimately eliminate these incidental killings.

After the expiration of the 2-year exemption period, no meaningful change in the tuna industry was made, and the dolphin killings continued. Animal welfare and environmental groups responded by suing the Department of Commerce for enforcement under the Act. They won and the tuna fishermen called a strike in protest.

After a number of hearings, quotas on the number of incidental dolphin "takings" were instituted, as well as other guidelines. In the meantime, the improvement of equipment and diligence on the part of tuna fishermen led to a reduction of incidental dolphin killings.

In 1990, to the delight of animal rights groups, the three major tuna canners—Starkist, Chicken of the Sea and Bumble Bee—announced that they would no longer purchase tuna which was caught in a manner which caused injury and death to dolphins.

CHAPTER 4:
LIVESTOCK AND THE MEATPACKING INDUSTRY

IN GENERAL

Prior to the enactment of the first humane slaughter laws, the slaughter procedures of livestock carried out in American meatpacking plants were among the most barbaric in the world. While yet alive, animals were frequently boiled, beaten with iron sledgehammers, subjected to electric shock, shackled and hung from the rafters, or knifed and left to die a slow death.

As these cruel practices came to public light, an effort to end these activities was set in motion, and legislation was introduced to outlaw such inhumane methods. Hearings were held at which testimony was taken from representatives of humane societies nationwide. Studies and investigations were conducted into slaughterhouse procedures.

THE FEDERAL HUMANE SLAUGHTER ACT

In 1960, the first federal Humane Slaughter Act was finally signed into law by President Eisenhower. The Act required America's meatpacking plants to institute humane practices in slaughtering animals.

In an effort to strengthen the 1960 legislation, a bill was introduced in 1978—The Federal Humane Slaughter Act of 1978. This Act sought to provide greater enforcement of the existing law. The Act mandated that every federally inspected meatpacking plant use humane methods in the slaughter and handling of all cattle, sheep, swine, goats, horses, mules, and all other equines. As set forth below, the Act provided an exception for livestock being slaughtered according to religious ritual.

The Act empowered the federal meat inspectors to withhold inspecting the meat of any plants which continued to employ inhumane practices in violation of the law. The threat of withholding meat inspection was a powerful economic incentive for the meatpacking industry to comply with the standards required under the law. The 1978 Act further banned the import of any meat which was slaughtered in an inhumane fashion.

A humane slaughter method is defined in the Act as: (1) a method whereby the animal is rendered insensible to pain by mechanical, electrical, chemical or other means that is rapid and effective, before being shackled, hoisted, thrown, cast or cut; or (2) a method in accordance with ritual requirements of the Jewish faith or any other religious faith whereby the animal suffers loss of consciousness by anemia of the brain caused by the simultaneous and instantaneous severance of the carotid arteries with a sharp instrument.

Critics of the Act argue that the protection offered does not go far enough because it is ultimately concerned with human interests instead of animal interests. For example, reducing injuries to animals is cost-effective because it means that more meat will pass USDA scrutiny. In addition, there is a reduction in the risk of injury to employees by anxious and distressed animals. Further, the overall result is lower meat production costs which is, of course, a benefit to humans.

Thus, it is argued that although the Act does call for "humane" treatment, it does not afford animals any additional protection because animal "rights" always defer to the wants and needs of humans.

The Act does not cover smaller meatpacking plants which are not federally inspected. It is up to the individual states to enact their own legislation to govern the humane slaughter and handling of livestock. The majority of states have enacted some sort of humane slaughter laws, largely based on the federal Act, and have charged certain state governmental authorities with enforcement in order to strengthen the effectiveness of the laws.

CHAPTER 5:
ANIMAL EXPERIMENTATION

HISTORICAL BACKGROUND

In large part due to strong opposition by scientific institutions, the United States was unable to enact any meaningful legislation concerning the treatment of animals used in laboratory experimentation until 1985. Although all jurisdictions had enacted some type of animal anti-cruelty statute, many routinely exempted animal experimentation. In addition, prosecutions for cruelty related to animal experimentation were rare even in those states which did not provide such an exemption.

Most recently, two laws designed to protect animals used in experimentation have been passed with the help of animal rights organizations who lobbied for their enactment. The ICCVAM Authorization Act permanently establishes the Interagency Coordinating Committee on the Validation of Alternative Methods (ICCVAM). This committee reviews alternatives to animal tests and recommends changes in testing procedures to the appropriate federal regulatory agencies. In addition, the animal rights organizations were also able to mobilize their members in order to effect the passage of the Chimpanzee Health Improvement, Maintenance, and Protection Act (CHIMP Act), which establishes a system of sanctuaries for government-owned chimpanzees who are no longer "needed" in federally funded research protocols.

Procurement Laws

Most of the animal experimentation legislation enacted in the mid-1940's through 1960 were known as "procurement laws." Procurement laws were not concerned with animal welfare. To the contrary, procurement laws generally forced municipal pounds, and animal shelters which received tax funds, to surrender dogs and cats for experimentation. The stated purpose for these laws was to help meet the scientific demand for research animals and to deter the rise in pet theft and resale to dealers who in turn resold the stolen pets to laboratories.

There was little concern, however, about the well-being of the seized animals. There were no safeguards written into the procurement laws concerning the duration the animals were to be used, nor the extent of pain they were permitted to endure.

The advocate for much of the procurement legislation was the National Society for Medical Research (NSMR). Although animal welfare societies attempted to fight these laws, they were overpowered by the dominant and influential biomedical community.

Some of the humane society shelters chose to forego government funds and/or pound contracts rather than continue to surrender animals for experimental purposes. Other groups, such as the American Society for the Prevention of Cruelty to Animals (ASPCA)—which had close ties to the research community—preferred to continue receiving tax funds, so it cooperated by surrendering large numbers of animals to laboratories.

Because there were no meaningful laboratory inspection requirements, there was widespread maltreatment of the seized animals. The animals were frequently subjected to painful surgery, and thereafter left to suffer and die, without food or water, in cramped and filthy living conditions.

This practice continued until the mid-1970's, when certain states began to repeal their procurement laws. In fact, some states made a complete turnaround by enacting legislation which prohibited the surrender of impounded animals for experimental research purposes.

Procurement laws were largely unsuccessful in decreasing the incidence of pet thefts. In fact, laboratories which were legally entitled to seize animals from shelters and pounds were still known to purchase animals from dealers. Despite this failed objective, a number of jurisdictions still have not repealed their procurement laws. Nevertheless, efforts to enact and strengthen laboratory inspection provisions began to appear in an attempt to provide the seized animals with some degree of protection.

THE FEDERAL ANIMAL WELFARE ACT

The Federal Animal Welfare Act contains the primary legislation enacted governing the use of animals in biomedical experimentation—a practice known as "vivisection." The text of the Act is set forth at Appendix 3.

The Act applies to any research facility. A research facility is defined as any school—excluding elementary and secondary schools—institution, organization, or person that (1) uses or intends to use live animals in research, tests, experiments, and that (2) purchases or transports live animals in commerce, or (3) receives funds under a grant, award, or loan, or contract from a department, agency, or instrumentality of the United States for the purpose of carrying out research, tests, or experiments.

The Improved Standards for Laboratory Animals Act

The most important amendments to the Act—The Improved Standards for Laboratory Animals Act—were enacted in 1985. These amendments required the establishment of an information service in the National Agricultural Library in cooperation with the National Library of Medicine. The information service maintains data which assists in (i) preventing unintended duplication of experiments and tests; (ii) finding alternatives to the use of laboratory animals in experiments; and (iii) instructing scientists and laboratory employees concerning the humane animal practices now required under the law.

Animal Care Committees

The amendments further require that each registered research facility appoint an Institutional Animal Care and Use Committee, which must include no fewer than three members who possess sufficient ability to assess the questions of animal, care, treatment, and practices in the experimental research presented to the Committee. At least one of the members must be a veterinarian; and one must be a non-affiliated individual to represent the community's concern for proper animal care and treatment.

The Act does require that a consultation with a veterinarian be held and all viable alternatives be considered prior to the start of an experiment that may cause pain to the animal. In addition, the Secretary of Agriculture has established certain standards concerning the (i) care rendered prior to and following the experiment; (ii) the use of painkillers and/or euthanasia; (iii) administration of anesthesia with paralytic drugs or the reason for withholding anesthesia or other pain relief; (iv) the unnecessary use of the same animal in more than one major surgical experiment; and (v) whether the experiment is duplicative. The Committee has the power to approve or suspend animal experimentation depending on the facility's compliance with these standards. The Act also sets forth monetary fines for violations.

The Committee is required to conduct inspections of the facility twice a year, and report on any deficiencies encountered. Facilities which do not cooperate in correcting reported deficiencies risk losing grant money and enforcement action by the Department of Agriculture.

Critics of the Act's power to truly protect animals argue that the 1985 amendments purport to recognize that animals involved in biomedical experiments have interests which should be protected, however, the Act still permits the animals to be used for any purpose that is deemed "necessary" to the experiment. This is so no matter how painful or strange the experiment may be. As the animal rights activists argue, experiments may depart from these standards if the research facility properly documents that such a deviation is "necessary" to the experiment.

ANIMAL EXPERIMENTATION IN THE CLASSROOM

The right of a student to abstain from animal experimentation in the classroom promotes both the right of the student—as a conscientious objector to harming animals—as well as the right of the animal to be free from pain. Lawsuits brought on behalf of students who object to animal experimentation in the classroom are generally rooted in the constitutional right to freedom of religion. Therefore, the student must generally show that the animal experimentation is at the behest of the a government actor—e.g., a public school; that the student's objection is based on a sincere religious belief, not simply a morally-based objection; that the requirement is placing a burden on the student's religious freedom; and that there is no compelling interest in requiring the student to engage in animal experimentation. Where it can be shown that there is a compelling interest, the interest must be satisfied in a manner which is the least restrictive to the student.

A sample complaint based on freedom of religion in a case entitled Kissinger v. Ohio State University is set forth at Appendix 4.

CHAPTER 6:
HUNTING AND WILDLIFE MANAGEMENT

IN GENERAL

To the nonhunter, the very act of traveling miles into the woods, rifle in hand, for the purpose of shooting "Bambi" between the eyes, is a barbaric form of entertainment. Many animal rights groups—from the hardcore activists to the mainstream animal welfare groups—denounce hunting and support its prohibition. They argue that hunting serves no practical purpose and causes unnecessary suffering and death to countless animals.

The hunter argues that the killings are justified because they use their prey for food. They further argue that they are in fact performing a service in that the animals would otherwise starve if it were not for population control.

According to *Animal Rights International*, hunters kill more than 175 million animals each year, and for every animal killed, two are left seriously injured to slowly die. Of human concern, hunters also accidentally kill an average of 400 people each year.

THE U.S. FISH AND WILDLIFE SERVICE

The U.S. Fish and Wildlife Service (USFWS) is generally responsible for overseeing hunting activities. Although hunters account for only 7 to 12 percent of the population, the Federal Government allocates approximately five hundred million dollars per year to support this "sport." A major portion of this tax revenue is used to artificially provide more game animals for hunters to kill.

According to *Friends of Animals*, governmental authorities routinely burn, cut down, defoliate and bulldoze hundreds of thousands of forested acres each year, so that sunlight is able to hit the forest floor and create browse food for deer. This method apparently stimulates the birth rate of deer. Another method used to provide more living targets for the hunters to kill and maim is the flooding of hundreds of thousands of acres in order to attract migrating geese and ducks.

CITIZEN INVOLVEMENT

In order to put an end to the unnecessary killing and maiming of millions of animals, the destruction of countless acres of natural habitat, and the dissipation of millions of tax dollars, a number of animal rights groups invite concerned citizens to take action. Those interested in taking an active role in the abolition of sport hunting may contact the *Committee to Abolish Sport Hunting* (C.A.S.H), Post Office Box 43, White Plains, New York 10605, for further information.

TRAPPING

Professional trappers are those who engage in the trapping business as their main source of income. When the price of fur rises, professional trappers are joined by many part-time or amateur fur trappers seeking to make a profit. Unfortunately, this leads to "overtrapping" which threatens to eliminate certain furbearing species. There are a number of furbearing animals which have already become endangered or extinct in certain states solely as a result of overtrapping.

Types of Traps

There are a number of methods used in trapping furbearing animals. The most humane trapping method employs cage traps which lure the animal inside, e.g. with non-exposed bait. As the animal crawls into the cage, it causes the lid to close and entrap the animal after it has entered. Exposed bait is generally prohibited due to the probability of attracting non-target animals, such as birds of prey. Nevertheless, if a non-target animal or domesticated pet is accidently caught in a cage trap, they are able to be freed without injury. Unfortunately, cage traps are not widely used among trappers.

One of the most offensive methods employed in the fur trapping industry involves the use of steel jaw leg traps to capture furbearing animals. Unfortunately, these traps have no way of distinguishing the type of animal they ensnare, thus, domesticated pets and other non-target animals have fallen victim to such traps.

The injuries to animals caught in the steel jaw leg trap are reportedly horrendous. This type of trap is known to cause traumatic leg amputations, fractures, broken bones, infections and excruciating pain to the ensnared animals. Although these traps have been banned in over 60 countries, there has been virtually no effort by the federal government or the majority of states to ban the use of these traps in the United States.

Due to the public outcry against the prolonged suffering endured by animals caught in the steel jaw leg trap, the Conibear trap—nicknamed the "killer trap"—was designed to bring immediate death to the animal. The Conibear trap employs two metal bars which, once engaged, are supposed to forcefully clamp down on the animal's neck. However, all too frequently, the trap does not kill, but maims and seriously injures the animals it catches.

A minority of states have tried to limit the use of steel jaw leg traps and/or killer traps by placing restrictions on the size of the trap, or by banning its use on land.

Another type of trap commonly used is a snare, which is available in different types and styles. A neck or body snare is a piece of uncoated wire which is designed to encircle the animal's neck or body, and tighten until it cuts through the animal's skin, causing death. Leg snares are designed to encircle the animal's leg and hold it in place. Although leg snares have traditionally been uncoated, modern leg snares have been developed which employ a coated cable to grasp the animals leg without cutting the animal's skin.

The laws among the states relating to snare use varies. Some states have banned the use of all snares, while other states permit the use of leg snares, but ban neck and body snares or restrict their size and/or placement.

Trap Visitation

Most states have enacted visitation regulations—i.e., rules concerning the intervals at which a trapper must check a trap—to ensure that trapped animals do not endure prolonged suffering, e.g. starvation, thirst or pain. A minority of states require trappers to check their traps a minimum of every 24 hours. A few states have no checking requirements at all.

Miscellaneous Restrictions

Depending on the state, additional restrictions on trapping may apply. A large number of states prohibit the use of poison as a means to capture some or all furbearing animals. Further, many states no longer permit trappers to destroy animal habitats—e.g. beaver dams—in order to force the animals out of hiding. In addition, many states have various restrictions on trap placement, such as the distance a trap must be from a residential area or recreational facility.

Because specific trapping laws vary widely among the states, the reader is advised to check the law of his or her own jurisdiction concerning specific rules and regulations.

HUNTER HARASSMENT STATUTES

Animal rights proponents seek to abolish hunting and trapping and, in doing so, some activists engage in activities designed to dissuade hunters and trappers from engaging in this sport. In order to protect the rights of the hunters to be free from harassment, a majority of states have enacted statutes that prohibit individuals from interfering with hunting.

A table of state hunter harassment statutes is set forth at Appendix 5.

The provisions of the hunter harassment statutes vary from state to state, thus the reader is advised to check the law of his or her own jurisdiction;. A representative law, enacted by the state of Massachusetts, is set forth at Appendix 6.

WILDLIFE MANAGEMENT

Deer Hunts

There has been much controversy lately over the method in which to manage wildlife populations, particularly deer, so that their number is not so great that they present a danger to the human population in adjacent areas. For example, complaints have been made that deer ruin the landscaping of homes by eating the shrubs. Complaints have also been made that deers pose a dangerous threat to drivers because they frequently jump out unexpectedly onto roads and highways in front of oncoming vehicles.

Many states have proposed permitting such over-populated areas to be open to hunters in order to control the number of deer inhabiting the area. Further, because such actions are considered management rather than hunting, the actions are not subjected to the usual hunting statutes and regulations and may take place at whatever times and places permitted by the state's gaming commission,

A municipality seeking a deer management permit must generally submit a Deer Management Plan that includes the scope of the deer problem, the various approaches considered and attempted by the municipality, a deer density estimate, a deer density "goal," and the target number of deer to be killed during the hunt.

Wildlife Contraception

Wildlife contraception is gaining recognition and acceptance as a possible way to control animal populations by either the administration of hormones or by vaccinations. However, there are concerns about the possible contamination of the meat of a game animal—e.g. venison—if hormones are given to the animal.

In addition, because of the necessity of capturing an animal to administer hormones, the preferred method of delivery appears to be vaccines, which can be delivered remotely. Nevertheless, animal contraception is beginning to emerge as a preferable, more humane alternative to the killing of large numbers of animals in order to control animal populations.

PROTECTION OF WILD HORSES

There has been a movement to protect wild horses on public lands in the western United States. It is believed that horses were indigenous to the Americas and roamed free at one point in history until they died out and were subsequently reintroduced to the region by the Spanish explorers. The Native Americans captured many wild horses. The last remaining herds of wild horses are centered in Nevada. This has caused a problem for cattlemen in the area who claim that the horses compete with cattle in grazing public lands. In order to solve this problem, cattlemen rounded up and slaughtered large numbers of wild horses. When this atrocity came to the public's attention, there was a strong outcry to protect the wild horses. In 1971, Congress passed the Wild and Free-Roaming Horses and Burros Act.

In its policy findings, Congress stated that such legislation was necessary because wild and free-roaming horses symbolized the historic pioneer spirit of the West, contributed to the diversity of life forms within the Nation, and enriched the lives of the American people. Insofar as it was recognized that these horses were disappearing, Congress enacted the Act in order to protect wild horses and burros from capture, branding, harassment and death.

The text of The Wild and Free-Roaming Horses and Burros Act is set forth at Appendix 7.

Nevertheless, large numbers of wild horses are still illegally killed and sold to slaughterhouses. Further, the Secretary of Agriculture has been given the authority to "manage" the wild horse populations if the public lands become overpopulated. The Secretary is authorized to round up excessive numbers of wild horses and offer them to the public for adoption, thus facilitating the abuse which the Act was designed to prevent.

CHAPTER 7:
SPORTS AND ENTERTAINMENT

ANIMALS IN CAPTIVITY

The primary argument for the maintenance of zoos is their usefulness in preventing species extinction through captive breeding programs. Although national wildlife parks purport to provide animals the same protection in a preserved natural habitat, zoos are viewed by many as an important backup. They offer a controlled atmosphere, which is particularly important for the preservation of endangered species, such as the great apes and large carnivores.

Most jurisdictions have laws which specify the manner in which captive wildlife must be maintained. Depending on the size and maturity of the animal, these regulations place limits on the number of animals which can be kept in a particular size cage. They often require certain types of apparatus to be placed in the cage, such as swinging bars for monkeys, or perching branches and nesting boxes for birds.

The American Association of Zoological Parks and Aquariums (AAZPA) maintains certain standards which zoos must meet in order to operate. In 1986, the AAZPA developed minimum standards for the housing of non-human primates in a zoological setting. In developing these standards, consideration was given to the social groupings found within the primate population, such as the need for young primates to bond with their parents during their developmental stage.

In addition, environmental requirements were considered, such as the temperature, lighting, ventilation, and sanitary condition of the exhibit areas; as well as the availability of fresh water and proper nourishment, and routine veterinarian services.

HORSE RACING

Horse racing is legal in the majority of jurisdictions, and betting on the outcome of the race is an overwhelmingly popular form of entertainment. Horse racing is generally conducted under the jurisdiction of a State

Racing Commission. There are three main types of horse racing, which include thoroughbred racing; harness racing; and steeplechase.

In thoroughbred racing, the jockey sits on the horse's back and races around an oval track. In harness racing, the jockey sits in a vehicle known as a sulky, which is pulled by the horse around the track. In steeplechasing, the jockey also sits on the horse's back, however, instead of racing around a track, the horse runs through a course which contains obstacles over which the horse must jump.

There are a number of common problems encountered in this sport which require monitoring and intervention by the appropriate authorities. For example, racing requires the horses to endure grueling workouts, which often lead to a horse's premature physical breakdown due to stress placed on their bones. In addition, the widespread practices of administering narcotics to race horses prior to the race, or of prodding the horse with electrical or mechanical devices during the race, have been outlawed, although jockeys are still generally permitted to use whips or spurs to nudge the animal into action.

ANIMAL FIGHTS

Despite laws designed to eliminate the practice of conducting animal fights for entertainment, the custom continues to endure as a popular underground "sport" among certain segments of society. Dogfights and cockfights are the most commonly held secret competitions. Motives for continuing this repulsive activity include the heavy gambling practices related to it, as well as the perverted pleasure spectators appear to get from viewing two animals tearing each other to shreds.

In 1976, in an effort to abolish this deplorable practice, Congress passed the Foley Bill, named after Congressman Thomas Foley, which amended the Federal Animal Welfare Act to prohibit animal fighting (7 U.S.C. 2156). In short, the amendment makes it illegal to (1) knowingly sponsor or exhibit an animal in a fighting venture for which the animal was moved in interstate or foreign commerce; (2) buy, sell, transport, deliver or receive such an animal; or to (3) use the U.S. mail, telegraph, telephone, radio or television operating in interstate or foreign commerce to promote an animal fighting venture. Violators are subject to a fine of up to Five Thousand ($5,000) Dollars and/or imprisonment up to one year.

Nevertheless, in an effort to get the bill passed, certain concessions were made which continue to permit gamecock fighting in those states which permit the activity. States in which gamecock fighting is legal include Arizona, Louisiana, Missouri, New Mexico and Oklahoma.

Dog fighting is illegal in all states. In addition, forty-two states deem dog fighting a felony, including Alabama, Alaska, Arizona, Arkansas, California, Colorado, Florida, Georgia, Illinois, Indiana, Kansas, Kentucky, Louisiana, Maine, Massachusetts, Michigan, Minnesota, Mississippi, Missouri, Montana, Nebraska, Nevada, New Hampshire, New Jersey, New Mexico, New York, North Carolina, North Dakota, Ohio, Oklahoma, Oregon, Pennsylvania, Rhode Island, South Carolina, South Dakota, Tennessee, Texas, Utah, Virginia, Washington, Wisconsin, and Wyoming.

The full text of Section 2156 of the Federal Animal Welfare Act is set forth at Appendix 3.

CHAPTER 8:
ENDANGERED SPECIES

IN GENERAL

Species and habitat endangerment and extinction is one of the most urgent environmental problems facing society today. Habitat extinction is a critical part of the problem because species cannot live without their supporting environment. Thus, habitat extinction is causally connected to animal extinction. In fact, the leading cause of species endangerment and extinction is loss of habitat, which is primarily caused by mankind.

Another major cause of species endangerment and extinction involves the accidental or intentional introduction of a species into a new setting, thereby disrupting the delicate ecological balance of the existing habitat.

The third leading cause of species endangerment and extinction is overexploitation. Overexploitation refers to the use of a particular species at a rate that leads to endangerment or extinction of that species.

For example, according to the African Wildlife Foundation, the volume of world trade in ivory from 1980 to 1985 was 800 tons per year. In order to meet such a demand, approximately 90,000 elephants had to be killed yearly. This caused a depletion in the African elephant population. In 1979, there were approximately 1,300,000 African elephants in existence, whereas there are presently less than 650,000.

Although species extinction is historically a natural occurrence, it has increased at an unprecedented rate primarily due to human activity which does not allow for species adaptation. As a result, it is estimated that hundreds of thousands of species may become extinct in the near future.

A table of endangered species categorized by state is set forth at Appendix 8.

THE ENDANGERED SPECIES ACT

In order to combat this problem, Congress enacted the Endangered Species Act in order to "conserve to the extent practicable the various species of fish or wildlife and plants facing extinction." They declared their authority to do so pursuant to certain existing international treaties and conventions.

The stated purpose of the Act is "to provide a means whereby the ecosystems upon which endangered species and threatened species depend may be conserved, to provide a program for the conservation of such endangered species and threatened species. . ."

The Act sets forth the procedure to be followed in determining whether a particular species or habitat is endangered or threatened. The Act also calls for the development and implementation of plans for the conservation and survival of listed endangered and threatened species, and sets forth restrictions regarding listed species.

The Act does, however, contain exemptions for the purpose of scientific experimentation pursuant to a permit issued by the Secretary—either the Secretary of the Interior or the Secretary of Commerce depending upon their jurisdiction—under established terms and conditions.

The text of the Endangered Species Act is set forth at Appendix 9.

THE U.S. FISH AND WILDLIFE SERVICE

The U.S. Fish and Wildlife Service ("USFWS") is a bureau within the Department of the Interior. Its stated mission is to conserve, protect, and enhance fish and wildlife and their habitats for the continuing benefit of the American people. The USFWS is primarily responsible for migratory birds, endangered species, certain marine mammals, freshwater and anadromous fish, the National Wildlife Refuge System, wetlands, conserving habitat, and controlling environmental contaminants.

Regional Offices

The USFWS is headquartered in Washington, D.C. where it oversees nationwide activities. The USFWS is divided into seven geographic regions. Its regional offices are involved in regional and local activities.

Region One: The Pacific Region—The Pacific Region includes California, Idaho, Nevada, Oregon and Washington.

Region Two: The Southwest Region—The Southwest Region includes Arizona, New Mexico, Oklahoma and Texas.

Region Three: The Great Lakes-Big Rivers Region—The Great Lakes-Big Rivers Region includes Illinois, Indiana, Iowa, Michigan, Missouri, Minnesota, Ohio and Wisconsin.

Region Four: The Southeast Region—The Southeast Region includes Alabama, Arkansas, Florida, Georgia, Kentucky, Louisiana, Mississippi, North Carolina, Puerto Rico/Virgin Islands, South Carolina and Tennessee.

Region Five: The Northeast Region—The Northeast Region includes Connecticut, Delaware, Maine, Maryland, Massachusetts, New Hampshire, New Jersey, New York, Pennsylvania, Rhode Island, Vermont, Virginia and West Virginia.

Region Six: The Mountain-Prairie Region—The Mountain-Prairie Region includes Colorado, Kansas, Montana, North Dakota, Nebraska, South Dakota, Utah and Wyoming.

Region Seven: The Alaska Region—The Alaska Region consists of the state of Alaska.

The USFWS Division of Endangered Species

In carrying out its responsibilities under the Endangered Species Act, the USFWS Division of Endangered Species maintains a list of those species determined to be threatened and/or endangered. This listing process is one of the basic functions performed by the Fish and Wildlife Service.

In order to list, reclassify, or delist a species, the USFWS must follow a strict legal process known as a "rulemaking" procedure. The rule is first proposed in the Federal Register, a U.S. government publication. After a public comment period, the USFWS decides if the rule should be approved, revised, or withdrawn.

This process can take up to a year, or longer in unusual circumstances. Participation by all interested parties, including the general public, the scientific community, other government agencies, and foreign governments, is encouraged.

Once an animal or plant is listed, all protective measures authorized by the Endangered Species Act apply to the species and its habitat. Such measures include: (i) protection from any adverse effects of Federal activities; (ii) restrictions on taking, transporting, or selling a species; (iii) authorization for the USFWS to develop and carry out recovery plans; (iv) the authority to purchase important habitat; and (v) Federal aid to State and Commonwealth wildlife agencies that have cooperative agreements with the USFWS.

The USFWS has developed a priority system designed to direct its efforts toward the plants and animals in greatest need of protection. The magnitude of threat is the most important consideration, followed by the immediacy of the threat and the taxonomic distinctiveness of the species. The most distinctive is a monotypic genus, then a full species, and lastly a sub-species, variety, or vertebrate population.

As of 1995, 447 species of animals were listed as threatened and endangered, and 28 species of animals were proposed for listing. 124 species were designated critical habitat; 7 species had proposed critical habitat designations; and 97 species of animals were USFWS candidate species.

A directory of regional contacts for the USFWS Endangered Species Program is set forth at Appendix 10.

CHAPTER 9:
COMPANION ANIMALS

IN GENERAL

Many people who live in rental housing are surprised to find out that their lease prohibits them from owning a pet, usually a dog or cat. Oftentimes, a tenant will have lived in their rental housing for a long period of time with their companion animal, ignorant of the lease provision, when they are suddenly faced with eviction because a new owner has taken over the building and is enforcing the no pets policy under the existing lease. As further discussed below, despite this "no pets" policy, tenants may have certain legal rights that apply in such situations. Nevertheless, insofar as this almanac is designed to present only a general discussion of the law, the reader is advised to check the law of his or her own jurisdiction in this regard.

APPLICABLE LAW

Whether or not a tenant will be permitted to keep a pet despite the land-lord's "no pet" policy depends in large part on the law which governs the specific problem. A tenant's rights may be regulated by federal, state or municipal laws. Federal law applies to everyone in the United States and the violation of a federal law is illegal in every state. Violating a federal law is illegal in every state. Federal law determines the minimum protection available to a tenant in rental housing and generally concerns a tenant's civil rights in housing, such as a prohibition against discriminatory practices. State law can provide further specific protections for tenants under the state constitution and statutes enacted by the state legislature however state law cannot provide a tenant with less protection than the federal law requires. Municipal and local laws provide even more specific regulations.

FEDERAL LEGISLATION

There are four federal laws which may impact a tenant's right to keep a companion animal in rental housing.

The Housing and Urban Rural Recovery Act of 1983

Under The Housing and Urban Rural Recovery Act, the owner or manager of any federally assisted rental housing that is designated for the elderly or disabled cannot prohibit a tenant from keeping a common household pet.

The Act provides that:

No owner or manager of any federally assisted rental housing for the elderly or handicapped may—

(1) as a condition of tenancy or otherwise, prohibit or prevent any tenant in such housing from owning common household pets or having common household pets living in the dwelling accommodations of such tenant in such housing; or

(2) restrict or discriminate against any such person in connection with admission to, or continued occupancy of, such housing by reason of the ownership of such pets by, or the presence of such pets in the dwelling accommodations of, such person.

Nevertheless, the statute does permit a landlord to remove an animal who is considered a threat or nuisance to others, thus the owner of a companion animal in such rental housing should make a special effort to ensure that their pet behaves appropriately and receives proper care.

In that connection, the Act provides that:

Nothing in this section may be construed to prohibit any owner or manager of federally assisted rental housing for the elderly or handicapped, or any local housing authority or other appropriate authority of the community where such housing is located, from requiring the removal of any such housing of any pet whose conduct or condition is duly determined to constitute a nuisance or a threat to the health or safety of the other occupants of such housing or of other persons in the community where such housing is located.

The Fair Housing Amendments Act of 1988

Under The Fair Housing Amendments Act, it is illegal to refuse to sell or rent a dwelling to a person because of race, color, religion, sex, familial status, or national origin. These prohibitions against discrimination form the basis for permitting persons with disabilities to keep a companion animal in their home when the animal is needed to provide assistance to the disabled tenant. For example, a landlord cannot refuse to rent to, or evict, a blind person because they own a seeing eye dog. Further, the law applies whether or not the disabled individual is the person named on the lease provided the disabled individual is legally living in the dwelling.

The Fair Housing Amendments Act applies to nearly all housing, whether the dwelling is for sale or rent, but generally excludes (i) buildings with four or fewer units if the landlord lives in the building; and (ii) private owners who own fewer than three single family homes.

The Americans With Disabilities Act of 1990

The Americans With Disabilities Act (ADA) also requires public agencies, or agencies receiving federal funds, to provide access for all individuals, regardless of disability. Disabled individuals who need their companion animal as part of their care, treatment or rehabilitation may also rely on this statute as a basis for keeping their pet in their rental home.

The Rehabilitation Act of 1973

In addition, the Rehabilitation Act—the predecessor to the ADA—provides similar protection to disabled persons when the landlord is connected with a federally funded program. Under the Rehabilitation Act, no disabled person can be discriminated against or excluded from participating in a program or activity receiving federal public assistance.

The United States Department of Housing and Urban Development (HUD)

The United States Department of Housing and Urban Development enforces the federal fair housing laws and provides information and assistance in making a complaint. The National HUD Discrimination Hotline is 1-800-669-9777/TDD: 1-800 927-9275. In addition, the Fair Housing Information Clearinghouse provides educational materials about fair housing regulations and can be reached at 1-800-343-3442/TDD: 1-800-290-1617.

STATE LAWS

As set forth above, a state can provide its citizens greater rights than those provided under federal law, but its protections cannot fall below the minimum federal standards. For example, a state may pass laws that give protection to the elderly or disabled, much like the federal legislation described above.

In addition, a court may apply the doctrine of "estoppel" in allowing a tenant to keep a pet where the landlord knew at an earlier time that the tenant had the pet but didn't seek to enforce the "no pet" provision of the lease. Under the estoppel doctrine, the landlord may not be permitted to make this claim at a later date if he ignored the behavior earlier, on the basis that he implicitly approved of the action by failing to take steps to correct it, thus waiving his claim by his inaction. Nevertheless, a tenant is not advised to acquire a pet if he or she knows this is a violation of the lease.

CHAPTER 10:
ANIMAL SACRIFICE

IN GENERAL

A number of religions in the United States practice animal sacrifice as part of their religious ceremonies. As further discussed below, most of the litigation that has resulted from such religious practices has focused on the Santeria religion.

SANTERIA

The proper name for the Santeria religion is Regla de Ocha, which means "The Rule of the Orisha." The popular name, "Santeria," means "The Way of the Saints." Santeria is of Caribbean origin. It incorporates the worship of the Orisha—the head guardian—and beliefs of the Yoruba and Bantu people in Southern Nigeria, Senegal and the Guinea Coast. These are combined with elements of worship from Roman Catholicism.

The origins of Santeria date back to the slave trade when Yoruba natives were forcibly transported from Africa to the Caribbean. They were typically baptized by the Roman Catholic church upon arrival, and their native practices were suppressed. Nevertheless, they kept their old beliefs alive by equating each "Orisha" of their traditional religions with a corresponding Christian Saint, e.g., Babalz Ayi became St. Lazarus—patron of the sick.

In America, Santeria is concentrated in the Hispanic populations of Florida, Puerto Rico, New Jersey, New York City and Los Angeles with estimates of worshipers ranging from 800,000 to over 5 million.

Animal Sacrifice

Although beliefs and practices within each faction of Santeria may differ significantly, the religion recognizes a supreme deity, the creator of the universe, and the lesser guardians known as Orisha. Each Orisha needs food, in the form of animal sacrifice, to remain effective. Thus, the animal sacrifice forms an integral part of the Santeria religion. The animal's blood is collected and offered to the Orisha. Chickens are the most common animal used in the ritual. It is believed that the sacrifice pleases the Saints, and brings good luck, purification and forgiveness of sins.

There has been considerable conflict between Santerians and animal rights groups because of the animal sacrifices. The Santerians defend their practices by claiming that the animals are killed in a humane manner and later eaten, just as the many of millions of animals slaughtered daily in North American commercial establishments. They also claim that the United States Constitution guarantees freedom of religious expression.

In 1993, the Santerians won an important U.S. Supreme Court victory over the City of Hialeah which sought to prohibit its practice of animal sacrifice as a violation of its animal cruelty statutes. This has, for now, established the constitutional right to practice animal sacrifice, at least in the manner carried out by the Santerians.

Following is the U.S. Supreme Court decision which found that the City of Hialeah could not prohibit the practitioners of the Santeria religion from performing animal sacrifices because such a prohibition violated their right to religious expression under the First Amendment.

Church of the Lukumi Bablu Aye, Inc. et. al. v. City of Hialeah

Certiorari to the United States Court of Appeals for the Eleventh Circuit No. 91-948, 936 F. 2d 586 (1993) (Argued November 4, 1992-Decided June 11, 1993)

Petitioner church and its congregants practice the Santeria religion, which employs animal sacrifice as one of its principal forms of devotion. The animals are killed by cutting their carotid arteries and are cooked and eaten following all Santeria rituals except healing and death rites. After the church leased land in respondent city and announced plans to establish a house of worship and other facilities there, the city council held an emergency public session and passed, among other enactments, Resolution 87-66, which noted city residents' "concern" over religious practices inconsistent with public morals, peace, or safety, and declared the city's "commitment" to prohibiting such practices;

> Ordinance 87-40, which incorporates the Florida animal cruelty laws and broadly punishes "[w]hoever . . . unnecessarily or cruelly . . . kills any animal," and has been interpreted to reach killings for religious reasons;

> Ordinance 87-52, which defines "sacrifice" as "to unnecessarily kill . . . an animal in a . . . ritual . . . not for the primary purpose of food consumption," and prohibits the "possess[ion], sacrifice, or slaugh-

ter" of an animal if it is killed in "any type of ritual" and there is an intent to use it for food, but exempts "any licensed [food] establishment" if the killing is otherwise permitted by law;

Ordinance 87-71, which prohibits the sacrifice of animals, and defines "sacrifice" in the same manner as Ordinance 87-52; and

Ordinance 87-72, which defines "slaughter" as "the killing of animals for food" and prohibits slaughter outside of areas zoned for slaughterhouses, but includes an exemption for "small numbers of hogs and/or cattle" when exempted by state law.

Petitioners filed this suit under 42 U. S. C. 1983, alleging violations of their rights under, inter alia, the Free Exercise Clause of the First Amendment. Although acknowledging that the foregoing ordinances are not religiously neutral, the District Court ruled for the city, concluding, among other things, that compelling governmental interests in preventing public health risks and cruelty to animals fully justified the absolute prohibition on ritual sacrifice accomplished by the ordinances, and that an exception to that prohibition for religious conduct would unduly interfere with fulfillment of the governmental interest because any more narrow restrictions would be unenforceable as a result of the Santeria religion's secret nature. The Court of Appeals affirmed.

Held: The judgment is reversed. Justice Kennedy delivered the opinion of the Court with respect to Parts I, II-A-1, II-A-3, II-B, III, and IV, concluding that the laws in question were enacted contrary to free exercise principles, and they are void.

(a) Under the Free Exercise Clause, a law that burdens religious practice need not be justified by a compelling governmental interest if it is neutral and of general applicability. *Employment Div., Dept. of Human Resources of Oregon v. Smith,* 494 U. S. 872. However, where such a law is not neutral or not of general application, it must undergo the most rigorous of scrutiny: It must be justified by a compelling governmental interest and must be narrowly tailored to advance that interest. Neutrality and general applicability are interrelated, and failure to satisfy one requirement is a likely indication that the other has not been satisfied.

(b) The ordinances' texts and operation demonstrate that they are not neutral, but have as their object the suppression of Santeria's central element, animal sacrifice. That this religious exercise has been targeted is evidenced by Resolution 87-66's statements of "concern" and "commitment," and by the use of the words "sacrifice" and "ritual" in Ordinances 87-40, 87-52, and 87-71. Moreover, the latter ordinances' various prohibitions, definitions, and exemptions demonstrate that they were "gerrymandered" with care to proscribe religious killings of animals by Santeria church members but to exclude almost all other animal killings. They also suppress much more religious conduct than is necessary to achieve their stated ends. The legitimate governmental interests in protecting the public health and preventing cruelty to animals could be addressed by restrictions stopping far short of a flat prohibition of all Santeria sacrificial practice, such as general regulations on the disposal of organic garbage, on the care of animals regardless of why they are kept, or on methods of slaughter. Although Ordinance 87-72 appears to apply to substantial nonreligious conduct and not to be overbroad, it must also be invalidated because it functions in tandem with the other ordinances to suppress Santeria religious worship.

(c) Each of the ordinances pursues the city's governmental interests only against conduct motivated by religious belief and thereby violates the requirement that laws burdening religious practice must be of general applicability. Ordinances 87-40, 87-52, and 87-71 are substantially underinclusive with regard to the city's interest in preventing cruelty to animals, since they are drafted with care to forbid few animal killings but those occasioned by religious sacrifice, while many types of animal deaths or kills for nonreligious reasons are either not prohibited or approved by express provision. The city's assertions that it is "self-evident" that killing for food is "important," that the eradication of insects and pests is "obviously justified," and that euthanasia of excess animals "makes sense" do not explain why religion alone must bear the burden of the ordinances. These ordinances are also substantially underinclusive with regard to the city's public health interests in preventing the disposal of animal carcasses in open public places and the consumption of uninspected meat, since neither interest is pursued by respondent with regard to conduct that is not motivated by religious conviction. Ordinance 87-72 is underinclusive on its face, since it does not regulate nonreligious slaughter for food in like manner, and respondent has not explained why the commercial slaughter of "small numbers" of cattle and hogs does not implicate its professed desire to prevent cruelty to animals and preserve the public health.

(d) The ordinances cannot withstand the strict scrutiny that is required upon their failure to meet the Smith standard. They are not narrowly tailored to accomplish the asserted governmental interests. All four are overbroad or underinclusive in substantial respects because the proffered objectives are not pursued with respect to analogous nonreligious conduct and those interests could be achieved by narrower ordinances that burdened religion to a far lesser degree. Moreover, where, as here, government restricts only conduct protected by the First Amendment and fails to enact feasible measures to restrict other conduct producing substantial harm or alleged harm of the same sort, the governmental interests given in justification of the restriction cannot be regarded as compelling.

Kennedy, J., delivered the opinion of the Court with respect to Parts I, III, and IV, in which Rehnquist, C. J., and White, Stevens, Scalia, Souter, and Thomas, JJ., joined, the opinion of the Court with respect to Part II-B, in which Rehnquist, C. J., and White, Stevens, Scalia, and Thomas, JJ., joined, the opinion of the Court with respect to Parts II-A-1 and II-A-3, in which Rehnquist, C. J., and Stevens, Scalia, and Thomas, JJ., joined, and an opinion with respect to Part II-A-2, in which Stevens, J., joined. Scalia, J., filed an opinion concurring in part and concurring in the judgment, in which Rehnquist, C. J., joined. Souter, J., filed an opinion concurring in part and concurring in the judgment. Blackmun, J., filed an opinion concurring in the judgment, in which O'Connor, J., joined.

APPENDIX 1:
NATIONAL ANIMAL RIGHTS ORGANIZATIONS

Name	Address	Phone	Fax	Email	URL	Mission
Action for Animals	SAO 176 HUB 207, Box 352238 Seattle, WA 98195	206-227-5752	n/a	afa@afa-online.org	http://www.afa-online .org	AFA strives to end animal suffering through educational outreach, demonstrations, and local media involvement
Action for Animals Network	PO Box 9039, Alexandria, VA 22304	703-461-3283	703-461-3283	anmlntwk@erols.com	http://www.enviroweb .org/aan	AAN focuses mainly on animals who suffer in the meat and dairy industries and in circuses

Name	Address	Phone	Fax	Email	URL	Mission
All For Animals	1324 State Street, #J109 Santa Barbara, CA 93101	805-682-3160	805-569-9810	info@allforanimals.com	http://www.allforanimals.com	pro-animal organization dedicated to informing and educating people about cruelty-free living and the rights of all animals
Alliance for Animals	122 State Street, #406, Madison, 53703	608-257-6333	608-257-6400	alliance@allanimals.org	http://www.allanimals.org	devoted to increasing public awareness of animal abuse and promoting the humane treatment of all animals
Alliance for the Wild Rockies	PO Box 8731, Missoula, MO 59807	406-721-5420	406-721-9917	awr@wildrockiesalliance.org	http://www.wildrockiesalliance.org	formed to save the Northern Rockies Bioregion from habitat destruction
American Anti-Vivisection Society	801 Old York Rd, Suite 204, Jenkintown, PA 19046-1685	215-887-0816	215-887-2088	aavsonline@aol.com	http://www.aavs.org	dedicated to ending the use of animals in research testing and education
Animal Defense League - New York City	PO Box 20878, New York, 10009	917-724-8126	n/a	NYC_ADL@bigfoot.com	http://members.aol.com/adlnycli/home.htm	nationally active, grassroots, animal liberation and defense organization
Animal Haven	35-22 Prince Street, Flushing, NY 11354	718-886-3683	n/a	animalhaveninc@aol.com	http://www.animalhavenshelter.org	a no-kill shelter for abandoned animals in New York City

Name	Address	Phone	Fax	Email	URL	Mission
American Humane Association	63 Inverness Drive East, Englewood, CO 80112-5117	303-792-9900	303-792-5333	animal@americanhumane.org	http://www.amerhumane.org	mission is to prevent cruelty, abuse, neglect and exploitation of animals
American Humane Association Film and TV Unit	15366 Dickens Street, Sylmar, 91403	818-501-0123	818-501-8725	geebrr@aol.com	http://www.AHAFilm.org	monitors the care and treatment of animals used in filmed media
Animallaw.com	NAVS 53 West Jackson Street, 15th floor, Chicago, IL 60604	312-427-6065	n/a	g_a_wachtel@yahoo.com	http://www.animallaw.com	a comprehensive online resource which disseminates legal and legislative information as it pertains to animal issues
Animal Legal Defense Fund	127 Fourth Street, Petaluma, CA 94952	707-769-7771	707-769-0785	info@aldf.org	http://www.aldf.org	leading animal rights law organization working nationally to defend animals from abuse and exploitation
Animal Liberation of Texas	PO Box 820872. Dallas, TX 75382	972-664-6760	214-342-8957	ALTdallas@aol.com	http://www.animalliberation.com	ALT's mission is to stop the torture and suffering of animals
Animal Lifeline	POBox 981, Waterford, NJ 08089	n/a	n/a	squash1098@earthlink.net	http://www.angelfire.com/nj2/animalifeline	dedicated to finding loving homes for pets
Animal Place	3448 Laguna Creek Trail, Vacaville, CA 95688-9724	707-449-4814	707-449-8775	AnimalPlace@aol.com	http://www.enviroweb.org/animal_place	a nonprofit sanctuary for abused and discarded farm animals

Name	Address	Phone	Fax	Email	URL	Mission
Animal Protection Institute	Sacramento, CA 95820	916-731-5521	916-731-4467	LawrenceCarter-Long @api4animals.org.	http://www.api4ani mals.org	dedicated to informing, educating, and advocating the humane treatment of all animals
Animal Refuge Foundation	3377 Spalding Rd, Sherman, TX 75092	903-564-7056	n/a	arf@arfhouse.com	http://www.arfhouse .com	a no-kill "care-for-life" canine sanctuary which provides refuge and care for unwanted abused and/or physically challenged canines
Animal Rescue Foundation	251 Underwood Road, PO Box 1032, Milledgeville, GA 31061	912-454-1273	n/a	arf@accucomm.net	http://www.animalre scuefoundation.org	mission includes finding responsible permanent homes as family pets for abandoned animals
Animal Rights Advocates of Western New York	PO Box 475, Buffalo, NY 14226	716-648-6423	716-648-6423	ARAofWNY@aol.com	http://www.geocities. com/arawny	dedicated to the elimination of animal abuse and exploitation
Animal Rights Coalition	3867 Winter Berry Road, Jacksonville, FL 32210	904-781-2620	n/a	emcue@juno.com	http://www.arc-.org	mission is to educate the public on animal issues
Animal Rescue and Adoption Society	2390 S. Delaware St., Denver, CO 80223	303-744-6076	303-744-6075	mehughes@du.edu	http://arascolorado.tr ipod.com	a no-kill non-profit cat shelter

Name	Address	Phone	Fax	Email	URL	Mission
Animal Shelter	PO Box 770707, Winter Garden, FL 34777-0707	407-877-PETS	407-877-3292	pets@animalshelter.org	http://www.animalshelter.org	a non-profit organization whose mission is to help care for homeless pets
Animal Welfare Institute	PO Box 3650, Washington, DC 20007	202-337-2332	202-338-9478	awi@awionline.org	http://www.awionline.org	mission is to reduce the pain and fear inflicted on animals by humans
Animal Welfare League	10305 Southwest Highway, Chicago Ridge, IL 60415	708)636-8586	708)636-9488	awl@wans.net.	http://www.animalwelfareleague.com	mission is to prevent cruelty to animals and provide quality homes for animals through an adoption program
Ark-Haven Animal Sanctuary	PO Box 1559, McMinnville, OR 97128	503-843-1196	n/a	bj@ark-haven.org	http://www.ark-haven.org	a no-kill sanctuary dedicated to the rescue, rehabilitation and long term care of abused and neglected dogs, cats, and farm animals
Association of Veterinarians for Animal Rights	PO Box 208, Davis, CA 95617-0208	530-759-8106	530-759-8116	AVAR@igc.org	http://www.avar.org	mission is to reform the way society treats all nonhumans
Badlands Animal League	4661-105 Ave. SW, Dickinson, ND 58601	n/a	n/a	bal@pop.ctctel.com	http://bdlsanlg.webjump.com	mission is to reduce the animal population through spay-neuter programs and the construction of a no-kill animal shelter

Name	Address	Phone	Fax	Email	URL	Mission
Best Friends Animal Sanctuary	5001 Angel Canyon Drive, Kanab, UT 84741-5001	435-644-2001	435-644-2078	info@bestfriends.org	http://www.bestfriends.org/index.htm	the nation's largest sanctuary for abused and abandoned cats and dogs and other animals
Bide-A-Wee	410 east 38th Street, New York, NY 10016	212-532-6395	n/a	bawpr@aol.com	http://www.bideawee.org	a non-profit animal shelter and humane society whose mission is to match responsible people with homeless pets
Cats Haven	PO Box 30206, Indianapolis, IN 46230	n/a	n/a	n/a	http://www.indy.net/~catshavn	a pro-life, no-kill shelter for cats and kittens who are in transition
Center For Captive Chimpanzee Care	PO Box 3746, Boynton Beach, FL 33424	561-963-8050	561-641-3246	info@savethechimps.org	http://www.savethechimps.org	mission is to create a sanctuary for the permanent, lifetime care for chimpanzees retired from research laboratories or who have been abandoned by owners no longer able to provide adequate care
Coalition for Animals	PO Box 611, Somerville, NJ 08876	908-281-0086	n/a	njcfa@worldnet.att.net	http://home.att.net/~njcfa	mission is to institute changes that will end animal exploitation and abuse

Name	Address	Phone	Fax	Email	URL	Mission
Companion Animal Protection Society	PMB 143, 2100 West Drake Road, Fort Collins, CO 80526	970-223-8300	970-223-8330	caps2@mindspring.com	http://www.caps-web.org	mission is ending the suffering of pet shop and puppy mill dogs
Cornell Coalition for Animal Defense	PO Box 39, Willard Straight Hall, Cornell University, Ithaca, NY 14853	607-279-6717	n/a	ccad@cornell.edu	http://www.rso.cornell.edu/ccad	an active group of animal liberation activists on the Cornell University campus
Defenders Of Animals	PO Box 5634, Weybosset Hill Station Providence, RI 02903-0634	401-738-3710	n/a	dennis@defendersofanimals.org	http://www.defendersofanimals.org	mission is to provide assistance to sick, injured and homeless animals
Doris Day Animal League	227 Massachusetts Ave. NE, Suite 100, Washington, DC 20002	202-546-1761	n/a	info@ddal.org	http://www.ddal.org	dedicated to animal protection issues
Dream Catcher Farm Horse Sanctuary	Rocky Mount, VA 24151	540-489-3805	n/a	equine@horsesanctuary.com	http://www.horsesanctuary.com	horse sanctuary for abused, neglected and elderly equine
Elephant Sanctuary	PO Box 393, Hohenwald, TN 38462	931-796-6500	931-796-4810	elephant@elephants.com	http://www.elephants.com	the nation's first natural habitat refuge developed specifically for endangered Asian elephants

Name	Address	Phone	Fax	Email	URL	Mission
Endangered Species Coalition	1101 14th Street NW, Suite 1200 Washington, DC 20005	202-682-9400	202-682-1331	esc@stopextinction.org	http://www.stopextinction.org	the coalition supports stronger protections for the nation's imperiled wildlife
FARM - Farm Animal Reform Movement	PO Box 30654, Bethesda, MD 20824	301-530-1737	n/a	farm@farm.org	http://www.farm.org	a national, tax-exempt, educational organization advocating a plant-based diet and rights for farmed animals
Felines, Inc.	PO Box 60616, Chicago, IL 60660	773-465-4132	773-465-6454	felinesinc@aol.com	http://www.felinesinc.org	mission is to care for and rehabilitate abandoned, abused and injured cats and kittens
Friends of Animals	777 Post Road, Darien, CT 06820	203-656-1522	n/a	icontact@friendsofanimals.org	http://www.friendsofanimals.org	a non-profit organization working to protect animals from cruelty and abuse
Green Acres Sanctuary	2867 Copper Kettle Hwy., Rockwood, PA 15557	814-926-4902	814-926-4902	info@greenacressanctuary.com	http://greenacressanctuary.com	a non-profit society for the prevention of cruelty to animals
Green Mountain Animal Defenders	PO Box 4577, Burlington, VT 05406	802-878-2230	n/a	SMacNair@gmad.net	http://gmad.net	a volunteer group dedicated to the humane treatment of all animals

Name	Address	Phone	Fax	Email	URL	Mission
Greyhound Adoption Service	16 Jak-Len Drive, Salisbury, MA	978-462-7973	n/a	schildkr@mediaone.net	http://members.aol.com/greycanine	a non-profit humane organization dedicated to finding loving, responsible homes for retired racing greyhounds
Greyhound Protection League	PO Box 669, Penn Valley, CA 95946	800-G-HOUNDS	800-446-8637, n/a	greyhounds_org@bigfoot.com	http://www.greyhounds.org	a non-profit organization dedicated to protecting greyhounds from the exploitation and abuses inherent in the greyhound racing industry
Habitat for Horses, Inc.	PO Box 213, Hitchcock, 77563	409-935-0277	409-935-0424	admin@habitatforhorses.org	http://www.habitatforhorses.org	a sanctuary for retired horses from across the nation
Heart and Soul Animal Sanctuary	369 Montezuma Avenue, #130, Santa Fe, NM 87105-2626	505-455-2774	n/a	safeanimals2@aol.com	http://www.animal-sanctuary.org	mission is to alleviate the suffering of all animals
Homes for Hounds	5081 SW Pacific Coast Hwy, Waldport, OR	541-563-3467	n/a	silver@newportnet.com	http://www.homesforhounds.homestead.com	an organization that finds homes for retired racing greyhounds
Horse Rescue	PO Box 232, Cushman, AR 72526	870-793-7534	870-793-5237	ozland@arkansas.net	http://myozland.tripod.com/ozlandhorserescue	a shelter for abused, neglected, or any other needy horses

Name	Address	Phone	Fax	Email	URL	Mission
Humane Society of the United States	2100 L Street NW, Washington, DC 20037	301-258-3072	301-258-3074	hwhite@hsus.org	http://www.hsus.org	the nation's largest animal protection organization
International Society for Animal Rights	965 Griffin Pond Road, Clarks Summit, PA 18411	717-586-2200	717-586-9580	ISAR@AOL.COM	http://www.i-s-a-r.com	mission is to expose and end the injustice of the exploitation of animals and the suffering inflicted on them
International Wildlife Coalition	70 East Falmouth Highway, East Falmouth, MA 02536	508.548.8328	508.548.8542	iwcadopt@cape.com	http://www.iwc.org	mission is to save endangered species, protect wild animals and preserve habitat and the environment
Jane Goodall Institute	PO Box 14890, Silver Spring, MD 20911	301-565-0086	301-565-3188	cschluter@janegoodall.org	http://www.janegoodall.org	mission is to take informed and compassionate action to improve the environment of all living things
Jungle Friends	13915 N. State Road 121, Gainesville, FL 32653	904-462-7779	n/a	info@junglefriends.org	http://www.junglefriends.org	a refuge for primates against exploitation, abuse, neglect and improper care
K - 9 Rescue	652 Oak Trail, Lockhart, TX 78644	512-376-2499	603-307-0274	belmal@juno.com	http://www.k-9rescue.com	mission is saving dogs at the local shelter from death row

Name	Address	Phone	Fax	Email	URL	Mission
Last Chance For Animals	8033 Sunset Blvd., # 35, Los Angeles, CA 90046	310-271-6096	310-271-1890	office@lcanimal.org	http://www.lcanimal.org	mission is to promote certain basic rights protecting animals from pain caused by humans
League of Humane Voters	PO Box 401, Congers, NY 10920	845-268-8685	n/a	mail@humanevoters.org	http://www.humanevoters.org	established to organize voters who are concerned about non-human animals
Marine Mammal Center	The Marine Mammal Center, Golden Gate National Recreation Area, Salito, California 94965	n/a	415-289-SEAL	n/a	http://www.tmmc.org	one of the largest marine mammal rehabilitation facilities in the world
Medical Research Modernization Committee	3200 Morley Rd., Shaker Heights, OH 44122	216-283-6702	216-283-6702	stkaufman@pol.net	http://www.mrmcmed.org	a national health advocacy group composed of physicians, scientists and other health care professionals who evaluate the benefits, risks and costs of medical research methods and technologies

Name	Address	Phone	Fax	Email	URL	Mission
Montana Large Animal Sanctuary	PO Box 939, Polson, MT 59860	406-883-1823	406-883-1825	belkay@digisys.net	http://www.envirolink.org/orgs/mlasr	provides a loving home for large animals that are unwanted or require special care
National Anti-Vivisection Society	53 W. Jackson, Suite 1552, Chicago, IL 60604	800-888-NAVS	n/a	navs@navs.org	http://www.navs.org	mission is to abolish the exploitation of animals used in research, education and product testing
National Humane Education Society	521-A East Market Street, Leesburg, VA 20176	703-777-8319	703-771-4048	n/a	http://www.nhes.org	a nonprofit organization whose mission is to foster a sentiment of kindness to animals in children and adults
North Shore Animal League	25 Davis Avenue, Port Washington, NY 11050	516-883-7575	n/a	nsal1@aol.com	http://www.nsal.org	the largest pet adoption agency in the world
Northwest Animal Rights Network	1704 East Galer, Seattle, WA 98112	206-323-7301	n/a	info@narn.org	http://www.narn.org	mission is to actively promote the equal consideration of animals in the Pacific Northwest
People for Animal Rights	PO Box 8707, Kansas City, MO 64114	816-767-1199	n/a	parinfo@parkc.org	http://www.parkc.org	mission is to eliminate all animal abuse and exploitation

Name	Address	Phone	Fax	Email	URL	Mission
People for the Ethical Treatment of Animals (PETA)	501 Front Street, Norfolk, VA 23510	757-622-7382	757-622-0457	info@peta-online.org	http://www.peta.org	the largest animal rights organization in the world dedicated to establishing and protecting the rights of all animals.
Pets Alive	363 Derby Road, Middletown, NY 10940	845-386-9738	n/a	petsaliv@warwick.net	http://www.petsalive.com	a no-kill animal shelter whose mission is to rescue, rehabilitate, and place animals in need
Reptile & Exotic Animal Rescue	12184 Cr 167, Tyler, TX 75703	n/a	n/a	ReptileRescue1@cs.com	http://www.reptilerescue.tsx.org	a small non-profit organization dedicated to saving reptiles, exotic mammals and wildlife
Rocky Mountain Animal Defense	2525 Arapahoe, Suite E4-335, Boulder, CO 80302	303-449-4422	n/a	rmad@rmad.org	http://www.rmad.org	mission is to help eliminate the human-imposed suffering of animals in the Rocky Mountain region
Society for The Protection of Animals	PO Box 1047, Fremont, OH 43420	419-334-5521	n/a	spa@spaohio.org	http://www.spaohio.org	a non-profit organization created to provide a pro-active solution for minimizing the stray cat/dog population in the area

Name	Address	Phone	Fax	Email	URL	Mission
St. Louis Animal Rights Team	PO Box 28501, St. Louis, MO 63146	314-851-0928	n/a	stlouisanimalrightsteam@visto.com	http://www.enviroweb.org/start	a nonprofit, educational
Student Organization for Animal Rights	925 E. 900 S., Salt Lake City, UT 84105-1401	801-321-UARC	n/a	soar@uarc.com	http://soar.uarc.com	mission is to teach people that it is both easy and necessary to adopt a lifestyle that does not advocate the needless murder and torture of animals
The Animal Group	PO Box 250707, Little Rock, AR 72225	501-537-4824	801-327-5649	TheAnimalGroup@hotmail.org	http://www.theanimalgroup.org	dedicated to promoting the humane treatment of animals and fostering respect, compassion and protection for all creatures
The Society for Animal Protective Legislation	PO Box 3719, Washington, DC 20007	202-337-2334	n/a	sapl@saplonline.org	http://www.saplonline.org	advocates legislation concerned with animal protection
Urban Wildlife Rescue	PO Box 201311, Denver, CO 80220	303-340-4911	303-363-8628	eartandme@visto.com	http://www.urbanwildliferescue.org	a non-profit organization dedicated to rescuing and rehabilitating wildlife
Voices For Animals	Stroudsburg, PA	570-992-6073	n/a	senne@ptd.net	http://voices.htmlplanet.com/main.html	small organization concerned with animal protection issues

Name	Address	Phone	Fax	Email	URL	Mission
Wildlife Advocacy Project	1601Connecticut Ave, NW #700, Washington, DC 20009	202-518-3700	202-588-5049	wildinfo@wildlifeadvocacy.org	http://www.wildlifeadvocacy.org	mission is to stop the abuse and exploitation of animals held in captivity
Wildlife Conservation Society	Bronx Zoo, 185th St. and Southern Blvd, Bronx, NY 10460	718-220-5197	n/a	feedback@wcs.org	http://www.wcs.org	mission is to save wildlife and wild lands throughout the world
World Animal Foundation	PO Box 30762, Middleburg Hts., OH 44130	530-685-6826	530-685-6826	CustomerService@WorldAnimalFoundation.com	http://www.WorldAnimalFoundation.com	mission is to preserve and protect the planet and the animal that inhabit it
World Wildlife Fund	1250 Twenty-Fourth Street N.W., PO Box 97180, Washington, DC 20037	1-800-CALL-WWF	n/a	n/a	http://www.worldwildlife.org	the largest privately supported international conservation organization in the world whose mission is to protect the world's wildlife and wildlands
21st Century Animal Resource and Education Services	16224 N. Linda Dr., PO Box 373, Dolan Springs, AZ 86441	520-767-4895	same	21stcares@eresq.net	http://www.21stcenturycares.org	an animal welfare organization dedicated to supporting and promoting various forms of humane education in our nation's schools

APPENDIX 2:
STATE ANIMAL ANTI-CRUELTY STATUTES

CODE OF ALABAMA 1975

§ 13A-11-14 CRUELTY TO ANIMALS.

(a) A person commits the crime of cruelty to animals if, except as otherwise authorized by law, he intentionally or recklessly:

(1) Subjects any animal to cruel mistreatment; or

(2) Subjects any animal in his custody to cruel neglect; or

(3) Kills or injures without good cause any animal belonging to another.

(b) Cruelty to animals is a Class B misdemeanor.

ALASKA STATUTES

§ 11.61.140 CRUELTY TO ANIMALS.

(a) A person commits the crime of cruelty to animals if the person

(1) intentionally inflicts severe and prolonged physical pain or suffering on an animal;

(2) recklessly neglects an animal and, as a result of that neglect, causes the death of the animal or causes severe pain or suffering to the animal; or

(3) kills an animal by the use of a decompression chamber.

(b) It is a defense to a prosecution under (a)(1) or (2) of this section that the conduct of the defendant

(1) conformed to accepted veterinary practice;

(2) was part of scientific research governed by accepted standards; or

(3) was necessarily incident to lawful hunting or trapping activities.

(c) In this section, "animal" means a vertebrate living creature not a human being, but does not include fish.

(d) Cruelty to animals is a class A misdemeanor.

ARIZONA REVISED STATUTES

§ 13-2910. CRUELTY TO ANIMALS OR POULTRY; CLASSIFICATION.

A. A person commits cruelty to animals if, except as otherwise authorized by law, such person recklessly:

  1. Subjects any animals or poultry under human custody or control to cruel mistreatment; or

  2. Subjects any animal or poultry under his custody or control to cruel neglect or abandonment; or

  3. Kills any animal or poultry under the custody or control of another without either legal privilege or consent of the owner.

B. It is a defense to subsection A of this section if any person exposes poison to be taken by a dog which has killed or wounded livestock or poison to be taken by predatory animals on premises owned, leased or controlled by him for the purpose of the protection of such person or his livestock or poultry, and the treated property is kept posted by the person who authorized or performed the treatment until such poison has been removed, and such poison is removed by the person exposing the poison after the threat to such person, his livestock or poultry has ceased to exist. The posting required shall be in such manner as to provide adequate warning to persons who enter the property by the point or points of normal entry. The warning notice which is posted shall be of such size that it is readable at a distance of fifty feet, shall contain a poison statement and symbol and shall state the word "Danger" or "Warning".

C. Cruelty to animals or poultry is a class 2 misdemeanor.

ARKANSAS CODE OF 1987

§ 5-62-101 CRUELTY TO ANIMALS.

(a) A person commits the offense of cruelty to animals if, except as authorized by law, he knowingly:

  (1) Abandons any animal;

  (2) Subjects any animal to cruel mistreatment;

  (3) Subjects any animal in his custody to cruel neglect; or

(4) Kills or injures any animal belonging to another without legal privilege or consent of the owner.

(b) Cruelty to animals is a Class A misdemeanor.

CALIFORNIA PENAL CODE

§ 597. CRUELTY TO ANIMALS.

(a) Except as provided in subdivision (c) of this section or Section 599c, every person who maliciously and intentionally maims, mutilates, tortures, or wounds a living animal, or maliciously and intentionally kills an animal, is guilty of an offense punishable by imprisonment in the state prison, or by a fine of not more than twenty thousand dollars ($20,000), or by both the fine and imprisonment, or, alternatively, by imprisonment in the county jail for not more than one year, or by a fine of not more than twenty thousand dollars ($20,000), or by both the fine and imprisonment.

(b) Except as otherwise provided in subdivision (a) or (c), every person who overdrives, overloads, drives when overloaded, overworks, tortures, torments, deprives of necessary sustenance, drink, or shelter, cruelly beats, mutilates, or cruelly kills any animal, or causes or procures any animal to be so overdriven, overloaded, driven when overloaded, overworked, tortured, tormented, deprived of necessary sustenance, drink, shelter, or to be cruelly beaten, mutilated, or cruelly killed; and whoever, having the charge or custody of any animal, either as owner or otherwise, subjects any animal to needless suffering, or inflicts unnecessary cruelty upon the animal, or in any manner abuses any animal, or fails to provide the animal with proper food, drink, or shelter or protection from the weather, or who drives, rides, or otherwise uses the animal when unfit for labor, is, for every such offense, guilty of a crime punishable as a misdemeanor or as a felony or alternatively punishable as a misdemeanor or a felony and by a fine of not more than twenty thousand dollars ($20,000).

(c) Every person who maliciously and intentionally maims, mutilates, or tortures any mammal, bird, reptile, amphibian, or fish as described in subdivision (d), is guilty of an offense punishable by imprisonment in the state prison, or by a fine of not more than twenty thousand dollars ($20,000), or by both the fine and imprisonment, or, alternatively, by imprisonment in the county jail for not more than one year, by a fine of not more than twenty thousand dollars ($20,000), or by both the fine and imprisonment.

(d) Subdivision (c) applies to any mammal, bird, reptile, amphibian, or fish which is a creature described as follows:

(1) Endangered species or threatened species as described in Chapter 1.5 (commencing with Section 2050) of Division 3 of the Fish and Game Code.

(2) Fully protected birds described in Section 3511 of the Fish and Game Code.

(3) Fully protected mammals described in Chapter 8 (commencing with Section 4700) of Part 3 of Division 4 of the Fish and Game Code.

(4) Fully protected reptiles and amphibians described in Chapter 2 (commencing with Section 5050) of Division 5 of the Fish and Game Code.

(5) Fully protected fish as described in Section 5515 of the Fish and Game Code.

This subdivision does not supersede or affect any provisions of law relating to taking of the described species, including, but not limited to, Section 12008 of the Fish and Game Code.

(e) For the purposes of subdivision (c), each act of malicious and intentional maiming, mutilating, or torturing a separate specimen of a creature described in subdivision (d) is a separate offense. If any person is charged with a violation of subdivision (c), the proceedings shall be subject to Section 12157 of the Fish and Game Code.

(f) Upon the conviction of a person charged with a violation of this section by causing or permitting an act of cruelty, as defined in Section 599b, all animals lawfully seized and impounded with respect to the violation by a peace officer, officer of a humane society, or officer of a pound or animal regulation department of a public agency shall be adjudged by the court to be forfeited and shall thereupon be awarded to the impounding officer for proper disposition. A person convicted of a violation of this section by causing or permitting an act of cruelty, as defined in Section 599b, shall be liable to the impounding officer for all costs of impoundment from the time of seizure to the time of proper disposition.

Mandatory seizure or impoundment shall not apply to animals in properly conducted scientific experiments or investigations performed under the authority of the faculty of a regularly incorporated medical college or university of this state.

COLORADO REVISED STATUTES

§ 18-9-202. CRUELTY TO ANIMALS—NEGLECT OF ANIMALS—OFFENSES.

(1)(a) A person commits cruelty to animals if he knowingly or with criminal negligence overdrives, overloads, overworks, tortures, torments, deprives of necessary sustenance, unnecessarily or cruelly beats, needlessly mutilates, needlessly kills, carries or confines in or upon any vehicles in a cruel or reckless manner, or otherwise mistreats or neglects any animal, or causes or procures it to be done, or, having the charge of custody of any animal, fails to provide it with proper food, drink, or protection from the weather, or abandons it.

(1)(b) Any person who intentionally abandons a dog or cat commits the offense of cruelty to animals.

(2)(a) Cruelty to animals is a class 1 misdemeanor.

(2)(b) In the case of any person incurring a second or subsequent conviction under the provisions of paragraph (a) of this subsection (2), a sentence of imprisonment within the minimum and maximum terms shall be mandatory and shall not be subject to suspension, nor shall such person be eligible for probation or parole for any part of such period. A plea of nolo contendere accepted by the court shall be considered a conviction for the purposes of this section.

(3) Nothing in this part 2 shall be construed to amend or in any manner change the authority of the wildlife commission, as established in title 33, C.R.S., or to prohibit any conduct therein authorized or permitted.

CONNECTICUT GENERAL STATUTES

§ 53-247. CRUELTY TO ANIMALS. INTENTIONAL KILLING OF POLICE ANIMAL.

(a) Any person who overdrives, drives when overloaded, overworks, tortures, deprives of necessary sustenance, mutilates or cruelly beats or kills or unjustifiably injures any animal, or who, having impounded or confined any animal, fails to give such animal proper care or neglects to cage or restrain any such animal from doing injury to itself or to another animal or fails to supply any such animal with wholesome air, food and water, or unjustifiably administers any poisonous or noxious drug or substance to any domestic animal or unjustifiably exposes any such drug or substance, with intent that the same shall be taken by an animal, or causes it to be done, or, having charge or custody of any animal, inflicts cruelty upon it or fails to provide it with proper food, drink or protection from the weather or abandons it or carries it or causes it to be carried in a cruel manner, or sets on foot, instigates, promotes or carries on or performs any act as assistant, umpire or principal in, or is a witness of, or in any way aids in or engages in the furtherance of, any fight between cocks or other birds, dogs or other animals, premeditated by any person owning, or having custody of, such birds or animals, or fights with or baits, harasses or worries any animal for the purpose of making it perform for amusement, diversion or exhibition, shall be fined not more than one thousand dollars or imprisoned not more than one year or both.

(b) Any person who intentionally kills any animal while such animal is in the performance of its duties under the supervision of a peace officer, as defined in section 53a-3, shall be fined not more than five thousand dollars or imprisoned not more than five years or both.

DELAWARE CODE

§ 1325 CRUELTY TO ANIMALS; CLASS A MISDEMEANOR; CLASS F FELONY.

(a) For the purpose of this section, the following words and phrases shall include, but not be limited to, the meanings respectively ascribed to them as follows:

(1) "Cruel" includes every act or omission to act whereby unnecessary or unjustifiable physical pain or suffering is caused or permitted.

(2) "Cruel mistreatment" includes any treatment whereby unnecessary or unjustifiable physical pain or suffering is caused or permitted.

(3) "Cruel neglect" includes neglect of an animal, which is under the care and control of the neglector, whereby pain or suffering is caused to the animal or abandonment of any domesticated animal by its owner or custodian.

(4) "Cruelty to animals" includes mistreatment of any animal or neglect of any animal under the care and control of the neglector, whereby unnecessary or unjustifiable physical pain or suffering is caused. By way of example this includes: Unjustifiable beating of an animal; overworking an animal; tormenting an animal; abandonment of an animal; failure to feed properly or give proper shelter or veterinary care to an animal.

(5) "Person" includes any individual, partnership, corporation or association living and/or doing business in the State.

(6) "Abandonment" includes completely forsaking or deserting an animal originally under one's custody without making reasonable ar-

rangements for custody of that animal to be assumed by another person.

(7) "Custody" includes the responsibility for the welfare of an animal subject to one's care and control whether one owns it or not.

(8) "Proper feed" includes providing each animal with daily food and water of sufficient quality and quantity to prevent unnecessary or unjustifiable physical pain or suffering by the animal.

(9) "Proper shelter" includes providing each animal with adequate shelter from the weather elements as required to prevent unnecessary or unjustifiable physical pain or suffering by the animal.

(10) "Proper veterinary care" includes providing each animal with veterinary care sufficient to prevent unnecessary or unjustifiable physical pain or suffering by the animal.

(11) "Animal" shall not include fish, crustacea or molluska.

(12) "Serious injury" shall include any injury to any animal which creates a substantial risk of death, or which causes prolonged impairment of health or prolonged loss or impairment of the function of any bodily organ.

(b) A person is guilty of cruelty to animals when the person intentionally or recklessly:

(1) Subjects any animal to cruel mistreatment; or

(2) Subjects any animal in the person's custody to cruel neglect; or

(3) Kills or injures any animal belonging to another person without legal privilege or consent of the owner; or

(4) Cruelly or unnecessarily kills or injures any animal whether belonging to the actor or another. This section does not apply to the killing of any animal normally or commonly raised as food for human consumption, provided that such killing is not cruel. A person acts unnecessarily if the act is not required to terminate an animal's suffering, to protect the life or property of the actor or another person or if other means of disposing of an animal exist which would not impair the health or well-being of that animal.

Paragraphs (1), (2) and (4) of this subsection are inapplicable to accepted veterinary practices and activities carried on for scientific research.

Cruelty to animals is a class A misdemeanor, unless the person intentionally kills or causes serious injury to any animal in violation of paragraph (4) of this subsection, in which case it is a class F felony.

(c) Any person convicted of a misdemeanor violation of this section shall be prohibited from owning or possessing any animal for 5 years after said conviction, except for animals grown, raised or produced within the State for resale, or for sale of a product thereof, where the person has all necessary licenses for such sale or resale, and receives at least 25 percent of the person's annual gross income from such sale or resale.

A violation of this subsection is subject to a fine in the amount of $1,000 in any court of competent jurisdiction and to forfeiture of any animal illegally owned in accordance with the provisions of 3 Del. C. s 7907.

(d) Any person convicted of a felony violation of this section shall be prohibited from owning or possessing any animal for 15 years after said conviction, except for animals grown, raised or produced within the State for resale, or for sale of a product thereof, where the person has all necessary licenses for such sale or resale, and receives at least 25 percent of the person's annual gross income from such sale or resale.

A violation of this subsection is subject to a fine in the amount of $5,000 in any court of competent jurisdiction and to forfeiture of any animal illegally owned in accordance with the provisions of 3 Del. C. s 7907.

(e) Any agent of the Delaware Society for the Prevention of Cruelty to Animals, or, in Kent County of this State, of the Kent County Society for the Prevention of Cruelty to Animals, may impound an animal owned or possessed in apparent violation of this section, consistent with 3 Del. C. s 7907.

(f) This section shall not apply to the lawful hunting or trapping of animals as provided by law.

DISTRICT OF COLUMBIA CODE 1981

§ 22-801 DEFINITION AND PENALTY.

Whoever overdrives, overloads, drives when overloaded, overworks, tortures, torments, deprives of necessary sustenance, cruelly beats, mutilates, or cruelly kills, or causes or procures to be so overdriven, overloaded, driven when overloaded, overworked, tortured, tormented, deprived of necessary sustenance, cruelly beaten, mutilated, or cruelly killed any animal, and whoever, having the charge or custody of any animal, either as owner or otherwise, inflicts unnecessary cruelty upon the same, or unnecessarily fails to provide the same with proper food, drink, shelter, or protection from the weather, shall for every such offense be punished by imprisonment in jail not exceeding 180 days, or by fine not exceeding $250, or by both such fine and imprisonment.

FLORIDA STATUTES

§ 828.12. CRUELTY TO ANIMALS.

(1) A person who unnecessarily overloads, overdrives, torments, deprives of necessary sustenance or shelter, or unnecessarily mutilates, or kills any animal, or causes the same to be done, or carries in or upon any vehicle, or otherwise, any animal in a cruel or inhumane manner, is guilty of a misdemeanor of the first degree, punishable as provided in s. 775.082 or by a fine of not more than $5,000, or both.

(2) A person who intentionally commits an act to any animal which results in the cruel death, or excessive or repeated infliction of unnecessary pain or suffering, or causes the same to be done, is guilty of a felony of the third degree, punishable as provided in s. 775.082 or by a fine of not more than $10,000, or both.

(3) A veterinarian licensed to practice in the state shall be held harmless from either criminal or civil liability for any decisions made or services rendered under the provisions of this section. Such a veterinarian is, therefore, under this subsection, immune from a lawsuit for his part in an investigation of cruelty to animals.

CODE OF GEORGIA

§ 16-12-4 CRUELTY TO ANIMALS.

(a) A person is guilty of a misdemeanor of cruelty to animals in the second degree when his act, omission, or neglect causes unjustifiable physical pain, suffering, or death to any living animal.

(b) A person is guilty of a misdemeanor of cruelty to animals in the first degree upon a second or subsequent violation of subsection (a) of this Code section and, upon conviction, may be punished by imprisonment not to exceed 12 months or a fine not to exceed $5,000.00 or both.

(c) This Code section does not apply to the killing of animals raised for the purpose of providing food nor does it apply to any person who hunts wild animals in compliance with the game and fish laws of this state. The killing or injuring of an animal for humane purposes or in the furtherance of medical or scientific research is justifiable.

HAWAII REVISED STATUTES

§ 711-1109 CRUELTY TO ANIMALS.

(1) A person commits the offense of cruelty to animals if the person intentionally, knowingly or recklessly:

(a) Overdrives, overloads, tortures, torments, cruelly beats or starves any animal or causes or procures the overdriving, overloading, torture, torment, cruel beating or starving of any animal;

(b) Mutilates, poisons, or kills without need any animal other than insects, vermin, or other pests;

(c) Keeps, uses or in any way is connected with or interested in the management of, or receives money for the admission of any person to, any place kept or used for the purpose of fighting or baiting any bull, bear, dog, cock or other animal, and every person who encourages, aids or assists therein, or who permits or suffers any place to be so kept or used;

(d) Carries or causes to be carried, in or upon any vehicle or other conveyance, any animal in a cruel or inhumane manner; or

(e) Assists another in the commission of any act of cruelty to any animal.

(2) Subsection (1)(a), (b), (d), (e) and the following subsection (3) are not applicable to accepted veterinary practices and to activities carried on for scientific research governed by standards of accepted educational or medicinal practices.

(3) Whenever any domestic animal is so severely injured that there is no reasonable probability that its life or usefulness can be saved, the animal may be immediately destroyed.

(4) Cruelty to animals is a misdemeanor.

IDAHO CODE

§ 25-3504 COMMITTING CRUELTY TO ANIMALS.

Every person who is cruel to any animal, or causes or procures any animal to be cruelly treated; and whoever, having the charge or custody of any animal, either as owner or otherwise, subjects any animal to cruelty, is, for every such offense, guilty of a misdemeanor and shall, upon conviction, be punished in accordance with section 25-3520A, Idaho Code.

ILLINOIS COMPILED STATUTES

§ 70/3.02. AGGRAVATED CRUELTY.

No person may intentionally commit an act that causes a companion animal to suffer serious injury or death. Aggravated cruelty does not include euthanasia of a companion animal through recognized methods approved by the Department of Agriculture.

INDIANA CODE

§ 35-46-3-12 TORTURE, MUTILATION OR KILLING OF VERTEBRATE ANIMAL.

(a) A person who knowingly or intentionally:

(1) tortures, beats, or mutilates a vertebrate animal resulting in serious injury or death to the animal; or

(2) kills a vertebrate animal without the authority of the owner of the animal;

commits cruelty to an animal, a Class A misdemeanor.

(b) It is a defense that the accused person reasonably believes the conduct was necessary to:

(1) prevent injury to the accused person or another person;

(2) protect the property of the accused person from destruction or substantial damage; or

(3) prevent a seriously injured vertebrate animal from prolonged suffering.

IOWA CODE

§ 717.2. LIVESTOCK NEGLECT.

1. A person who impounds or confines livestock, in any place, and does any of the following commits the offense of livestock neglect:

a. Fails to provide livestock with care consistent with customary animal husbandry practices.

b. Deprives livestock of necessary sustenance.

c. Injures or destroys livestock by any means which causes pain or suffering in a manner inconsistent with customary animal husbandry practices.

2. A person who commits the offense of livestock neglect is guilty of a simple misdemeanor. A person who intentionally commits the offense of livestock neglect which results in serious injury to or the death of livestock is guilty of a serious misdemeanor. However, a person shall not be guilty of more than one offense of livestock neglect punishable as a serious misdemeanor, when care or sustenance is not provided to multiple head of livestock during any period of uninterrupted neglect.

3. This section does not apply to an institution, as defined in section 145B.1, or a research facility, as defined in section 162.2, provided that the institution or research facility performs functions within the scope of accepted practices and disciplines associated with the institution or research facility.

KANSAS STATUTES

§ 21-4310. CRUELTY TO ANIMALS.

(a) Cruelty to animals is:

(1) Intentionally killing, injuring, maiming, torturing or mutilating any animal;

(2) abandoning or leaving any animal in any place without making provisions for its proper care; or

(3) having physical custody of any animal and failing to provide such food, potable water, protection from the elements, opportunity for exercise and other care as is needed for the health or well-being of such kind of animal.

(b) The provisions of this section shall not apply to:

(1) Normal or accepted veterinary practices;

(2) bona fide experiments carried on by commonly recognized research facilities;

(3) killing, attempting to kill, trapping, catching or taking of any animal in accordance with the provisions of chapter 32 or chapter 47 of the Kansas Statutes Annotated;

(4) rodeo practices accepted by the rodeo cowboys' association;

(5) the humane killing of an animal which is diseased or disabled beyond recovery for any useful purpose, or the humane killing of animals for population control, by the owner thereof or the agent of such owner residing outside of a city or the owner thereof within a city if no animal shelter, pound or licensed veterinarian is within the city, or by a licensed veterinarian at the request of the owner thereof, or by any offi-

cer or agent of an incorporated humane society, the operator of an animal shelter or pound, a local or state health officer or a licensed veterinarian three business days following the receipt of any such animal at such society, shelter or pound;

(6) with respect to farm animals, normal or accepted practices of animal husbandry;

(7) the killing of any animal by any person at any time which may be found outside of the owned or rented property of the owner or custodian of such animal and which is found injuring or posing a threat to any person, farm animal or property; or

(8) an animal control officer trained by a licensed veterinarian in the use of a tranquilizer gun, using such gun with the appropriate dosage for the size of the animal, when such animal is vicious or could not be captured after reasonable attempts using other methods.

(c) Cruelty to animals is a class A nonperson misdemeanor.

KENTUCKY REVISED STATUTES

§ 525.125. CRUELTY TO ANIMALS IN THE FIRST DEGREE.

(1) The following persons are guilty of cruelty to animals in the first degree whenever a four-legged animal is caused to fight for pleasure or profit:

(a) The owner of the animal;

(b) The owner of the property on which the fight is conducted if the owner knows of the fight;

(c) Anyone who participates in the organization of the fight.

(2) Activities of animals engaged in hunting, field trials, dog training, and other activities authorized either by a hunting license or by the Department of Fish and Wildlife shall not constitute a violation of this section.

(3) Cruelty to animals in the first degree is a Class D felony.

§ 525.130. CRUELTY TO ANIMALS IN THE SECOND DEGREE.

(1) A person is guilty of cruelty to animals in the second degree when except as authorized by law he intentionally or wantonly:

(a) Subjects any animal to or causes cruel or injurious mistreatment through abandonment, participates other than as provided in KRS 525.125 in causing it to fight for pleasure or profit, (including, but not limited to being a spectator or vendor at an event where a four (4) legged animal is caused to fight for pleasure or profit) mutilation, beating, torturing, tormenting, failing to provide adequate food, drink, space, or health care, or by any other means; or

(b) Subjects any animal in his custody to cruel neglect; or

(c) Kills any animal.

(2) Nothing in this section shall apply to the killing of animals:

(a) Pursuant to a license to hunt, fish, or trap;

(b) Incident to the processing as food or for other commercial purposes;

(c) For humane purposes;

(d) For any other purpose authorized by law.

(3) Activities of animals engaged in hunting, field trials, dog training, and other activities authorized either by a hunting license or by the Department of Fish and Wildlife shall not constitute a violation of this section.

(4) Cruelty to animals in the second degree is a Class A misdemeanor.

LOUISIANA REVISED STATUTES

§ 102.1. CRUELTY TO ANIMALS; SIMPLE AND AGGRAVATED.

A. (1) Any person who intentionally or with criminal negligence commits any of the following shall be guilty of simple cruelty to animals:

(a) Overdrives, overloads, drives when overloaded, or overworks a living animal.

(b) Torments, cruelly beats, or unjustifiably injures any living animal, whether belonging to himself or another.

(c) Having charge, custody, or possession of any animal, either as owner or otherwise, unjustifiably fails to provide it with proper food, proper drink, proper shelter, or proper veterinary care.

(d) Abandons any animal. A person shall not be considered to have abandoned an animal if he delivers to an animal control center an animal which he found running at large.

(e) Impounds or confines or causes to be impounded or confined in a pound or other place, a living animal and fails to supply it during such confinement with proper food, proper drink, and proper shelter.

(f) Carries, or causes to be carried, a living animal in or upon a vehicle or otherwise, in a cruel or inhumane manner.

(g) Unjustifiably administers any poisonous or noxious drug or substance to any domestic animal or unjustifiably exposes any such drug or substance, with intent that the same shall be taken or swallowed by any domestic animal.

(h) Injures any animal belonging to another person without legal privilege or consent of the owner.

(i) Mistreats any living animal by any act or omission whereby unnecessary or unjustifiable physical pain, suffering, or death is caused to or permitted upon the animal.

(j) Causes or procures to be done by any person any act enumerated in this Subsection.

A. (2)(a) Whoever commits the crime of simple cruelty to animals shall be fined not more than one thousand dollars, or imprisoned for not more than six months, or both.

(b) In addition to any other penalty imposed, a person who commits the crime of cruelty to animals shall be ordered to perform five eight-hour days of court-approved community service. The community service requirement shall not be suspended.

B. (1) Any person who intentionally or with criminal negligence tortures, maims, mutilates, or maliciously kills any living animal, whether belonging to himself or another, shall be guilty of aggravated cruelty to animals.

B. (2) Any person who causes or procures to be done by any person any act designated in this Subsection shall also be guilty of aggravated cruelty to animals.

B. (3) Whoever commits the crime of aggravated cruelty to animals shall be fined not less than one thousand dollars nor more than twenty-five thousand dollars or imprisoned, with or without hard labor, for not less than one year nor more than ten years, or both.

B. (4) For purposes of this Subsection, where more than one animal is tortured, maimed, mutilated, or maliciously killed, each act comprises a separate offense.

C. This Section shall not apply to the lawful hunting or trapping of wildlife as provided by law, herding of domestic animals, accepted veterinary practices, and activities carried on for scientific or medical research governed by accepted standards.

D. For purposes of this Section, fowl shall not be defined as animals. Only the following birds shall be identified as animals for purposes of this Section:

(1) Order Psittaciformes-parrots, parakeets, lovebirds, macaws, cockatiels or cockatoos.

(2) Order Passeriformes-canaries, starlings, sparrows, flycatchers, mynah or myna.

MAINE REVISED STATUTES

§ 4011. CRUELTY TO ANIMALS.

1. Cruelty to animals. Except as provided in subsection 1-A, a person, including an owner or the owner's agent, is guilty of cruelty to animals if that person:

A. Kills or attempts to kill any animal belonging to another person without the consent of the owner or without legal privilege;

B. Except for a licensed veterinarian or a person certified under Title 17, section 1042, kills or attempts to kill an animal by a method that does not cause instantaneous death;

C. If that person is a licensed veterinarian or a person certified under Title 17, section 1042, kills or attempts to kill an animal by a method that causes undue suffering. The commissioner shall adopt rules that define "undue suffering";

D. Injures, overworks, tortures, torments, abandons or cruelly beats or mutilates an animal; gives drugs to an animal with an intent to harm the animal; gives poison or alcohol to an animal; or exposes a poison with intent that it be taken by an animal. The owner or occupant of property is privileged to use reasonable force to eject a trespassing animal;

E. Deprives an animal that the person owns or possesses of necessary sustenance, necessary medical attention, proper shelter, protection from the weather or humanely clean conditions; or

F. Keeps or leaves a domestic animal on an uninhabited or barren island lying off the coast of the State during the month of December, January, February or March without providing necessary sustenance and proper shelter.

1-A. Animal cruelty. Except as provided in paragraphs A and B, a person is guilty of cruelty to animals if that person kills or attempts to kill a cat or dog.

A. A licensed veterinarian or a person certified under Title 17, section 1042 may kill a cat or dog according to the methods of euthanasia under Title 17, chapter 42, subchapter IV.]

B. A person who owns a cat or dog, or the owner's agent, may kill that owner's cat or dog by shooting with a firearm provided the following conditions are met.

(1) The shooting is performed by a person 18 years of age or older using a weapon and ammunition of suitable caliber and other characteristics to produce instantaneous death by a single shot.

(2) Death is instantaneous.

(3) Maximum precaution is taken to protect the general public, employees and other animals.

(4) Any restraint of the cat or dog during the shooting does not cause undue suffering to the cat or dog.

2. Affirmative defenses. It is an affirmative defense to this section that:

A. The conduct was performed by a licensed veterinarian or was a part of scientific research governed by accepted standards;

B. The conduct was designed to control or eliminate rodents, ants or other common pests on the defendant's own property; or

C. The conduct involved the use of live animals as bait or in the training of other animals in accordance with the laws of the Department of Inland Fisheries and Wildlife, Title 12, Part 10.

Evidence of proper care of any animal shall not be admissible in the defense of alleged cruelty to other animals.

TITLE 17. CRIMES

§ 1031. CRUELTY TO ANIMALS.

1. Cruelty to animals. Except as provided in subsection 1-A, a person, including an owner or the owner's agent, is guilty of cruelty to animals if that person:

A. Kills or attempts to kill any animal belonging to another person without the consent of the owner or without legal privilege;

B. Except for a licensed veterinarian or a person certified under section 1042, kills or attempts to kill an animal by a method that does not cause instantaneous death;

C. If that person is a licensed veterinarian or a person certified under section 1042, kills or attempts to kill an animal by a method that causes undue suffering. The commissioner shall adopt rules that define "undue suffering";

D. Injures, overworks, tortures, torments, abandons or cruelly beats or mutilates an animal; gives drugs to an animal with an intent to harm the animal; gives poison or alcohol to an animal; or exposes a poison with intent that it be taken by an animal. The owner or occupant of property is privileged to use reasonable force to eject a trespassing animal;

E. Deprives an animal that the person owns or possesses of necessary sustenance, necessary medical attention, proper shelter, protection from the weather or humanely clean conditions; or

F. Keeps or leaves a domestic animal on an uninhabited or barren island lying off the coast of the State during the month of December, January, February or March without providing necessary sustenance and proper shelter;

G. Hunts or sells for the purpose of hunting any animal, except as permitted pursuant to Title 7, Chapter 202-A and Title12, Part 10;

H. Injects, inserts or causes ingestion of any substance used solely to enhance the performance of an animal by altering the animal's detriment, including but not limited to excessive levels of sodium bicarbonate in equines used for competition;

I. Commits bestiality on an animal . . .;

J. Kills or tortures an animal to frighten or intimidate a person or forces a person to injure or kill an animal.

1-A. Animal cruelty. Except as provided in paragraphs A and B, a person is guilty of cruelty to animals if that person kills or attempts to kill a cat or dog.

A. A licensed veterinarian or a person certified under section 1042 may kill a cat or dog according to the methods of euthanasia under chapter 42, subchapter IV.

B. A person who owns a cat or dog, or the owner's agent, may kill that owner's cat or dog by shooting with a firearm provided the following conditions are met.

(1) The shooting is performed by a person 18 years of age or older using a weapon and ammunition of suitable caliber and other characteristics to produce instantaneous death by a single shot.

(2) Death is instantaneous.

(3) Maximum precaution is taken to protect the general public, employees and other animals.

(4) Any restraint of the cat or dog during the shooting does not cause undue suffering.

1-B. Aggravated cruelty to animals. A person is guilty of aggravated cruelty to animals if that person, in a manner manifesting a depraved indifference to animal life or suffering, intentionally, knowingly or recklessly:

A. Causes extreme physical pain to an animal;

B. Kills an animal; or

C. Physically tortures an animal.

2. Affirmative defense. It is an affirmative defense to prosecution under this section that:

A. The defendant's conduct conformed to accepted veterinary practice or was a part of scientific research governed by accepted standards;

B. The defendant's conduct or that of his agent was designed to control or eliminate rodents, ants or other common pests on his own property; or

C. The defendant's conduct involved the use of live animals as bait or in the training of other animals in accordance with the laws of the Department of Inland Fisheries and Wildlife, Title 12, Part 10.

Evidence of proper care of any animal shall not be admissible in the defense of alleged cruelty to other animals.

3. Penalty. Except as provided under Para A; cruelty to animals under subsection 1 or 1-A is a Class D crime. [Sections A-G omitted]

3-A. Penalty for aggravated cruelty to animals. Aggravated cruelty to animals under subsection 1-B is a Class C crime . . .

4. Criminal or civil prosecution. A person may be arrested or detained for the crime of cruelty to animals in accordance with the rules of criminal procedure. No person may be arrested or detained for the civil violation of cruelty to animals. The attorney for the State shall elect to charge a defendant with the crime of cruelty to animals under this section or the civil violation of cruelty to animals under Title 7, section 4011. In making this election, the attorney for the State shall consider the severity of the cruelty displayed, the number of animals involved, any prior convictions or adjudications of animal cruelty entered against the defendant and such other factors as may be relevant to a determination of whether criminal or civil sanctions will best accomplish the goals of the animal welfare laws in the particular case before the attorney for the State. The election and determination required by this subsection shall not be subject to judicial review. The factors involved in such election and determination are not elements of the criminal offense or civil violation of animal cruelty and are not subject to proof or disproof as prerequisites or conditions for conviction under this subsection or adjudication under Title 7, section 4011.

CODE OF MARYLAND

§ 59 CRUELTY TO ANIMALS A MISDEMEANOR.

(a) Cruelty.—Any person who

(1) overdrives, overloads, deprives of necessary sustenance, tortures, torments, or cruelly beats; or

(2) causes, procures or authorizes these acts; or

(3) having the charge or custody of an animal, either as owner or otherwise, inflicts unnecessary suffering or pain upon the animal, or unnecessarily fails to provide the animal with nutritious food in sufficient quantity, necessary veterinary care, proper drink, air, space, shelter or protection from the weather; or

(4) uses or permits to be used any bird, fowl, or cock for the purpose of fighting with any other animal, which is commonly known as cockfighting, is guilty of a misdemeanor punishable by a fine not exceeding $1,000 or by imprisonment not to exceed 90 days, or both.

(b) Mutilation.—Any person who

(1) intentionally mutilates or cruelly kills an animal, or causes, procures, or authorizes the cruel killing or intentional mutilation of an animal; or

(2) uses or permits a dog to be used in or arranges or conducts a dogfight, is guilty of a misdemeanor punishable by a fine not exceeding $5,000 or by imprisonment not to exceed 3 years, or both.

(c) Customary and normal veterinary and agricultural husbandry practices.—Customary and normal veterinary and agricultural husbandry practices including but not limited to dehorning, castration, docking tails, and limit feeding, are not covered by the provisions of this section. In the case of activities in which physical pain may unavoidably be caused to animals, such as food processing, pest elimination, animal training, and hunting, cruelty shall mean a failure to employ the most humane method reasonably available. It is the intention of the General Assembly that all animals, whether they be privately owned, strays, domesticated, feral, farm, corporately or institutionally owned, under private, local, State, or federally funded scientific or medical activities, or otherwise being situated in Maryland shall be protected from intentional cruelty, but that no person shall be liable for criminal prosecution for normal human activities to which the infliction of pain to an animal is purely incidental and unavoidable.

MASSACHUSETTS GENERAL LAWS

§ 77. CRUELTY TO ANIMALS.

Whoever overdrives, overloads, drives when overloaded, overworks, tortures, torments, deprives of necessary sustenance, cruelly beats, mutilates or kills an animal, or causes or procures an animal to be overdriven, overloaded, driven when overloaded, overworked, tortured, tormented, deprived of necessary sustenance, cruelly beaten, mutilated or killed; and whoever uses in a cruel or inhuman manner in a race, game, or contest, or in training therefor, as lure or bait a live animal, except an animal if used as lure or bait in fishing; and whoever, having the charge or custody of an animal, either as owner or otherwise, inflicts unnecessary cruelty upon it, or unnecessarily fails to provide it with proper food, drink, shelter, sanitary environment, or protection from the weather, and whoever, as owner, possessor, or person having the charge or custody of an animal, cruelly drives or works it when unfit for labor, or willfully abandons it, or carries it or causes it to be carried in or upon a vehicle, or otherwise, in an unnecessarily cruel or inhuman manner or in a way and manner which might endanger the animal carried thereon, or knowingly and willfully authorizes or permits it to be subjected to unnecessary torture, suffering or cruelty of any kind shall be punished by a fine of not more than one thousand dollars or by imprisonment for not more than one year, or both.

In addition to any other penalty provided by law, upon conviction for any violation of this section or of sections seventy-seven A, seventy-eight, seventy-eight A, seventy-nine A, seventy-nine B, eighty A, eighty B, eighty C, eighty D, eighty F, eighty-six, eighty-six A, eighty-six B or ninety-four the defendant may, after an appropriate hearing to determine the defendant's fitness for continued custody of the abused animal, be ordered to surrender or forfeit to the custody of any society, incorporated under the laws of the commonwealth for the prevention of cruelty to animals or for the care and protection of homeless or suffering animals, the animal whose treatment was the basis of such conviction.

MICHIGAN COMPILED LAWS

§ 750.50. DEFINITIONS; CRIMES AGAINST ANIMALS, CRUEL TREATMENT, ABANDONMENT, FAILURE TO PROVIDE ADEQUATE CARE; PENALTIES, MISDEMEANOR, PAYMENT OF COSTS; EXCEPTIONS.

(1) As used in this section and section 50b:

(a) "Adequate care" means the provision of sufficient food, water, shelter, sanitary conditions, and veterinary medical attention in order to maintain an animal in a state of good health.

(b) "Animal" means any vertebrate other than a human being.

(c) "Livestock" has the meaning attributed to the term in the animal industry act of 1987, Act No. 466 of the Public Acts of 1988, being sections 287.701 to 287.747 of the Michigan Compiled Laws.

(d) "Person" means an individual, partnership, limited liability company, corporation, association, governmental entity, or other legal entity.

(e) "Neglect" means to fail to sufficiently and properly care for an animal to the extent that the animal's health is jeopardized.

(f) "Sanitary conditions" means space free from health hazards including excessive animal waste, overcrowding of animals, or other conditions that endanger the animal's health. This definition does not include a condition resulting from a customary and reasonable practice pursuant to farming or animal husbandry.

(g) "Shelter" means adequate protection from the elements suitable for the age and species of animal and weather conditions to maintain the animal in a state of good health, including structures or natural features such as trees and topography.

(h) "State of good health" means freedom from disease and illness, and in a condition of proper body weight and temperature for the age and species of the animal, unless the animal is undergoing appropriate treatment.

(i) "Water" means potable water that is suitable for the age and species of animal, made regularly available unless otherwise directed by a veterinarian licensed to practice veterinary medicine.

(2) An owner, possessor, or person having the charge or custody of an animal shall not do any of the following:

(a) Fail to provide an animal with adequate care.

(b) Cruelly drive, work, or beat an animal, or cause an animal to be cruelly driven, worked, or beaten.

(c) Carry or cause to be carried in or upon a vehicle or otherwise any live animal having the feet or legs tied together, other than an animal being transported for medical care, or a horse whose feet are hobbled to protect the horse during transport or in any other cruel and inhumane manner.

(d) Carry or cause to be carried a live animal in or upon a vehicle or otherwise without providing a secure space, rack, car, crate, or cage, in which livestock may stand, and in which all other animals may stand, turn around, and lie down during transportation, or while awaiting slaughter. As used in this subdivision, for purposes of transportation of sled dogs, "stand" means sufficient vertical distance to allow the animal to stand without its shoulders touching the top of the crate or transportation vehicle.

(e) Abandon an animal or cause an animal to be abandoned, in any place, without making provisions for the animal's adequate care, unless premises are temporarily vacated for the protection of human life during a disaster. An animal that is lost by an owner or custodian while traveling, walking, hiking or hunting shall not be regarded as abandoned under this section when the owner or custodian has made a reasonable effort to locate the animal.

(f) Willfully or negligently allow any animal, including one who is aged, diseased, maimed, hopelessly sick, disabled, or nonambulatory to suffer unnecessary neglect, torture, or pain .

(3) A person who violates subsection (2) is guilty of a misdemeanor, punishable by imprisonment for not more than 93 days, or by a fine of not more than $1,000.00, or community service not to exceed 200 hours, or any combination of these penalties.

(4) As a part of the sentence for a violation of subsection (2), the court may order the defendant to pay the costs of the prosecution and the costs of the care, housing, and veterinary medical care for the animal, as applicable. If the court does not order a defendant to pay all of the applicable costs listed in this subsection, or orders only partial payment of these costs, the court shall state on the record the reason for that action.

(5) As a part of the sentence for a violation of subsection (2), the court may, as a condition of probation, order the defendant not to own or possess an animal for a period of time not to exceed the period of probation.

(6) A person who owns or possesses an animal in violation of an order issued under subsection (5) is subject to revocation of probation.

(7) This section does not prohibit the lawful use of an animal, including, but not limited to, the following:

(a) Fishing.

(b) Hunting, trapping, or wildlife control.

(c) Horse racing.

(d) The operation of a zoological park or aquarium.

(e) Pest or rodent control.

(f) Scientific research.

(g) Farming or animal husbandry.

MINNESOTA STATUTES

§ 343.21. OVERWORKING OR MISTREATING ANIMALS; PENALTY.

Subdivision 1. Torture. No person shall overdrive, overload, torture, cruelly beat, neglect, or unjustifiably injure, maim, mutilate, or kill any animal, or cruelly work any animal when it is unfit for labor, whether it belongs to that person or to another person.

Subdivision 2. Nourishment; shelter. No person shall deprive any animal over which the person has charge or control of necessary food, water, or shelter.

Subdivision 3. Enclosure. No person shall keep any cow or other animal in any enclosure without providing wholesome exercise and change of air.

Subdivision 4. Low feed. No person shall feed any cow on food which produces impure or unwholesome milk.

Subdivision 5. Abandonment. No person shall abandon any animal.

Subdivision 6. Temporary abandonment. No person shall allow any maimed, sick, infirm, or disabled animal to lie in any street, road, or other public place for more than three hours after receiving notice of the animal's condition.

Subdivision 7. Cruelty. No person shall willfully instigate or in any way further any act of cruelty to any animal or animals, or any act tending to produce cruelty to animals.

Subdivision 8. Caging. No person shall cage any animal for public display purposes unless the display cage is constructed of solid material on three sides to protect the caged animal from the elements and unless the horizontal dimension of each side of the cage is at least four times the length of the caged animal. The provisions of this subdivision do not apply to the Minnesota state agricultural society, the Minnesota state fair, or to the county agricultural societies, county fairs, to any agricultural display of caged animals by any political subdivision of the state of Minnesota, or to district, regional or national educational livestock or poultry exhibitions. The provisions of this subdivision do not apply to captive wildlife, the exhibition of which is regulated by section 97A.041.

Subdivision 9. Penalty. A person who fails to comply with any provision of this section is guilty of a misdemeanor. A person convicted of a second or subsequent violation of subdivision 1 or 7 within five years of a previous violation of subdivision 1 or 7 is guilty of a gross misdemeanor.

Subdivision 10. Restrictions. If a person is convicted of violating this section, the court shall require that pet or companion animals, as defined in section 346.36, subdivision 6, that have not been seized by a peace officer or agent and are in the custody of the person must be turned over to a peace officer or other appropriate officer or agent unless the court determines that the person is able and fit to provide adequately for an animal. If the evidence indicates lack of proper and reasonable care of an animal, the burden is on the person to affirmatively demonstrate by clear and convincing evidence that the person is able and fit to have custody of and provide adequately for an animal. The court may limit the person's further possession or custody of pet or companion animals, and may impose other conditions the court considers appropriate, including, but not limited to:

(1) imposing a probation period during which the person may not have ownership, custody, or control of a pet or companion animal;

(2) requiring periodic visits of the person by an animal control officer or agent appointed pursuant to section 343.01, subdivision 1;

(3) requiring performance by the person of community service in a humane facility; and

(4) requiring the person to receive behavioral counseling.

MISSISSIPPI CODE 1972

§ 97-41-1. LIVING CREATURES NOT TO BE CRUELLY TREATED.

If any person shall override, overdrive, overload, torture, torment, unjustifiably injure, deprive of necessary sustenance, food, or drink; or cruelly beat or needlessly mutilate; or cause or procure to be overridden, overdriven, overloaded, tortured, unjustifiably injured, tormented, or deprived of necessary sustenance, food or drink; or to be cruelly beaten or needlessly mutilated or killed, any living creature, every such offender shall, for every offense, be guilty of a misdemeanor.

MISSOURI STATUTES

§ 578.009. ANIMAL NEGLECT—PENALTIES.

1. A person is guilty of animal neglect when he has custody or ownership or both of an animal and fails to provide adequate care or adequate control, including, but not limited to, knowingly abandoning an animal in any place without making provisions for its adequate care which results in substantial harm to the animal.

2. Animal neglect is a class C misdemeanor upon first conviction and for each offense, punishable by imprisonment or a fine not to exceed five hundred dollars, or both, and a class B misdemeanor punishable by imprisonment or a fine not to exceed one thousand dollars, or both upon the second and all subsequent convictions. All fines and penalties for a first conviction of animal neglect may be waived by the court provided that the person found guilty of animal neglect shows that adequate, permanent remedies for the neglect have been made. Reasonable costs incurred for the care and maintenance of neglected animals may not be waived.

§ 578.012. ANIMAL ABUSE—PENALTIES.

1. A person is guilty of animal abuse when a person:

(1) Intentionally or purposely kills an animal in any manner not allowed by or expressly exempted from the provisions of sections 578.005 to 578.023 and 273.030, RSMo:

(2) Purposely or intentionally causes injury or suffering to an animal; or

(3) Having ownership or custody of an animal knowingly fails to provide adequate care or adequate control.

2. Animal abuse is a class A misdemeanor, unless the defendant has previously plead guilty to or has been found guilty of animal abuse or the suffering involved in subdivision (2) of subsection 1 of this section is the result of torture and mutilation consciously inflicted while the animal was alive, in which case it is a class D felony.

3. For purposes of this section, "animal" shall be defined as a mammal.

MONTANA CODE

§ 45-8-211. CRUELTY TO ANIMALS—EXCEPTION.

(1) A person commits the offense of cruelty to animals if without justification the person knowingly or negligently subjects an animal to mistreatment or neglect by:

(a) overworking, beating, tormenting, injuring, or killing any animal;

(b) carrying or confining any animal in a cruel manner;

(c) failing to provide an animal in the person's custody with:

(i) proper food, drink, or shelter; or

(ii) in cases of immediate, obvious, serious illness or injury, licensed veterinary or other appropriate medical care;

(d) abandoning any helpless animal or abandoning any animal on any highway, railroad, or in any other place where it may suffer injury, hunger, or exposure or become a public charge; or

(e) promoting, sponsoring, conducting, or participating in an animal race of more than 2 miles, except a sanctioned endurance race.

(2) (a)A person convicted of the offense of cruelty to animals shall be fined not to exceed $500 or be imprisoned in the county jail for a term not to exceed 6 months, or both. A person convicted of a second or subsequent offense of cruelty to animals shall be fined not to exceed $1,000 or be imprisoned in the state prison for a term not to exceed 2 years, or both.

(b) If the convicted person is the owner, the person may be required to forfeit to the county in which the person is convicted any animal affected. This provision does not affect the interest of any secured party or other person who has not participated in the offense.

(3) In addition to the sentence provided in subsection (2), the court may:

(a) require the defendant to pay all reasonable costs incurred in providing necessary veterinary attention and treatment for any animal affected; and

(b) prohibit or limit the defendant's ownership, possession, or custody of animals, as the court believes appropriate during the term of the sentence.

(4) Nothing in this section prohibits:

(a) a person from humanely destroying an animal for just cause; or

(b) the use of commonly accepted agricultural and livestock practices on livestock.

NEBRASKA REVISED STATUTES OF 1943

§ 28-1009. CRUELTY TO ANIMALS; HARASSMENT OF A POLICE ANIMAL; PENALTY.

(1) A person commits cruelty to animals if he or she abandons, cruelly mistreats, or cruelly neglects an animal. Cruelty to animals is a Class II misdemeanor for the first offense and a Class I misdemeanor for any subsequent offense.

(2) A person commits harassment of a police animal if he or she knowingly and intentionally teases or harasses a police animal in order to distract, agitate, or harm the police animal for the purpose of preventing such animal from performing its legitimate official duties. Harassment of a police animal is a Class IV misdemeanor unless the harassment is the proximate cause of the death of the police animal, in which case it is a Class IV felony.

NEW HAMPSHIRE STATUTES

§ 644:8. CRUELTY TO ANIMALS.

I. In this section, "cruelty" shall include, but not be limited to, acts or omissions injurious or detrimental to the health, safety or welfare of any animal, including the abandoning of any animal without proper provision for its care, sustenance, protection or shelter.

II. In this section, "animal" means a domestic animal, a household pet or a wild animal in captivity.

III. A person is guilty of a misdemeanor for a first offense, and of a class B felony for a second or subsequent offense, who:

(a) Without lawful authority negligently deprives or causes to be deprived any animal in his possession or custody necessary care, sustenance or shelter;

(b) Negligently beats, cruelly whips, tortures, mutilates or in any other manner mistreats or causes to be mistreated any animal;

(c) Negligently overdrives, overworks, drives when overloaded, or otherwise abuses or misuses any animal intended for or used for labor;

(d) Negligently transports any animal in his possession or custody in a manner injurious to the health, safety or physical well-being of such animal;

(e) Negligently abandons any animal previously in his possession or custody by causing such animal to be left without supervision or adequate provision for its care, sustenance or shelter; or

(f) Otherwise negligently permits or causes any animal in his possession or custody to be subjected to cruelty, inhumane treatment or unnecessary suffering of any kind.

III-a. A person is guilty of a class B felony who purposely beats, cruelly whips, tortures, or mutilates any animal or causes any animal to be beaten, cruelly whipped, tortured, or mutilated.

IV. In addition to being guilty of crimes as provided in paragraphs III and III-a, any person charged with cruelty to animals may have his animal confiscated by the arresting officer and, upon said person's conviction of cruelty to animals, the court may dispose of said animal in any manner it decides. The costs, if any, incurred in boarding and treating the animal, pending disposition of the case, and in disposing of the animal, upon a conviction of said person for cruelty to animals, shall be borne by the person so convicted.

IV-a. (a) Except as provided in subparagraph (b) any appropriate law enforcement officer, animal control officer, or officer of a duly licensed humane society may take into temporary protective custody any animal when there is probable cause to believe that it has been abused or neglected in violation of paragraphs III or III-a when there is a clear and imminent danger to the animal's health or life and there is not sufficient time to obtain a court order. Such officer shall leave a written notice indicating the type and number of animals taken into protective custody, the name of the officer, the time and date taken, the reason it was taken, the procedure to have the animal returned and any other relevant information. Such notice shall be left at the location where the animal was taken into custody. The officer shall provide for proper care and housing of any animal taken into protective custody under this paragraph. If, after 7 days, the animal has not been returned or claimed, the officer shall petition the municipal or district court seeking either permanent custody or a one-week extension of custody or shall file charges under this section. If a week's extension is granted by the court and after a period of 14 days the animal remains unclaimed, the title and custody of the animal shall rest with the officer on behalf of his department or society. The department or society may dispose of the animal in any lawful and humane manner as if it were the rightful owner. If after 14 days the officer or his department determines that charges should be filed under this section, he shall petition the court.

(b) For purposes of subparagraph (a) the appropriate law enforcement officer for domestic animals, as defined in RSA 436:1, II, or livestock, as defined in RSA 427:38, III, shall be a veterinarian licensed under RSA 332-B or the state veterinarian.

V. A veterinarian licensed to practice in the state shall be held harmless from either criminal or civil liability for any decisions made for services rendered under the provisions of this section or RSA 435:11-16. Such a veterinarian is, therefore, under this paragraph, protected from a lawsuit for his part in an investigation of cruelty to animals.

NEW JERSEY STATUTES

§ 4:22-17. CRUELTY IN GENERAL; DISORDERLY PERSONS OFFENSE.

A person who shall:

a. Overdrive, overload, drive when overloaded, overwork, torture, torment, deprive of necessary sustenance, unnecessarily or cruelly beat or otherwise abuse, or needlessly mutilate or kill, a living animal or creature;

b. Cause or procure any of such acts to be done; or

c. Inflict unnecessary cruelty upon a living animal or creature of which he has charge either as owner or otherwise, or unnecessarily fail to provide it with proper food, drink, shelter or protection from the weather—

Shall be guilty of a disorderly persons offense.

§ 4:22-18. CARRYING ANIMAL IN CRUEL MANNER; DISORDERLY PERSONS OFFENSE.

A person who shall carry, or cause to be carried, a living animal or creature in or upon a vehicle or otherwise, in a cruel or inhumane manner, shall be guilty of a disorderly persons offense.

§ 4:22-26. ACTS CONSTITUTING CRUELTY IN GENERAL; PENALTY.

A person who shall:

a. Overdrive, overload, drive when overloaded, overwork, torture, torment, deprive of necessary sustenance, or cruelly beat or otherwise abuse or needlessly mutilate or kill a living animal or creature;

b. Cause or procure to be done by his agent, servant, employee or otherwise an act enumerated in subsection "a." of this section;

c. Inflict unnecessary cruelty upon a living animal or creature of which he has charge or custody either as owner or otherwise, or unnecessarily fail to provide it with proper food, drink, shelter or protection from the weather;

d. Receive or offer for sale a horse which by reason of disability, disease or lameness, or any other cause, could not be worked without violating the provisions of this article;

e. Keep, use, be connected with or interested in the management of, or receive money or other consideration for the admission of a person to, a place kept or used for the purpose of fighting or baiting a living animal or creature;

f. Be present and witness, pay admission to, encourage, aid or assist in an activity enumerated in subsection "e." of this section;

g. Permit or suffer a place owned or controlled by him to be used as provided in subsection "e." of this section;

h. Carry, or cause to be carried, a living animal or creature in or upon a vehicle or otherwise, in a cruel or inhuman manner;

i. Use a dog or dogs for the purpose of drawing or helping to draw a vehicle for business purposes;

j. Impound or confine or cause to be impounded or confined in a pound or other place a living animal or creature, and shall fail to supply it during such confinement with a sufficient quantity of good and wholesome food and water;

k. Abandon a maimed, sick, infirm or disabled animal or creature to die in a public place;

l. Willfully sell, or offer to sell, use, expose, or cause or permit to be sold or offered for sale, used or exposed, a horse or other animal having the disease known as glanders or farcy, or other contagious or infectious disease dangerous to the health or life of human beings or animals, or who shall, when any such disease is beyond recovery, refuse, upon demand, to deprive the animal of life;

m. Own, operate, manage or conduct a roadside stand or market for the sale of merchandise along a public street or highway; or a shopping mall, or a part of the premises thereof; and keep a living animal or creature confined, or allowed to roam in an area whether or not the area is enclosed, on these premises as an exhibit; except that this subsection shall not be applicable to: a pet shop licensed pursuant to P.L.1941, c. 151 (C. 4:19-15.1 et seq.); a person who keeps an animal, in a humane manner, for the purpose of the protection of the premises; or a recognized breeders' association, a 4-H club, an educational agricultural program, an equestrian team, a humane society or other similar charitable or nonprofit organization conducting an exhibition, show or performance;

n. Keep or exhibit a wild animal at a roadside stand or market located along a public street or highway of this State; a gasoline station; or a shopping mall, or a part of the premises thereof;

o. Sell, offer for sale, barter or give away or display live baby chicks, ducklings or other fowl or rabbits, turtles or chameleons which have been dyed or artificially colored or otherwise treated so as to impart to them an artificial color;

p. Use any animal, reptile, or fowl for the purpose of soliciting any alms, collections, contributions, subscriptions, donations, or payment of money except in connection with exhibitions, shows or performances conducted in a bona fide manner by recognized breeders' associations, 4-H clubs or other similar bona fide organizations;

q. Sell or offer for sale, barter, or give away living rabbits, turtles, baby chicks, ducklings or other fowl under two months of age, for use as household or domestic pets;

r. Sell, offer for sale, barter or give away living baby chicks, ducklings or other fowl, or rabbits, turtles or chameleons under two months of age for any purpose not prohibited by subsection q. of this section and who shall fail to provide proper facilities for the care of such animals;

s. Artificially mark sheep or cattle, or cause them to be marked, by cropping or cutting off both ears, cropping or cutting either ear more than one inch from the tip end thereof, or half cropping or cutting both ears or either ear more than one inch from the tip end thereof, or who shall have or keep in his possession sheep or cattle, which he claims to own, marked contrary to this subsection unless they were bought in market or of a stranger;

t. Abandon a domesticated animal;

u. For amusement or gain, cause, allow, or permit the fighting or baiting of a living animal or creature;

v. Own, possess, keep, train, promote, purchase, or knowingly sell a living animal or creature for the purpose of fighting or baiting that animal or creature; or

w. Gamble on the outcome of a fight involving a living animal or creature—

Shall forfeit and pay a sum not to exceed $250.00, except in the case of a violation of subsection "t." a mandatory sum of $500, and $1,000 if the violation occurs on or near a roadway, to be sued for and recovered, with costs, in a civil action by any person in the name of the New Jersey Society for the Prevention of Cruelty to Animals.

NEW MEXICO STATUTES 1978

§ 30-18-1 CRUELTY TO ANIMALS.

Cruelty to animals consists of:

A. torturing, tormenting, depriving of necessary sustenance, cruelly beating, mutilating, cruelly killing or overdriving any animal;

B. unnecessarily failing to provide any animal with proper food or drink; or

C. cruelly driving or working any animal when such animal is unfit for labor.

Whoever commits cruelty to animals is guilty of a petty misdemeanor.

CONSOLIDATED LAWS OF NEW YORK

§ 353. OVERDRIVING, TORTURING AND INJURING ANIMALS; FAILURE TO PROVIDE PROPER SUSTENANCE.

A person who overdrives, overloads, tortures or cruelly beats or unjustifiably injures, maims, mutilates or kills any animal, whether wild or tame, and whether belonging to himself or to another, or deprives any animal of necessary sustenance, food or drink, or neglects or refuses to furnish it such sustenance or drink, or causes, procures or permits any animal to be overdriven, overloaded, tortured, cruelly beaten, or unjustifiably injured, maimed, mutilated or killed, or to be deprived of necessary food or drink, or who wilfully sets on foot, instigates, engages in, or in any way furthers any act of cruelty to any animal, or any act tending to produce such cruelty, is guilty of a misdemeanor, punishable by imprisonment for not more than one year, or by a fine of not more than one thousand dollars, or by both.

Nothing herein contained shall be construed to prohibit or interfere with any properly conducted scientific tests, experiments or investigations, involving the use of living animals, performed or conducted in laboratories or institutions, which are approved for these purposes by the state commissioner of health. The state commissioner of health shall prescribe the rules under which such approvals shall be granted, including therein standards regarding the care and treatment of any such animals. Such rules shall be published and copies thereof conspicuously posted in each such laboratory or institution. The state commissioner of health or his duly authorized representative shall have the power to inspect such laboratories or institutions to insure compliance with such rules and standards. Each such approval may be revoked at any time for failure to comply with such rules and in any case the approval shall be limited to a period not exceeding one year.

NEVADA REVISED STATUTES

§ 574.100. OVERDRIVING, TORTURING, INJURING OR ABANDONING ANIMALS; FAILURE TO PROVIDE PROPER SUSTENANCE; PENALTY.

Except in any case involving a willful or malicious act for which a greater penalty is provided by NRS 206.150, a person who:

1. Overdrives, overloads, tortures or cruelly beats or unjustifiably injures, maims, mutilates or kills any animal, whether belonging to himself or to another;

2. Deprives any animal of necessary sustenance, food or drink, or neglects or refuses to furnish it such sustenance or drink;

3. Causes, procures or permits any animal to be overdriven, overloaded, tortured, cruelly beaten, or unjustifiably injured, maimed, mutilated or killed, or to be deprived of necessary food or drink;

4. Willfully sets on foot, instigates, engages in, or in any way furthers an act of cruelty to any animal, or any act tending to produce such cruelty; or

5. Abandons an animal in circumstances other than those prohibited in NRS 574.110, is guilty of a misdemeanor.

GENERAL STATUTES OF NORTH CAROLINA

§ 14-360 CRUELTY TO ANIMALS; CONSTRUCTION OF SECTION.

If any person shall willfully overdrive, overload, wound, injure, torture, torment, deprive of necessary sustenance, cruelly beat, needlessly mutilate or kill or cause or procure to be overdriven, overloaded, wounded, injured, tortured, tormented, deprived of necessary sustenance, cruelly beaten, needlessly mutilated or killed as aforesaid, any useful beast, fowl or animal, every such offender shall for every such offense be guilty of a Class 1 misdemeanor. In this section, and in every law which may be enacted relating to animals, the words "animal" and "dumb animal" shall be held to include every living creature; the words "torture," "torment" or "cruelty" shall be held to include every act, omission or neglect whereby unjustifiable physical pain, suffering or death is caused or permitted. Such terms shall not be construed to prohibit the lawful taking of animals under the jurisdiction and regulation of the Wildlife Resources Commission.

NORTH DAKOTA CENTURY CODE

§ 36-21.1-02 OVERWORKING OR MISTREATING ANIMALS.

1. No person may overdrive, overload, torture, cruelly beat, neglect, or unjustifiably injure, maim, mutilate, or kill any animal, or cruelly work any animal when unfit for labor.

2. No person may deprive any animal over which he has charge or control of necessary food, water, or shelter.

3. No person may keep any animal in any enclosure without exercise and wholesome change of air.

4. No person may abandon any animal.

5. No person may allow any maimed, sick, infirm, or disabled animal of which he is the owner, or of which he has custody, to lie in any street, road, or other public place for more than three hours after notice.

6. No person may willfully instigate, or in any way further, any act of cruelty to any animal or animals, or any act tending to produce such cruelty.

7. No person may cage any animal for public display purposes unless the display cage is constructed of solid material on three sides to protect the caged animal from the elements, and unless the horizontal dimension of each side of the cage is at least four times the length of the caged animal. The provisions of this subsection do not apply to the North Dakota state fair association, to agricultural fair associations, to any agricultural display of caged animals by any political subdivision, or to district, regional, or national educational livestock or poultry exhibitions. Zoos which have been approved by the health district or the governing body of the political subdivision which has jurisdiction over the zoos are exempt from the provisions of this subsection.

8. Repealed by S.L. 1975, ch. 106, s 397.

OHIO REVISED CODE

§ 959.13 CRUELTY TO ANIMALS.

(A) No person shall:

(1) Torture an animal, deprive one of necessary sustenance, unnecessarily or cruelly beat, needlessly mutilate or kill, or impound or confine an animal without supplying it during such confinement with a sufficient quantity of good wholesome food and water;

(2) Impound or confine an animal without affording it, during such confinement, access to shelter from wind, rain, snow, or excessive direct sunlight if it can reasonably be expected that the animal would otherwise become sick or in some other way suffer. Division (A)(2) of this section does not apply to animals impounded or confined prior to slaughter. For the purpose of this section, shelter means a man-made enclosure, windbreak, sunshade, or natural windbreak or sunshade that is developed from the earth's contour, tree development, or vegetation.

(3) Carry or convey an animal in a cruel or inhuman manner;

(4) Keep animals other than cattle, poultry or fowl, swine, sheep, or goats in an enclosure without wholesome exercise and change of air, nor or [sic] feed cows on food that produces impure or unwholesome milk;

(5) Detain livestock in railroad cars or compartments longer than twenty-eight hours after they are so placed without supplying them with necessary food, water, and attention, nor permit such stock to be so crowded as to overlie, crush, wound, or kill each other.

(B) Upon the written request of the owner or person in custody of any particular shipment of livestock, which written request shall be separate and apart from any printed bill of lading or other railroad form, the length of time in which such livestock may be detained in any cars or compartments without food, water, and attention, may be extended to thirty-six hours without penalty therefor. This section does not prevent the dehorning of cattle.

(C) All fines collected for violations of this section shall be paid to the society or association for the prevention of cruelty to animals, if there be such in the county, township, or municipal corporation where such violation occurred.

OKLAHOMA STATUTES

§ 1685. CRUELTY TO ANIMALS.

Any person who shall willfully or maliciously overdrive, overload, torture, destroy or kill, or cruelly beat or injure, maim or mutilate, any animal in subjugation or captivity, whether wild or tame, and whether belonging to himself or to another, or deprive any such animal of necessary food, drink or shelter; or who shall cause, procure or permit any such animal to be so overdriven, overloaded, tortured, destroyed or killed, or cruelly beaten or injured, maimed or mutilated, or deprived of necessary food, drink or shelter; or who shall willfully set on foot, instigate, engage in, or in any way further any act of cruelty to any animal, or any act tending to produce such cruelty, shall be punished by imprisonment in the penitentiary not exceeding five (5) years, or by imprisonment in the county jail not exceeding one (1) year, or by fine not exceeding Five Hundred Dollars ($500.00); and any officer finding an animal so maltreated or abused shall cause the same to be taken care of, and the charges therefor shall be a lien upon such animal, to be collected thereon as upon a pledge or a lien.

1995 OREGON REVISED STATUTES

§ 167.315. ANIMAL ABUSE IN THE SECOND DEGREE.

(1) A person commits the crime of animal abuse in the second degree if, except as otherwise authorized by law, the person intentionally, knowingly or recklessly causes physical injury to an animal.

(2) Any practice of good animal husbandry is not a violation of this section.

(3) Animal abuse in the second degree is a Class B misdemeanor.

§ 167.320. ANIMAL ABUSE IN THE FIRST DEGREE.

(1) A person commits the crime of animal abuse in the first degree if, except as otherwise authorized by law, the person intentionally, knowingly or recklessly:

(a) Causes serious physical injury to an animal; or

(b) Cruelly causes the death of an animal.

(2) Any practice of good animal husbandry is not a violation of this section.

(3) Animal abuse in the first degree is a Class A misdemeanor.

§ 167.322. AGGRAVATED ANIMAL ABUSE IN THE FIRST DEGREE.

(1) A person commits the crime of aggravated animal abuse in the first degree if the person:

(a) Maliciously kills an animal; or

(b) Intentionally or knowingly tortures an animal.

(2) Aggravated animal abuse in the first degree is a Class C felony.

(3) As used in this section, "maliciously" means intentionally acting with a depravity of mind and reckless and wanton disregard of life.

§ 167.325. ANIMAL NEGLECT IN THE SECOND DEGREE.

(1) A person commits the crime of animal neglect in the second degree if, except as otherwise authorized by law, the person intentionally, knowingly, recklessly or with criminal negligence fails to provide minimum care for an animal in such person's custody or control.

(2) Animal neglect in the second degree is a Class B misdemeanor.

§ 167.330. ANIMAL NEGLECT IN THE FIRST DEGREE.

(1) A person commits the crime of animal neglect in the first degree if, except as otherwise authorized by law, the person intentionally, knowingly, recklessly or with criminal negligence:

(a) Fails to provide minimum care for an animal in such person's custody or control; and

(b) Such failure to provide care results in serious physical injury or death to the animal.

(2) Animal neglect in the first degree is a Class A misdemeanor.

§ 167.335. EXEMPTION FROM ORS 167.315 TO 167.330.

Unless gross negligence can be shown, the provisions of ORS 167.315 to 167.330 shall not apply to:

(1) The treatment of livestock being transported by owner or common carrier;

(2) Animals involved in rodeos or similar exhibitions;

(3) Commercially grown poultry;

(4) Animals subject to good animal husbandry practices;

(5) The killing of livestock according to the provisions of ORS 603.065;

(6) Animals subject to good veterinary practices as described in ORS 686.030;

(7) Lawful fishing, hunting and trapping activities;

(8) Wildlife management practices under color of law; and

(9) Lawful scientific or agricultural research or teaching that involves the use of animals.

§ 167.340. ANIMAL ABANDONMENT.

(1) A person commits the crime of animal abandonment if the person intentionally, knowingly, recklessly or with criminal negligence leaves a domesticated animal at a location without providing for the animal's continued care.

(2) It is no defense to the crime defined in subsection (1) of this section that the defendant abandoned the animal at or near an animal shelter, veterinary clinic or other place of shelter if the defendant did not make reasonable arrangements for the care of the animal.

(3) Animal abandonment is a Class C misdemeanor.

PENNSYLVANIA STATUTES AND CONSOLIDATED STATUTES

§ 5511. CRUELTY TO ANIMALS.

(a) Killing, maiming or poisoning domestic animals or zoo animals, etc.—

(1) A person commits a misdemeanor of the second degree if he willfully and maliciously:

(i) Kills, maims or disfigures any domestic animal of another person or any domestic fowl of another person.

(ii) Administers poison to or exposes any poisonous substance with the intent to administer such poison to any domestic animal of another person or domestic fowl of another person.

(iii) Harasses, annoys, injures, attempts to injure, molests or interferes with a dog guide for an individual who is blind, a hearing dog for an individual who is deaf or audibly impaired or a service dog for an individual who is physically limited.

Any person convicted of violating the provisions of this paragraph shall be sentenced to pay a fine of not less than $500.

(2) A person commits a felony of the third degree if he willfully and maliciously:

(i) Kills, maims or disfigures any zoo animal in captivity.

(ii) Administers poison to or exposes any poisonous substance with the intent to administer such poison to any zoo animal in captivity.

(2.1) (i) A person commits a misdemeanor of the second degree if he willfully and maliciously:

(A) Kills, maims, mutilates, tortures or disfigures any dog or cat, whether belonging to himself or otherwise.

(B) Administers poison to or exposes any poisonous substance with the intent to administer such poison to any dog or cat, whether belonging to himself or otherwise.

(ii) Any person convicted of violating the provisions of this paragraph shall be sentenced to pay a fine of not less than $1,000 or to imprisonment for not more than two years, or both. A subsequent conviction under this paragraph shall be a felony of the third degree. This paragraph shall apply to dogs and cats only.

(iii) The killing of a dog or cat by the owner of that animal is not malicious if it is accomplished in accordance with the act of December 22, 1983 (P.L. 303, No. 83), referred to as the Animal Destruction Method Authorization Law.

(3) This subsection shall not apply to:

(i) the killing of any animal taken or found in the act of actually destroying any domestic animal or domestic fowl;

(ii) the killing of any animal or fowl pursuant to the act of June 3, 1937 (P.L. 1225, No. 316), known as The Game Law, or Pa.C.S. ss 2384 (relating to declaring dogs public nuisances) and 2385 (relating to destruction of dogs declared public nuisances), or the regulations promulgated thereunder; or

(iii) such reasonable activity as may be undertaken in connection with vermin control or pest control.

(b) Regulating certain actions concerning fowl or rabbits.—A person commits a summary offense if he sells, offers for sale, barters, or gives away baby chickens, ducklings, or other fowl, under one month of age, or rabbits under two months of age, as pets, toys, premiums or novelties or if he colors, dyes, stains or otherwise changes the natural color of baby chickens, ducklings or other fowl, or rabbits or if he brings or transports the same into this Commonwealth. This section shall not be construed to prohibit the sale or display of such baby chickens, ducklings, or other fowl, or such rabbits, in proper facilities by persons engaged in the business of selling them for purposes of commercial breeding and raising.

(c) Cruelty to animals.—A person commits a summary offense if he wantonly or cruelly illtreats, overloads, beats, otherwise abuses any animal, or neglects any animal as to which he has a duty of care, whether belonging to himself or otherwise, or abandons any animal, or deprives any animal of necessary sustenance, drink, shelter or veterinary care, or access to clean and sanitary shelter which will protect the animal against inclement weather and preserve the animal's body heat and keep it dry. This subsection shall not apply to activity undertaken in normal agricultural operation.

(d) Selling or using disabled horse.—A person commits a summary offense if he offers for sale or sells any horse, which by reason of debility, disease or lameness, or for other cause, could not be worked or used without violating the laws against cruelty to animals, or leads, rides, drives or transports any such horse for any purpose, except that of conveying the horse to the nearest available appropriate facility for its humane keeping or destruction or for medical or surgical treatment.

(e) Transporting animals in cruel manner.—A person commits a summary offense if he carries, or causes, or allows to be carried in or upon any cart, or other vehicle whatsoever, any animal in a cruel or inhumane manner. The person taking him into custody may take charge of the animal and of any such vehicle and its contents, and deposit the same in some safe place of custody, and any necessary expenses which may be incurred for taking charge of and keeping the same, and sustaining any such animal, shall be a lien thereon, to be paid before the same can lawfully be recovered, or the said expenses or any part thereof remaining unpaid may be recovered by the person incurring the same from the owner of said creature in any action therefor.

For the purposes of this section, it shall not be deemed cruel or inhumane to transport live poultry in crates so long as not more than 15 pounds of live poultry are allocated to each cubic foot of space in the crate.

(f) Hours of labor of animals.—A person commits a summary offense if he leads, drives, rides or works or causes or permits any other person to lead, drive, ride or work any horse, mare, mule, ox, or any other animal, whether belonging to himself or in his possession or control, for more than 15 hours in any 24 hour period, or more than 90 hours in any one week.

Nothing in this subsection contained shall be construed to warrant any persons leading, driving, riding or walking any animal a less period than

15 hours, when so doing shall in any way violate the laws against cruelty to animals.

(g) Cruelty to cow to enhance appearance of udder.—A person commits a summary offense if he kneads or beats or pads the udder of any cow, or willfully allows it to go unmilked for a period of 24 hours or more, for the purpose of enhancing the appearance or size of the udder of said cow, or by a muzzle or any other device prevents its calf, if less than six weeks old, from obtaining nourishment, and thereby relieving the udder of said cow, for a period of 24 hours.

(h) Cropping ears of dog; prima facie evidence of violation.—A person commits a summary offense if he crops or cuts off, or causes or procures to be cropped or cut off, the whole, or part of the ear or ears of a dog or shows or exhibits or procures the showing or exhibition of any dog whose ear is or ears are cropped or cut off, in whole or in part, unless the person showing such dog has in his possession either a certificate of veterinarian stating that such cropping was done by the veterinarian or a certificate of registration from a county treasurer, showing that such dog was cut or cropped before this section became effective.

The provisions of this section shall not prevent a veterinarian from cutting or cropping the whole or part of the ear or ears of a dog when such dog is anesthetized, and shall not prevent any person from causing or procuring such cutting or cropping of a dog's ear or ears by a veterinarian.

The possession by any person of a dog with an ear or ears cut off or cropped and with the wound resulting therefrom unhealed, or any such dog being found in the charge or custody of any person or confined upon the premises owned by or under the control of any person, shall be prima facie evidence of a violation of this subsection by such person except as provided for in this subsection.

The owner of any dog whose ear or ears have been cut off or cropped before this section became effective may, if a resident of this Commonwealth, register such dog with the treasurer of the county where he resides, and if a nonresident of this Commonwealth, with the treasurer of any county of this Commonwealth, by certifying, under oath, that the ear or ears of such dog were cut or cropped before this section became effective, and the payment of a fee of $1 into the county treasury. The said treasurer shall thereupon issue to such person a certificate showing such dog to be a lawfully cropped dog.

(h.1) Animal fighting.—A person commits a felony of the third degree if he:

(1) for amusement or gain, causes, allows or permits any animal to engage in animal fighting;

(2) receives compensation for the admission of another person to any place kept or used for animal fighting;

(3) owns, possesses, keeps, trains, promotes, purchases or knowingly sells any animal for animal fighting;

(4) in any way knowingly encourages, aids or assists therein;

(5) wagers on the outcome of an animal fight;

(6) pays for admission to an animal fight or attends an animal fight as a spectator; or

(7) knowingly permits any place under his control or possession to be kept or used for animal fighting.

This subsection shall not apply to activity undertaken in a normal agricultural operation.

(i) Power to initiate criminal proceedings.—An agent of any society or association for the prevention of cruelty to animals, incorporated under the laws of the Commonwealth, shall have the same powers to initiate criminal proceedings provided for police officers by the Pennsylvania Rules of Criminal Procedure. An agent of any society or association for the prevention of cruelty to animals, incorporated under the laws of this Commonwealth, shall have standing to request any court of competent jurisdiction to enjoin any violation of this section.

(j) Seizure of animals kept or used for animal fighting.—Any police officer or agent of a society or association for the prevention of cruelty to animals incorporated under the laws of this Commonwealth, shall have power to seize any animal kept, used, or intended to be used for animal fighting. When the seizure is made, the animal or animals so seized shall not be deemed absolutely forfeited, but shall be held by the officer or agent seizing the same until a conviction of some person is first obtained for a violation of subsection (h.1). The officer or agent making such seizure shall make due return to the issuing authority, of the number and kind of animals or creatures so seized by him. Where an animal is thus seized, the police officer or agent is authorized to provide such care as is reasonably necessary, and where any animal thus seized is found to be disabled, injured or diseased beyond reasonable hope of recovery, the police officer or agent is authorized to provide for the humane destruction of the animal. In addition to any other penalty provided by law, the authority imposing sentence upon a conviction for any violation of subsection (h.1) shall order the forfeiture or surrender of any abused, neglected or deprived animal of the defendant to any society or association for the prevention of cruelty to animals duly incorporated under the laws of this Commonwealth and shall require that the owner pay the cost of the keeping, care and destruction of the animal.

(k) Killing homing pigeons.—A person commits a summary offense if he shoots, maims or kills any antwerp or homing pigeon, either while on flight or at rest, or detains or entraps any such pigeon which carries the name of its owner.

(l) Search warrants.—Where a violation of this section is alleged, any issuing authority may, in compliance with the applicable provisions of the Pennsylvania Rules of Criminal Procedure, issue to any police officer or any agent of any society or association for the prevention of cruelty to animals duly incorporated under the laws of this Commonwealth a search warrant authorizing the search of any building or any enclosure in which any violation of this section is occurring or has occurred, and authorizing the seizure of evidence of the violation including, but not limited to, the animals which were the subject of the violation. Where an animal thus seized is found to be neglected or starving, the police officer or agent is authorized to provide such care as is reasonably necessary, and where any animal thus seized is found to be disabled, injured or diseased beyond reasonable hope of recovery, the police officer or agent is authorized to provide for the humane destruction of the animal. The cost of the keeping, care and destruction of the animal shall be paid by the owner thereof and claims for the costs shall constitute a lien upon the animal. In addition to any other penalty provided by law, the authority imposing sentence upon a conviction for any violation of this section may require that the owner pay the cost of the keeping, care and destruction of the animal. No search warrant shall be issued based upon an alleged violation of this section which authorizes any police officer or agent or other person to enter upon or search premises where scientific research work is being conducted by, or under the supervision of, graduates of duly accredited scientific schools or where biological products are being produced for the care or prevention of disease.

(m) Forfeiture.—In addition to any other penalty provided by law, the authority imposing sentence upon a conviction for any violation of this section may order the forfeiture or surrender of any abused, neglected or deprived animal of the defendant to any society or association for the prevention of cruelty to animals duly incorporated under the laws of this Commonwealth.

(m.1) Fine for summary offense.—In addition to any other penalty provided by law, a person convicted of a summary offense under this section shall pay a fine of not less than $50 nor more than $750 or to imprisonment for not more than 90 days, or both.

(n) Skinning of and selling or buying pelts of dogs and cats.—A person commits a summary offense if he skins a dog or cat or offers for sale or exchange or offers to buy or exchange the pelt or pelts of any dog or cat.

(o) Representation of humane society by attorney.—Upon prior authorization and approval by the district attorney of the county in which the proceeding is held, an association or agent may be represented in any proceeding under this section by any attorney admitted to practice before the Supreme Court of Pennsylvania and in good standing. Attorney's fees shall be borne by the humane society or association which is represented.

(o.1) Construction of section.—The provisions of this section shall not supersede the act of December 7, 1982 (P.L. 784, No. 225), known as the Dog Law.

(p) Applicability of section.—This section shall not apply to, interfere with or hinder any activity which is authorized or permitted pursuant to the act of June 3, 1937 (P.L.1225, No. 316), known as The Game Law or Title 34 (relating to game).

(q) Definitions.—As used in this section, the following words and phrases shall have the meanings given to them in this subsection:

"Animal fighting." Fighting or baiting any bull, bear, dog, cock or other creature.

"Audibly impaired." The inability to hear air conduction thresholds at an average of 40 decibels or greater in the better ear.

"Blind." Having a visual acuity of 20/200 or less in the better eye with correction or having a limitation of the field of vision such that the widest diameter of the visual field subtends an angular distance not greater than 20 degrees.

"Deaf." Totally impaired hearing or hearing with or without amplification which is so seriously impaired that the primary means of receiving spoken language is through other sensory input, including, but not limited to, lip reading, sign language, finger spelling or reading.

"Domestic animal." Any dog, cat, equine animal, bovine animal, sheep, goat or porcine animal.

"Domestic fowl." Any avis raised for food, hobby or sport.

"Normal agricultural operation." Normal activities, practices and procedures that farmers adopt, use or engage in year after year in the production and preparation for market of poultry, livestock and their products in the production and harvesting of agricultural, agronomic, horticultural, silvicultural and aquicultural crops and commodities.

"Physically limited." Having limited ambulation, including, but not limited to, a temporary or permanent impairment or condition that causes an individual to use a wheelchair or walk with difficulty or insecurity, affects sight or hearing to the extent that an individual is insecure or exposed to danger, causes faulty coordination or reduces mobility, flexibility, coordination or perceptiveness.

"Zoo animal." Any member of the class of mammalia, aves, amphibia or reptilia which is kept in a confined area by a public body or private individual for purposes of observation by the general public.

GENERAL LAWS OF RHODE ISLAND 1956

§ 4-1-2 OVERWORK, MISTREATMENT, OR FAILURE TO FEED ANIMALS—"SHELTER" DEFINED.

(A) Whoever shall overdrive, overload, drive when overloaded, overwork, torture, torment, deprive of necessary sustenance, cruelly beat, mutilate or cruelly kill, or cause or procure to be so overdriven, overloaded, driven when overloaded, overworked, tortured, tormented, deprived of necessary sustenance, cruelly beaten, mutilated or cruelly killed, any animal, and whoever, having the charge or custody of any animal, either as owner or otherwise, shall inflict cruelty upon that animal, or shall willfully fail to provide that animal with proper food, drink, shelter or protection from the weather, shall, for every such offense, be imprisoned not exceeding eleven (11) months, or be fined not less than fifty dollars ($50.00) nor exceeding five hundred dollars ($500), or be both imprisoned and fined as aforesaid.

(B) Every owner, possessor or person having charge of any animal may upon conviction of a violation of this section be ordered to forfeit all rights to ownership of the animal to the animal control officer of the city or town in which the offense occurred or to a humane society which owns and operates the shelter which provided the subject animal shelter subsequent to any confiscation of said animal pursuant to this section.

(C) "Shelters", as used in this chapter, shall mean a structure used to house any animal, and which will provide sufficient protection from inclement elements for the health and well-being of the animal.

§ 4-1-3 UNNECESSARY CRUELTY.

Every owner, possessor or person having the charge or custody of any animal, who shall cruelly drive or work that animal when unfit for labor, or cruelly abandon that animal, or who shall carry that animal, or cause that animal to be carried, in or upon any vehicle or otherwise in a cruel or inhuman manner, or wilfully authorize or permit that animal to be subjected to unnecessary torture, suffering or cruelty of any kind, or who shall place or cause to have placed on any animal any substance that may produce irritation or pain, or that shall be declared a hazardous substance by the U.S. Food and Drug Administration or by the Rhode Island Department of Health, shall be punished for every such offense in the manner provided in § 4-1-2; provided however, that this section shall not be deemed to include any drug having curative and therapeutic effect for disease in animals and which is prepared and intended for veterinary use.

CODE OF LAWS OF SOUTH CAROLINA 1976

§ 47-1-40. ILL-TREATMENT OF ANIMALS GENERALLY.

(A) Whoever overloads, overdrives, overworks, or ill-treats any animal, or deprives any animal of necessary sustenance or shelter, or inflicts unnecessary pain or suffering upon any animal, or causes these things to be done, for every offense is guilty of a misdemeanor and, upon conviction, must be punished by imprisonment not exceeding sixty days or by a fine of not less than one hundred dollars nor more than four hundred dollars for a first offense; by imprisonment not exceeding ninety days or by a fine not exceeding eight hundred dollars, or both, for a second offense; or by imprisonment not exceeding two years or by a fine not exceeding two thousand dollars, or both, for a third or subsequent offense. Notwithstanding any other provision of law, a first offense under this subsection shall be tried in magistrate's court.

(B) Whoever tortures, torments, needlessly mutilates, cruelly kills, or inflicts excessive or repeated unnecessary pain or suffering upon any animal or causes the acts to be done for any of the offenses is guilty of a misdemeanor and, upon conviction, must be punished by imprisonment of not less than one hundred eighty days and not to exceed two years and by a fine of five thousand dollars.

(C) This section does not apply to fowl, accepted animal husbandry practices of farm operations, the training of animals, the practice of veterinary medicine, or activity authorized by Title 50.

SOUTH DAKOTA CODIFIED LAWS

§ 9-29-11 CRUELTY TO ANIMALS.

Every municipality shall have power to prohibit and punish cruelty to animals.

§ 40-1-1 DEFINITION OF TERMS.

Terms used in chapters 40-1 and 40-2, mean:

(1) "Abandonment," giving up with the intent of never again regaining one's interests in, or rights to, an animal other than placing ownership with a responsible party;

(2) "Animal," any mammal, bird, reptile, amphibian or fish, except humans;

(3) "Board," the South Dakota animal industry board;

(4) "Captive wild animal," any wild animal held in man-made confinement or physically altered to limit movement and facilitate capture;

(5) "Domestic animal," any animal that through long association with man, has been bred to a degree which has resulted in genetic changes affecting the temperament, color, conformation or other attributes of the species to an extent that makes it unique and different from wild individuals of its kind;

(6) "Exotic animal," any animal not occurring naturally in the United States either currently or historically;

(7) "Impoundment," taking physical control and custody of an animal;

(8) "Non-domestic animal," any animal that is not domestic;

(9) "Other livestock," any agricultural or commercial animal owned, bred or raised for profit, but not including dogs, cats, rabbits or other household pets;

(10) "Wild animal," any animal not in captivity, other than a domestic animal; and

(11) "Zoological animal," any animal in any zoo or intended to be used in a zoo.

§ 40-1-2. OVERWORK, TORTURE, STARVING OR CRUELTY TO ANIMAL PROHIBITED.

§ 40-1-2.2 MISTREATMENT, TORTURE OR CRUELTY OF ANIMALS DEFINED.

For the purposes of this chapter and chapter 40-2, the mistreatment, torture or cruelty of an animal is any act or omission whereby unnecessary, unjustifiable or unreasonable physical pain or suffering is caused, permitted or allowed to continue including acts of mutilation.

§40-1-2.3 NEGLECT DEFINED.

For the purposes of this chapter and chapter 40-2, the neglect of an animal is the failure to provide food, water, protection from the elements, adequate sanitation, adequate facilities or care generally considered to be standard and accepted for an animal's health and well-being consistent with the species, breed, physical condition and type of animal.

§ 40-1-2.4 INHUMANE TREATMENT DEFINED.

For the purposes of this chapter and chapter 40-2, the inhumane treatment of an animal is any act of mistreatment, torture, cruelty, neglect, abandonment, mutilation or inhumane slaughter of an animal that is not consistent with generally accepted training, use and husbandry procedures for the species, breed, physical condition and type of animal.

TENNESSEE CODE

§ 39-14-202 CRUELTY TO ANIMALS.

(a) A person commits an offense who intentionally or knowingly:

(1) Tortures, maims or grossly overworks an animal;

(2) Fails unreasonably to provide necessary food, water, care or shelter for an animal in the person's custody;

(3) Abandons unreasonably an animal in the person's custody;

(4) Transports or confines an animal in a cruel manner; or

(5) Inflicts burns, cuts, lacerations, or other injuries or pain, by any method, including blistering compounds, to the legs or hooves of horses in order to make them sore for any purpose including, but not limited to, competition in horse shows and similar events.

(b) It is a defense to prosecution under this section that the person was engaged in accepted veterinary practices, medical treatment by the owner or with the owner's consent, or bona fide experimentation for scientific research.

(c) Whenever any person is taken into custody by any officer for violation of subdivision (a)(4), the officer may take charge of the vehicle or conveyance, and its contents, used by the person to transport the animal. The officer shall deposit these items in a safe place for custody. Any necessary expense incurred for taking charge of and sustaining the same shall be a lien thereon, to be paid before the same can lawfully be recovered; or the expenses, or any part thereof, remaining unpaid may be recovered by the person incurring the same of the owners of the animal in an action therefor.

(d) In addition to the penalty imposed in subsection (f), the court making the sentencing determination for a person convicted under this section shall order the person convicted to surrender custody and forfeit the animal or animals whose treatment was the basis of the conviction. Custody shall be given to a humane society incorporated under the laws of this state. The court may prohibit the person convicted from having custody of other animals for any period of time the court determines to be reasonable, or impose any other reasonable restrictions on the person's custody of animals as necessary for the protection of the animals.

(e)(1) Nothing in this section shall be construed as prohibiting the owner of a farm animal or someone acting with the consent of the owner of such animal from engaging in usual and customary practices which are accepted by colleges of agriculture or veterinary medicine with respect to such animal.

(2) It is an offense for a person other than an officer, agent or member of a society described in s 39-14-210 to knowingly interfere with the performance of any such agricultural practices permitted by subdivision (e)(1).

(3) An offense under subdivision (e)(2) is a Class B misdemeanor.

(f) An offense under this section is a Class A misdemeanor.

TEXAS STATUTES AND CODES

§ 42.09. CRUELTY TO ANIMALS.

(a) A person commits an offense if he intentionally or knowingly:

(1) tortures or seriously overworks an animal;

(2) fails unreasonably to provide necessary food, care, or shelter for an animal in his custody;

(3) abandons unreasonably an animal in his custody;

(4) transports or confines an animal in a cruel manner;

(5) kills, injures, or administers poison to an animal, other than cattle, horses, sheep, swine, or goats, belonging to another without legal authority or the owner's effective consent;

(6) causes one animal to fight with another;

(7) uses a live animal as a lure in dog race training or in dog coursing on a racetrack; or

(8) trips a horse.

(b) It is a defense to prosecution under this section that the actor was engaged in bona fide experimentation for scientific research.

(c) For purposes of this section:

(1) "Animal" means a domesticated living creature and wild living creature previously captured. "Animal" does not include an uncaptured wild creature or a wild creature whose capture was accomplished by conduct at issue under this section.

(2) "Trip" means to use an object to cause a horse to fall or lose its balance.

(d) An offense under this section is a Class A misdemeanor.

(e) It is a defense to prosecution under Subsection (a)(5) that the animal was discovered on the person's property in the act of or immediately after injuring or killing the person's goats, sheep, cattle, horses, swine, or poultry and that the person killed or injured the animal at the time of this discovery.

(f) It is a defense to prosecution under Subsection (a)(8) that the actor tripped the horse for the purpose of identifying the ownership of the horse or giving veterinary care to the horse.

UTAH CODE, 1953

§ 76-9-301 CRUELTY TO ANIMALS.

(1) A person is guilty of cruelty to animals if the person intentionally, knowingly, recklessly, or with criminal negligence:

(a) fails to provide necessary food, care, or shelter for an animal in his custody;

(b) abandons an animal in the person's custody;

(c) transports or confines an animal in a cruel manner;

(d) injures an animal;

(e) causes any animal, not including a dog, to fight with another animal of like kind for amusement or gain; or

(f) causes any animal, including a dog, to fight with a different kind of animal or creature for amusement or gain.

(2) A violation of Subsection (1) is:

(a) a class B misdemeanor if committed intentionally or knowingly; and

(b) a class C misdemeanor if committed recklessly or with criminal negligence.

(3) A person is guilty of aggravated cruelty to an animal if the person:

(a) tortures an animal;

(b) administers poison or poisonous substances to an animal without having a legal privilege to do so;

(c) kills or causes to be killed an animal without having a legal privilege to do so.

(4) A violation of Subsection (3) is:

(a) a class A misdemeanor if committed intentionally or knowingly;

(b) a class B misdemeanor if committed recklessly; and

(c) a class C misdemeanor if committed with criminal negligence.

(5) It is a defense to prosecution under this section that the conduct of the actor towards the animal was:

(a) by a licensed veterinarian using accepted veterinary practice;

(b) directly related to bona fide experimentation for scientific research, provided that if the animal is to be destroyed, the manner employed will not be unnecessarily cruel unless directly necessary to the veterinary purpose or scientific research involved;

(c) permitted under Section 18-1-3;

(d) by a person who humanely destroys any animal found suffering past recovery for any useful purpose; or

(e) by a person who humanely destroys any apparently abandoned animal found on the person's property.

(6) For purposes of Subsection (5)(d), before destroying the suffering animal, the person who is not the owner of the animal shall obtain:

(a) the judgment of a veterinarian of the animal's nonrecoverable condition;

(b) the judgment of two other persons called by the person to view the unrecoverable condition of the animal in the person's presence;

(c) the consent from the owner of the animal to the destruction of the animal; or

(d) a reasonable conclusion that the animal's suffering is beyond recovery, through the person's own observation, if the person is in a location or circumstance where the person is unable to contact another person.

(7) This section does not affect or prohibit the training, instruction, and grooming of animals, so long as the methods used are in accordance with accepted husbandry practices.

(8)(a) This section does not affect or prohibit the use of an electronic locating or training collar by the owner of an animal for the purpose of lawful animal training, lawful hunting practices, or protecting against loss of that animal.

(b) County and municipal governments may not prohibit the use of an electronic locating or training collar.

(9) Upon conviction under this section, the court may in its discretion, in addition to other penalties:

(a) order the defendant to be evaluated to determine the need for psychiatric or psychological counseling, to receive counseling as the court determines to be appropriate, and to pay the costs of the evaluation and counseling;

(b) require the defendant to forfeit any rights the defendant has to the animal subjected to a violation of this section and to repay the reasonable costs incurred by any person or agency in caring for each animal subjected to violation of this section;

(c) order the defendant to no longer possess or retain custody of any animal, as specified by the court, during the period of the defendant's probation or parole or other period as designated by the court; and

(d) order the animal to be placed for the purpose of adoption or care in the custody of a county and municipal animal control agency, an animal welfare agency registered with the state, sold at public auction, or humanely destroyed.

(10) This section does not prohibit the use of animals in lawful training.

(11) As used in this section:

(a) "Abandons" means to intentionally deposit, leave, or drop off any live animal:

(i) without providing for the care of that animal; or

(ii) in a situation where conditions present an immediate, direct, and serious threat to the life, safety, or health of the animal.

(b) (i) "Animal" means a live, nonhuman vertebrate creature.

(ii) "Animal" does not include animals kept or owned for agricultural purposes and cared for in accordance with accepted husbandry practices, animals used for rodeo purposes, and does not include protected and unprotected wildlife as defined in Section 23-13-2.

(c) "Custody" means ownership, possession, or control over an animal.

(d) "Legal privilege" means an act authorized by state law, including Division of Wildlife Resources statutes and rules, and conducted in conformance with local ordinances.

(e) "Necessary food, care, and shelter" means appropriate and essential food and other needs of the animal, including veterinary care, and adequate protection against extreme weather conditions.

VERMONT STATUTES

§ 352. CRUELTY TO ANIMALS.

(a) A person commits the crime of cruelty to animals if the person:

(1) intentionally kills any animal belonging to another person without first obtaining legal authority or consent of the owner, or attempts to kill or kills an animal with or without the owner's consent by a means causing undue suffering;

(2) overworks, overloads, tortures, torments, abandons, administers poison to, cruelly beats or mutilates an animal, exposes a poison with intent that it be taken by an animal;

(3) ties, tethers, or restrains an animal, either a pet or livestock, in a manner that is inhumane or is detrimental to its welfare. Accepted agricultural methods are exempted;

(4) deprives an animal which a person owns, possesses or acts as an agent for, of adequate food, water, shelter, rest or sanitation, or necessary medical attention, or transports an animal in overcrowded vehicles;

(5) owns, possesses, keeps or trains an animal engaged in an exhibition of fighting, or possesses, keeps or trains any animal with intent that it be engaged in an exhibition of fighting, or permits any such act to be done on premises under his or her charge or control;

(6) acts as judge or spectator at events of animal fighting or bets or wagers on the outcome of such fight;

(7) as poundkeeper, officer, agent of a humane society or as an owner or employee of an establishment for treatment, board or care of an animal, knowingly receives, sells, transfers or otherwise conveys an animal in his or her care for the purpose of research or vivisection;

(8) intentionally torments or harasses an animal owned or engaged by a police department or public agency of the state or its political subdivisions, or interferes with the lawful performance of a police animal;

(9) knowingly sells, offers for sale, barters or displays living baby chicks, ducklings or other fowl which have been dyed, colored or otherwise treated so as to impart to them an artificial color, or fails to provide poultry with proper brooder facilities;

(10) fails to ensure that a crate or other container used to transport, hold or ship in commerce live poultry is maintained in sanitary condition and so constructed as to provide sufficient ventilation and warmth; or

(11) uses a live animal as bait or lure in a race, game or contest, or in training animals in a manner inconsistent with Part 4 of Title 10 or the rules adopted thereunder.

(b) Except as provided in subsection (c) of this section, an affirmative defense to prosecution may be raised under this section when:

(1) except for vivisection or research under subdivision (a)(7) of this section, the defendant was a veterinarian whose conduct conformed to accepted veterinary practice for the area, or was a scientist whose conduct was a part of scientific research governed by accepted procedural standards subject to review by an institutional care and use committee;

(2) the defendant's conduct was designed to control or eliminate rodents, ants or other common pests on the defendant's own property;

(3) the defendant was a person appropriately licensed to utilize pesticides under chapter 87 of Title 6;

(4) the defendant humanely euthanized any animal as a representative of a duly organized humane society, animal shelter or town pound according to rules of this subchapter, or as a veterinarian destroying animals under chapter 193 or sections 3511 and 3513 of Title 20; or

(5) a state agency was implementing a rabies control program.

(c) An affirmative defense to a charge of abandonment under this section shall not be recognized where a person abandons an animal at or near an animal shelter or veterinary clinic, or other place of shelter, without making reasonable arrangements for the care of the animal.

(d) The authority to enforce this chapter shall not be construed in a manner inconsistent with the animal control or disease control eradication programs in Title 6, or chapters 191, 193, 194 and 195 of Title 20 or the provisions of Part 4 of Title 10, or the rules adopted thereunder.

CODE OF VIRGINIA

§ 3.1-796.122 CRUELTY TO ANIMALS; PENALTY.

A. Any person who—

(i) overrides, overdrives, overloads, tortures, ill-treats, abandons, willfully inflicts inhumane injury or pain not connected with bona fide scientific or medical experimentation, or cruelly or unnecessarily beats, maims, mutilates, or kills any animal, whether belonging to himself or another; or

(ii) deprives any animal of necessary sustenance, food, drink or shelter; or

(iii) willfully sets on foot, instigates, engages in, or in any way furthers any act of cruelty to any animal; or

(iv) carries or causes to be carried in or upon any vehicle, vessel or otherwise any animal in a cruel, brutal, or inhumane manner, so as to produce torture or unnecessary suffering; or

(v) causes any of the above things, or being the owner of such animal permits such acts to be done by another, shall be guilty of a Class 1 misdemeanor. Prosecution for violations of this subsection shall commence within five years after commission of the offense. Prosecutions of this subsection regarding agricultural animals, as defined in s 3.1-796.66, shall commence within one year after commission of the offense.

B. Any person who abandons any dog, cat or other domesticated animal in any public place including the right-of-way of any public highway, road or street or on the property of another shall be guilty of a Class 3 misdemeanor.

C. Nothing in this section shall be construed to prohibit the dehorning of cattle.

D. For the purposes of this section and ss 3.1-796.109, 3.1-796.111, 3.1-796.113 through 3.1-796.115, and 3.1-796.125, the word animal shall be construed to include birds and fowl.

REVISED CODE OF WASHINGTON

§ 16.52.205. ANIMAL CRUELTY IN THE FIRST DEGREE.

A person is guilty of animal cruelty in the first degree when, except as authorized in law, he or she intentionally—

(a) inflicts substantial pain on,

(b) causes physical injury to, or

(c) kills an animal by a means causing undue suffering, or forces a minor to inflict unnecessary pain, injury, or death on an animal.

Animal cruelty in the first degree is a class C felony.

§ 16.52.207. ANIMAL CRUELTY IN THE SECOND DEGREE.

(1) A person is guilty of animal cruelty in the second degree if, under circumstances not amounting to first degree animal cruelty, the person knowingly, recklessly, or with criminal negligence inflicts unnecessary suffering or pain upon an animal.

(2) An owner of an animal is guilty of animal cruelty in the second degree if, under circumstances not amounting to first degree animal cruelty, the owner knowingly, recklessly, or with criminal negligence:

(a) Fails to provide the animal with necessary food, water, shelter, rest, sanitation, ventilation, space, or medical attention and the animal suffers unnecessary or unjustifiable physical pain as a result of the failure; or

(b) Abandons the animal.

(3) Animal cruelty in the second degree is a misdemeanor.

(4) In any prosecution of animal cruelty in the second degree, it shall be an affirmative defense, if established by the defendant by a preponderance of the evidence, that the defendant's failure was due to economic distress beyond the defendant's control.

WEST VIRGINIA CODE 1966

§ 19-20-12 DOGS, OTHER ANIMALS AND REPTILES PROTECTED BY LAW; UNLAWFUL KILLING THEREOF; AGGRIEVED OWNER'S REMEDY; PENALTIES; PENALTIES FOR UNLAWFUL STEALING OF PETS.

(a) Any dog which is registered, kept and controlled as provided in this article or any dog, cat, other animal or any reptile which is owned, kept and maintained as a pet by any person, irrespective of age, shall be protected by law; and any person who shall intentionally and unlawfully kill, injure or poison any such dog, cat, other animal or any reptile as specified above, or shall, in any other manner, intentionally and unlawfully cause the death or injury of any such dog, cat, other animal or any reptile shall be guilty of a misdemeanor, and, upon conviction thereof, shall be ordered to provide public service for not less than thirty nor more than ninety days, or fined not more than three hundred dollars, or both. Any person whose dog, cat, other animal or reptile as specified herein shall be killed or injured wrongfully or unlawfully by any other person shall have a right of action against the person who shall so kill or injure such dog, cat, animal or reptile but in no case involving a dog can recovery be had in excess of the assessed value of such dog.

(b) Any person who shall intentionally and unlawfully steal a dog, cat, other animal or reptile as specified in subsection (a) of this section, shall be guilty of a misdemeanor, and, upon conviction thereof, shall be ordered to provide public service for not less than thirty nor more than ninety days or fined not less than three hundred nor more than five hundred dollars, or both. Any person violating the provisions of this subsection shall, for the second or subsequent offense, be guilty of a misdemeanor, and, upon conviction thereof, shall be confined in the county jail for a period of not less than ninety days nor more than six months, or shall be ordered to provide public service for not more than one year, and fined not less than five hundred nor more than one thousand dollars. In no case can any action or prosecution relating to a dog under the provisions of this section be maintained if the dog concerned shall not have been duly registered pursuant to the provisions of this article or owned and kept pursuant to the provisions of this section or owned and kept pursuant to the provisions of this section at the time the cause of action shall have arisen.

(c) The commissioner of agriculture is hereby authorized to designate such reasonable number of his present employees as may be necessary to investigate alleged incidents of the unlawful stealing of dogs, other domestic animals or reptiles, alleged incidents of cruelty to such animals or reptiles and the alleged incidents of the unlawful stealing of such animals or reptiles for the purpose of sale to medical or other research companies. Such deputies shall make the results of their investigations known to any law-enforcement officers who have authority to enforce the provisions of this article.

(d) It shall be the duty of all members of the department of public safety, sheriffs and police officers to aid in the enforcement of the provisions of this article, and, for services rendered in the enforcement thereof, such persons shall be entitled to fees in the amounts set forth in section eight [s

19-20-8]. Such fees shall be paid by the county commission from the dog and kennel fund.

WISCONSIN STATUTES

§ 951.02. MISTREATING ANIMALS.

No person may treat any animal, whether belonging to the person or another, in a cruel manner. This section does not prohibit bona fide experiments carried on for scientific research or normal and accepted veterinary practices.

WYOMING STATUTES 1977

§ 6-3-203 CRUELTY TO ANIMALS; PENALTIES; LIMITATION ON MANNER OF DESTRUCTION.

(a) A person commits cruelty to animals if, without lawful authority, he knowingly:

(i) Overrides, overdrives, overloads, drives when overloaded, overworks, tortures or torments an animal or deprives an animal of necessary sustenance;

(ii) Unnecessarily or cruelly beats, injures, mutilates or kills an animal; or

(iii) Carries an animal in a cruel or inhumane manner.

(b) A person commits cruelty to animals if he has the charge and custody of any animal and unnecessarily fails to provide it with the proper food, drink or protection from the weather, or cruelly abandons the animal, or in the case of immediate, obvious, serious illness or injury, fails to provide the animal with appropriate care.

(c) A person commits aggravated cruelty to animals if he:

(i) Repealed by Laws 1987, ch. 91, s 2.

(ii) Owns, possesses, keeps or trains fowls or dogs with the intent to allow the dog or fowl to engage in an exhibition of fighting with another dog or fowl;

(iii) Repealed by Laws 1987, ch. 91, s 2.

(iv) For gain causes or allows any dog or fowl to fight with another dog or fowl;

(v) Knowingly permits any act prohibited under paragraphs (ii) or

(iv) of this subsection on any premises under his charge or control; or

(vi) Promotes any act prohibited under paragraphs (ii) or (iv) of this subsection.

(d) A person shall not destroy an animal by the use of a high-altitude decompression chamber or a carbon monoxide gas chamber utilizing a gasoline engine. This subsection is uniformly applicable to all cities and towns.

(e) Cruelty to animals is a misdemeanor punishable by imprisonment for not more than six (6) months, a fine of not more than seven hundred fifty dollars ($750.00), or both except that a subsequent offense, or aggravated cruelty to animals as defined by paragraphs (c)(ii), (iv), (v) and (vi) of this section is a high misdemeanor punishable by not more than one (1) year imprisonment, a fine of not more than five thousand dollars ($5,000.00), or both.

(f) Nothing in subsection (c) of this section may be construed to prohibit:

(i) The use of dogs in the management of livestock by the owner of the livestock, his employees or agents or other persons in lawful custody of the livestock;

(ii) The use of dogs or raptors in hunting; or

(iii) The training of dogs or raptors or the use of equipment in the training of dogs or raptors for any purpose not prohibited by law;

(iv) A person from humanely destroying an animal;

(v) The use of commonly accepted agricultural and livestock practices on livestock; or

(vi) Rodeo events, whether the event is performed in a rodeo, jackpot or otherwise.

(g) A person commits cruelty to animals if he is knowingly present at any place where an exhibition of fighting of fowls or dogs is occurring for amusement or gain.

(h) If a person convicted of cruelty to animals under this section is also the owner of the animal, the court may require the person to forfeit ownership of the animal to the county in which the person is convicted. This subsection shall not affect the interest of any secured party or other person who has not participated in the offense.

(j) In addition to any sentence and penalties imposed under subsections (e) and (h) of this section, the court may:

(i) Require the defendant to pay all reasonable costs incurred in providing necessary food and water, veterinary attention and treatment for any animal affected; and

(ii) Prohibit or limit the defendant's ownership, possession or custody of animals, as the court deems appropriate.

(k) Each animal affected by the defendant's conduct may constitute a separate count for the purposes of prosecution, conviction, sentencing and penalties under this section.

APPENDIX 3:
FEDERAL ANIMAL WELFARE ACT
(7 U.S.C. §§ 2131 et seq.)

§ 2131. TITLE AND FINDINGS

(a) This Act may be cited as the "Animal Welfare Act."

(b) The Congress finds that animals and activities which are regulated under this Act are either in interstate or foreign commerce or substantially affect such commerce or the free flow thereof, and that regulation of animals and activities a provided in this Act is necessary to prevent and eliminate burdens upon such commerce and to effectively regulate such commerce, in order:

(1) to insure that animals intended for use in research facilities or for exhibition purposes or for use as pets are provided humane care and treatment;

(2) to assure the humane treatment of animals during transportation in commerce; and

(3) to protect the owners of animals from the theft of their animals by preventing the sale or use of animals which have been stolen.

The Congress further finds that it is essential to regulate, as provided in this Act, the transportation, purchase, sale, housing, care, handling, and treatment of animals by carriers or by persons or organizations engaged in using them for research or experimental purposes or for exhibition purposes or holding them for sale as pets or for any such purpose or use. The congress further finds that:

(1) the use of animals is instrumental in certain research and education for advancing knowledge of cures and treatment for diseases and injuries which afflict both humans and animals;

(2) methods of testing that do not use animals are being and continue to be developed which are faster, less expensive, and more accurate

than traditional animal experiments for some purposes and further opportunities exist for the development of these methods of testing;

(3) measures which eliminate or minimize the unnecessary duplication of experiments on animals can result in more productive use of Federal funds; and

(4) measures which help meet the public concern for laboratory animal care and treatment are important in assuring that research will continue to progress.

§ 2132. DEFINITIONS. [OMITTED]

§ 2133. LICENSING OF DEALERS AND EXHIBITORS

The Secretary shall issue licenses to dealers and exhibitors upon application therefor in such form and manner as he may prescribe and upon payment of such fee established pursuant to 2153 of this title: Provided, That no such license shall be issued until the dealer or exhibitor shall have demonstrated that his facilities comply with the standards promulgated by the Secretary pursuant to section 2143 of this title: Provided, however, That any retail pet store or other person who derives less than a substantial portion of his income (as determined by the Secretary) from the breeding and raising of dogs or cats on his own premises and sells any such dog or cat to a dealer or research facility shall not be required to obtain a license as a dealer or exhibitor under this chapter. The Secretary is further authorized to license, as dealers or exhibitors, persons who do not qualify as dealers or exhibitors within the meaning of this chapter upon such persons' complying with the requirements specified above and agreeing, in writing, to comply with all the requirements of this chapter and the regulations promulgated by the Secretary hereunder.

§ 2134. VALID LICENSE FOR DEALERS AND EXHIBITORS REQUIRED

No dealer or exhibitor shall sell or offer to sell or transport or offer for transportation, in commerce, to any research facility or for exhibition or for use as a pet any animal, or buy, sell, offer to buy or sell, transport or offer for transportation, in commerce, to or from another dealer or exhibitor under this chapter any animal, unless and until such dealer or exhibitor shall have obtained a license from the Secretary and such license shall not have been suspended or revoked.

§ 2135. TIME PERIOD FOR DISPOSAL OF DOGS OR CATS BY DEALERS OR EXHIBITORS

No dealer or exhibitor shall sell or otherwise dispose of any dog or cat within a period of five business days after the acquisition of such animal or within such other period as may be specified by the Secretary: Provided, That operators of auction sales subject to section 2142 of this title shall not be required to comply with the provisions of this section.

§ 2136. REGISTRATION OF RESEARCH FACILITIES, HANDLERS, CARRIERS AND UNLICENSED EXHIBITORS

Every research facility, every intermediate handler, every carrier, and every exhibitor not licensed under section 2133 of this title shall register with the Secretary in accordance with such rules and regulations as he may prescribe.

§ 2137. PURCHASE OF DOGS OR CATS BY RESEARCH FACILITIES PROHIBITED EXCEPT FROM AUTHORIZED OPERATORS OF AUCTION SALES AND LICENSED DEALERS OR EXHIBITORS

It shall be unlawful for any research facility to purchase any dog or cat from any person except an operator of an auction sale subject to section 2142 of this title or a person holding a valid license as a dealer or exhibitor issued by the Secretary pursuant to this chapter unless such person is exempted from obtaining such license under section 2133 of this title.

§ 2138. PURCHASE OF DOGS OR CATS BY UNITED STATES GOVERNMENT FACILITIES PROHIBITED EXCEPT FROM AUTHORIZED OPERATORS OF AUCTION SALES AND LICENSED DEALERS OR EXHIBITORS

No department, agency, or instrumentality of the United States which uses animals for research or experimentation or exhibition shall purchase or otherwise acquire any dog or cat for such purposes from any person except an operator of an auction sale subject to section 2142 of this title or a person holding a valid license as a dealer or exhibitor issued by the Secretary pursuant to this chapter unless such person is exempted from obtaining such license under section 2133 of this title.

§ 2139. PRINCIPAL-AGENT RELATIONSHIP ESTABLISHED

When construing or enforcing the provisions of this chapter, the act, omission, or failure of any person acting for or employed by a research facility, a dealer, or an exhibitor or a person licensed as a dealer or an exhibitor pursuant to the second sentence of section 2133 of this title, or an operator of an auction sale subject to section 2142 of this title, or an intermediate handler, or a carrier, within the scope of his employment or office, shall be deemed the act, omission, or failure of such research facility, dealer, exhibitor, licensee, operator of an auction sale, intermediate handler, or carrier, as well as of such person.

§ 2140. RECORDKEEPING BY DEALERS, EXHIBITORS, RESEARCH FACILITIES, INTERMEDIATE HANDLERS, AND CARRIERS

Dealers and exhibitors shall make and retain for such reasonable period of time as the Secretary may prescribe, such records with respect to the purchase, sale, transportation, identification, and previous ownership of animals as the Secretary may prescribe. Research facilities shall make and retain such records only with respect to the purchase, sale, transportation, identification, and previous ownership of live dogs and cats. At the request of the Secretary, any regulatory agency of the Federal Government which requires records to be maintained by intermediate handlers and carriers with respect to the transportation, receiving, handling, and delivery of animals on forms prescribed by the agency, shall require there to be included in such forms, and intermediate handlers and carriers shall include in such forms, such information as the Secretary may require for the effective administration of this chapter. Such information shall be retained for such reasonable period of time as the Secretary may prescribe. If regulatory agencies of the Federal Government do not prescribe requirements for any such forms, intermediate handlers and carriers shall make and retain for such reasonable period as the Secretary may prescribe such records with respect to the transportation, receiving, handling, and delivery of animals as the Secretary may prescribe. Such records shall be made available at all reasonable times for inspection and copying by the Secretary.

§ 2141. MARKING AND IDENTIFICATION OF ANIMALS

All animals delivered for transportation, transported, purchased, or sold, in commerce, by a dealer or exhibitor shall be marked or identified at such time and in such humane manner as the Secretary may prescribe: Provided, That only live dogs and cats need be so marked or identified by a research facility.

§ 2142. HUMANE STANDARDS AND RECORDKEEPING REQUIREMENTS AT AUCTION SALES

The Secretary is authorized to promulgate humane standards and recordkeeping requirements governing the purchase, handling, or sale of animals, in commerce, by dealers, research facilities, and exhibitors at auction sales and by the operators of such auction sales. The Secretary is also authorized to require the licensing of operators of auction sales where any dogs or cats are sold, in commerce, under such conditions as he may prescribe, and upon payment of such fee as prescribed by the Secretary under 2153 of this title.

§ 2143. STANDARDS AND CERTIFICATION PROCESS FOR HUMANE HANDLING, CARE, TREATMENT AND TRANSPORTATION OF ANIMALS

a. Promulgation of standards, rules, regulations, and orders; requirements; research facilities; State authority

1. The Secretary shall promulgate standards to govern the humane handling, care, treatment, and transportation of animals by dealers, research facilities, and exhibitors.

2. The standards described in paragraph (1) shall include minimum requirements—

A. for handling, housing, feeding, watering, sanitation, ventilation, shelter from extremes of weather and temperatures, adequate veterinary care, and separation by species where the Secretary finds necessary for humane handling, care, or treatment of animals; and

B. for exercise of dogs, as determined by an attending veterinarian in accordance with general standards promulgated by the Secretary, and for a physical environment adequate to promote the psychological well-being of primates.

3. In addition to the requirements under paragraph (2), the standards described in paragraph (1) shall, with respect to animals in research facilities, include requirements—

A. for animal care, treatment, and practices in experimental procedures to ensure that animal pain and distress are minimized, including adequate veterinary care with the appropriate use of anesthetic, analgesic, tranquilizing drugs, or euthanasia;

B. that the principal investigator considers alternatives to any procedure likely to produce pain to or distress in an experimental animal;

C. in any practice which could cause pain to animals—

i. that a doctor of veterinary medicine is consulted in the planning of such procedures;

ii. for the use of tranquilizers, analgesics, and anesthetics;

iii. for pre-surgical and post-surgical care by laboratory workers, in accordance with established veterinary medical and nursing procedures;

iv. against the use of paralytics without anesthesia; and

v. that the withholding of tranquilizers, anesthesia, analgesia, or euthanasia when scientifically necessary shall continue for only the necessary period of time;

D. that no animal is used in more than one major operative experiment from which it is allowed to recover except in cases of—

i. scientific necessity; or

ii .other special circumstances as determined by the Secretary; and

E. that exceptions to such standards may be made only when specified by research protocol and that any such exception shall be detailed and explained in a report outlined under paragraph (7) and filed with the Institutional Animal Committee.

4. The Secretary shall also promulgate standards to govern the transportation in commerce, and the handling, care, and treatment in connection therewith, by intermediate handlers, air carriers, or other carriers, of animals consigned by any dealer, research facility, exhibitor, operator of an auction sale, or other person, or any department, agency, or instrumentality of the United States or of any State or local government, for transportation in commerce. The Secretary shall have authority to promulgate such rules and regulations as he determines necessary to assure humane treatment of animals in the course of their transportation in commerce including requirements such as those with respect to containers, feed, water, rest, ventilation, temperature, and handling.

5. In promulgating and enforcing standards established pursuant to this section, the Secretary is authorized and directed to consult experts, including outside consultants where indicated.

6.A. Nothing in this chapter—

i. except as provided in paragraphs (7) of this subsection, shall be construed as authorizing the Secretary to promulgate rules, regulations, or orders with regard to the design, outlines, or guidelines of actual research or experimentation by a research facility as determined by such research facility;

ii. except as provided subparagraphs (A) and (C)(ii) through (v) of paragraph (3) and paragraph (7) of this subsection, shall be construed as authorizing the Secretary to promulgate rules, regulations, or orders with regard to the performance of actual research or experimentation by a research facility as determined by such research facility; and

iii. shall authorize the Secretary, during inspection, to interrupt the conduct of actual research or experimentation.

6.B. No rule, regulation, order, or part of this chapter shall be construed to require a research facility to disclose publicly or to the Institutional Animal Committee during its inspection, trade secrets or commercial or financial information which is privileged or confidential.

7.A. The Secretary shall require each research facility to show upon inspection, and to report at least annually, that the provisions of this chapter are being followed and that professionally acceptable standards governing the care, treatment, and use of animals are being followed by the research facility during actual research or experimentation.

7.B. In complying with subparagraph (A), such research facilities shall provide—

i. information on procedures likely to produce pain or distress in any animal and assurances demonstrating that the principal investigator considered alternatives to those procedures;

ii. assurances satisfactory to the Secretary that such facility is adhering to the standards described in this section; and

iii. an explanation for any deviation from the standards promulgated under this section.

b. Paragraph (1) shall not prohibit any State (or a political subdivision of such State) from promulgating standards in addition to those standards promulgated by the Secretary under paragraph (1).

c. Research facility Committee; establishment, membership, functions, etc.

1. The Secretary shall require that each research facility establish at least one Committee. Each Committee shall be appointed by the chief executive officer of each such research facility and shall be composed of not fewer than three members. Such members shall possess sufficient ability to assess animal care, treatment, and practices in experimental

research as determined by the needs of the research facility and shall represent society's concerns regarding the welfare of animal subjects used at such facility. Of the members of the Committee—

A. at least one member shall be a doctor of veterinary medicine;

B. at least one member—

i. shall not be affiliated in any way with such facility other than as a member of the Committee;

ii. shall not be a member of the immediate family of a person who is affiliated with such facility; and

iii. is intended to provide representation for general community interests in the proper care and treatment of animals; and

C. in those cases where the Committee consists of more than three members, not more than three members shall be from the same administrative unit of such facility.

2. A quorum shall be required for all formal actions of the Committee, including inspections under paragraph (3).

3. The Committee shall inspect at least semiannually all animal study areas and animal facilities of such research facility and review as part of the inspection—

A. practices involving pain to animals, and

B. the condition of animals, to ensure compliance with the provisions of this chapter to minimize pain and distress to animals. Exceptions to the requirement of inspection of such study areas may be made by the Secretary if animals are studied in their natural environment and the study area is prohibitive to easy access.

4.A. The Committee shall file an inspection certification report of each inspection at the research facility. Such report shall—

i. be signed by a majority of the Committee members involved in the inspection;

ii. include reports of any violation of the standards promulgated, or assurances required, by the Secretary, including any deficient conditions of animal care or treatment, any deviations of research practices from originally approved proposals that adversely affect animal welfare, any notification to the facility regarding such conditions, and any corrections made thereafter;

iii. include any minority views of the Committee; and

iv. include any other information pertinent to the activities of the Committee.

4.B. Such report shall remain on file for at least three years at the research facility and shall be available for inspection by the Animal and Plant Health Inspection Service and any funding Federal agency.

4.C. In order to give the research facility an opportunity to correct any deficiencies or deviations discovered by reason of paragraph (3), the Committee shall notify the administrative representative of the research facility of any deficiencies or deviations from the provisions of this chapter. If, after notification and an opportunity for correction, such deficiencies or deviations remain uncorrected, the Committee shall notify (in writing) the Animal and Plant Health Inspection Service and the funding Federal agency of such deficiencies or deviations.

5. The inspection results shall be available to Department of Agriculture inspectors for review during inspections. Department of Agriculture inspectors shall forward any Committee inspection records which include reports of uncorrected deficiencies or deviations to the Animal and Plant Health Inspection Service and any funding Federal agency of the project with respect to which such uncorrected deficiencies and deviations occurred.

d. Federal research facilities; establishment, composition, and responsibilities of Federal Committee

In the case of Federal research facilities, a Federal Committee shall be established and shall have the same composition and responsibilities provided in subsection (b) of this section, except that the Federal Committee shall report deficiencies or deviations to the head of the Federal agency conducting the research rather than to the Animal and Plant Health Inspection Service. The head of the Federal agency conducting the research shall be responsible for—

1. all corrective action to be taken at the facility; and

2. the granting of all exceptions to inspection protocol.

e. Training of scientists, animal technicians, and other personnel involved with animal care and treatment at research facilities

Each research facility shall provide for the training of scientists, animal technicians, and other personnel involved with animal care and treatment in such facility as required by the Secretary. Such training shall include instruction on—

1. the humane practice of animal maintenance and experimentation;

2. research or testing methods that minimize or eliminate the use of animals or limit animal pain or distress;

3. utilization of the information service at the National Agricultural Library, established under subsection (e) of this section; and

4. methods whereby deficiencies in animal care and treatment should be reported.

f. Establishment of information service at National Agricultural Library; service functions

The Secretary shall establish an information service at the National Agricultural Library. Such service shall, in cooperation with the National Library of Medicine, provide information—

1. pertinent to employee training;

2. which could prevent unintended duplication of animal experimentation as determined by the needs of the research facility; and

3. on improved methods of animal experimentation, including methods which could—

A. reduce or replace animal use; and

B. minimize pain and distress to animals, such as anesthetic and analgesic procedures.

g. Suspension or revocation of Federal support for research projects; prerequisites; appeal procedure

In any case in which a Federal agency funding a research project determines that conditions of animal care, treatment, or practice in a particular project have not been in compliance with standards promulgated under this chapter, despite notification by the Secretary or such Federal agency to the research facility and an opportunity for correction, such agency shall suspend or revoke Federal support for the project. Any research facility losing Federal support as a result of actions taken under the preceding sentence shall have the right of appeal as provided in sections 701 through 706 of Title 5.

h. Veterinary certificate; contents; exceptions

No dogs or cats, or additional kinds or classes of animals designated by regulation of the Secretary, shall be delivered by any dealer, research facility, exhibitor, operator of an auction sale, or department, agency, or instrumentality of the United States or of any State or local government, to any intermediate handler or carrier for transportation in commerce, or received by any such handler or carrier for such transportation from any such person, department, agency, or instrumentality, unless the animal is accompanied by a certificate issued by a veterinarian licensed to practice veterinary medicine, certifying that he inspected the animal on a specified date, which shall not be more than ten days before such delivery, and, when so inspected, the animal appeared free of any infectious disease or physical abnormality which would endanger the animal or animals or other animals or endanger public health: Provided, however, That the Secretary may by regulation provide exceptions to this certification requirement, under such conditions as he may prescribe in the regulations, for animals shipped to research facilities for purposes of research, testing or experimentation requiring animals not eligible for such certification. Such certificates received by the intermediate handlers and the carriers shall be retained by them, as provided by regulations of the Secretary, in accordance with section 2140 of this title.

i. Age of animals delivered to registered research facilities; power of Secretary to designate additional classes of animals and age limits

No dogs or cats, or additional kinds or classes of animals designated by regulation of the Secretary, shall be delivered by any person to any intermediate handler or carrier for transportation in commerce except to registered research facilities if they are less than such age as the Secretary may by regulation prescribe. The Secretary shall designate additional kinds and classes of animals and may prescribe different ages for particular kinds or classes of dogs, cats, or designated animals, for the purposes of this section, when he determines that such action is necessary or adequate to assure their humane treatment in connection with their transportation in commerce.

j. Prohibition of C.O.D. arrangements for transportation of animals in commerce; exceptions

No intermediate handler or carrier involved in the transportation of any animal in commerce shall participate in any arrangement or engage in any practice under which the cost of such animal or the cost of the transportation of such animal is to be paid and collected upon delivery of the animal to the consignee, unless the consignor guarantees in writing the payment of transportation charges for any animal not claimed within a period of 48 hours after notice to the consignee of arrival of the animal, including, where necessary, both the return transportation charges and an amount sufficient to reimburse the carrier for all out-of-pocket expenses incurred for the care, feeding, and storage of such animals.

§ 2144. HUMANE STANDARDS FOR ANIMALS BY UNITED STATES GOVERNMENT FACILITIES

Any department, agency, or instrumentality of the United States having laboratory animal facilities shall comply with the standards and other requirements promulgated by the Secretary for a research facility under sections 2143(a), (f), (g), and (h) of this title. Any department, agency, or instrumentality of the United States exhibiting animals shall comply with the standards promulgated by the Secretary under sections 2143(a), (f), (g), and (h) of this title.

§ 2145. CONSULTATION AND COOPERATION WITH FEDERAL, STATE, AND LOCAL GOVERNMENTAL BODIES BY SECRETARY OF AGRICULTURE

a. The Secretary shall consult and cooperate with other Federal departments, agencies, or instrumentalities concerned with the welfare of animals used for research, experimentation or exhibition, or administration of statutes regulating the transportation in commerce or handling in connection therewith of any animals when establishing standards pursuant to section 2143 of this title and in carrying out the purposes of this chapter. The Secretary shall consult with the Secretary of Health and Human Services prior to issuance of regulations. Before promulgating any standard governing the air transportation and handling in connection therewith, of animals, the Secretary shall consult with the Secretary of Transportation who shall have the authority to disapprove any such standard if he notifies the Secretary, within 30 days after such consultation, that changes in its provisions are necessary in the interest of flight safety. The Surface Transportation Board, the Secretary of Transportation, and the Federal Maritime Commission, to the extent of their respective lawful authorities, shall take such action as is appropriate to implement any standard established by the Secretary with respect to a person subject to regulation by it.

b. The Secretary is authorized to cooperate with the officials of the various States or political subdivisions thereof in carrying out the purposes of this chapter and of any State, local, or municipal legislation or ordinance on the same subject.

§ 2146. ADMINISTRATION AND ENFORCEMENT BY SECRETARY

a. Investigations and inspections

The Secretary shall make such investigations or inspections as he deems necessary to determine whether any dealer, exhibitor, intermediate handler, carrier, research facility, or operator of an auction sale subject to section 2142 of this title, has violated or is violating any provision of this chapter or any regulation or standard issued thereunder, and for such purposes, the Secretary shall, at all reasonable times, have access to the places of business and the facilities, animals, and those records required to be kept pursuant to section 2140 of this title of any such dealer, exhibitor, intermediate handler, carrier, research facility, or operator of an auction sale. The Secretary shall inspect each research facility at least once each year and, in the case of deficiencies or deviations from the standards promulgated under this chapter, shall conduct such follow-up inspections as may be necessary until all deficiencies or deviations from such standards are corrected. The Secretary shall promulgate such rules and regulations as he deems necessary to permit inspectors to confiscate or destroy in a humane manner any animal found to be suffering as a result of a failure to comply with any provision of this chapter or any regulation or standard issued thereunder if (1) such animal is held by a dealer, (2) such animal is held by an exhibitor, (3) such animal is held by a research facility and is no longer required by such research facility to carry out the research, test, or experiment for which such animal has been utilized, (4) such animal is held by an operator of an auction sale, or (5) such animal is held by an intermediate handler or a carrier.

b. Penalties for interfering with official duties

Any person who forcibly assaults, resists, opposes, impedes, intimidates, or interferes with any person while engaged in or on account of the performance of his official duties under this chapter shall be fined not more than $5,000, or imprisoned not more than three years, or both. Whoever, in the commission of such acts, uses a deadly or dangerous weapon shall be fined not more than $10,000, or imprisoned not more than ten years, or both. Whoever kills any person while engaged in or on account of the performance of his official duties under this chapter shall be punished as provided under sections 1111 and 1114 of Title 18.

c. Procedures

For the efficient administration and enforcement of this chapter and the regulations and standards promulgated under this chapter, the provisions (including penalties) of sections 46, 48, 49 and 50 of Title 15 (except paragraph (c) through (h) of section 46 and the last paragraph of section 49 of Title 15), and the provisions of Title II of the Organized Crime Control Act of 1970, are made applicable to the jurisdiction, powers, and duties of the Secretary in administering and enforcing the provisions of this chapter and to any person, firm, or corporation with respect to whom such authority is exercised. The Secretary may prosecute any inquiry necessary to his duties under this chapter in any part of the United States, including any territory, or possession thereof, the District of Columbia, or the Commonwealth of Puerto Rico. The powers conferred by said sections 49 and 50 of Title 15 on the district courts of the United States may be exercised for the purposes of this chapter by any district court of the United States. The United States district courts, the District Court of Guam, the District Court of the Virgin Islands, the highest court of American Samoa, and the United States courts of the other territories, are vested with jurisdiction specifically to enforce, and to prevent and restrain violations of this chapter, and shall have jurisdiction in all other kinds of cases arising under this chapter, except as provided in section 2149(c) of this title.

§ 2147. INSPECTION BY LEGALLY CONSTITUTED LAW ENFORCEMENT AGENCIES

The Secretary shall promulgate rules and regulations requiring dealers, exhibitors, research facilities, and operators of auction sales subject to section 2142 of this title to permit inspection of their animals and records at reasonable hours upon request by legally constituted law enforcement agencies in search of lost animals.

§ 2148. REPEALED.

Pub. L. 91-579, 19, Dec. 24, 1970, 84 Stat. 1564

§ 2149. VIOLATIONS BY LICENSEES

a. Temporary license suspension; notice and hearing; revocation

If the Secretary has reason to believe that any person licensed as a dealer, exhibitor, or operator of an auction sale subject to section 2142 of this title, has violated or is violating any provision of this chapter, or any of the rules or regulations or standards promulgated by the Secretary hereunder, he may suspend such person's license temporarily, but not to exceed 21 days, and after notice and opportunity for hearing, may suspend for such additional period as he may specify, or revoke such license, if such violation is determined to have occurred.

b. Civil penalties for violation of any section, etc.; separate offenses; notice and hearing; appeal; considerations in assessing penalty; compromise of penalty; civil action by Attorney General for failure to pay penalty; district court jurisdiction; failure to obey cease and desist order

Any dealer, exhibitor, research facility, intermediate handler, carrier, or operator of an auction sale subject to section 2142 of this title, that violates any provision of this chapter, or any rule, regulation, or standard promulgated by the Secretary thereunder, may be assessed a civil penalty by the

Secretary of not more than $2,500 for each such violation, and the Secretary may also make an order that such person shall cease and desist from continuing such violation. Each violation and each day during which a violation continues shall be a separate offense. No penalty shall be assessed or cease and desist order issued unless such person is given notice and opportunity for a hearing with respect to the alleged violation, and the order of the Secretary assessing a penalty and making a cease and desist order shall be final and conclusive unless the affected person files an appeal from the Secretary's order with the appropriate United States Court of Appeals. The Secretary shall give due consideration to the appropriateness of the penalty with respect to the size of the business of the person involved, the gravity of the violation, the person's good faith, and the history of previous violations. Any such civil penalty may be compromised by the Secretary. Upon any failure to pay the penalty assessed by a final order under this section, the Secretary shall request the Attorney General to a civil action in a district court of the United States or other United States court for any district in which such person is found or resides or transacts business, to collect the penalty, and such court shall have jurisdiction to hear and decide any such action. Any person who knowingly fails to obey a cease and desist order made by the Secretary under this section shall be subject to a civil penalty of $1,500 for each offense, and each day during which such failure continues shall be deemed a separate offense.

c. Appeal of final order by aggrieved person; limitations; exclusive jurisdiction of United States Courts of Appeals

Any dealer, exhibitor, research facility, intermediate handler, carrier, or operator of an auction sale subject to section 2142 of this title, aggrieved by a final order of the Secretary issued pursuant to this section may, within 60 days after entry of such an order, seek review of such order in the appropriate United States Court of Appeals in accordance with the provisions of sections 2341, 2343 through 2350 of Title 28, and such court shall have exclusive jurisdiction to enjoin, set aside, suspend (in whole or in part), or to determine the validity of the Secretary's order.

d. Criminal penalties for violation; initial prosecution brought before United States magistrate judges; conduct of prosecution by attorneys of United States Department of Agriculture

Any dealer, exhibitor, or operator of an auction sale subject to section 2142 of this title, who knowingly violates any provision of this chapter shall, on conviction thereof, be subject to imprisonment for not more than 1 year, or a fine of not more than $2,500, or both. Prosecution of such violations shall, to the maximum extent practicable, be brought before United States magistrates as provided in section 636 of Title 28, and sections 3401 and 3402 of Title 18, and, with the consent of the Attorney General, may be conducted, at both trial and upon appeal to district court, by attorneys of the United States Department of Agriculture.

§ 2150. REPEALED.

Pub.L. 94-279, 14, Apr. 22, 1976, 90 Stat. 421

§ 2151. RULES AND REGULATIONS

The Secretary is authorized to promulgate such rules, regulations, and orders as he may deem necessary in order to effectuate the purposes of this chapter.

§ 2152. SEPARABILITY

If any provision of this chapter or the application of any such provision to any person or circumstances shall be held invalid, the remainder of this chapter and the application of any such provision to persons or circumstances other than those as to which it is held invalid shall not be affected thereby.

§ 2153. FEES AND AUTHORIZATION OF APPROPRIATIONS

The Secretary shall charge, assess, and cause to be collected reasonable fees for licenses issued. Such fees shall be adjusted on an equitable basis taking into consideration the type and nature of the operations to be licensed and shall be deposited and covered into the Treasury as miscellaneous receipts. There are hereby authorized to be appropriated such funds as Congress may from time to time provide: Provided, That there is authorized to be appropriated to the Secretary of Agriculture for enforcement by the Department of Agriculture of the provisions of section 2156 of this title an amount not to exceed $100,000 for the transition quarter ending September 30, 1976, and not to exceed $400,000 for each fiscal year thereafter.

§ 2154. EFFECTIVE DATES

The regulations referred to in sections 2140 and 2143 of this title shall be prescribed by the Secretary as soon as reasonable but not later than six months from August 24, 1966. Additions and amendments thereto be prescribed from time to time as may be necessary or advisable. Compliance by dealers with the provisions of this chapter and such regulations shall commence ninety days after the promulgation of such regulations. Compliance by research facilities with the provisions of this chapter and such regulations shall commence six months after the promulgation of such regulations, except that the Secretary may grant extensions of time to research facilities which do not comply with the prescribed by the Secretary pursuant to section 2143 of this title provided that the Secretary determines that there is evidence that the research facilities will meet such standards within a reasonable time. Notwithstanding the other provisions of this section, compliance by intermediate handlers, and carriers, and other persons with those provisions of this chapter, as amended by the Animal Welfare Act Amendments of 1976, and those regulations promulgated thereunder, which relate to actions of intermediate handlers and carriers, shall commence 90 days after promulgation of regulations under section 2143 of this title, as amended, with respect to intermediate handlers and carriers, and such regulations shall be promulgated no later than 9 months after April 22, 1976; and compliance by dealers, exhibitors, operators of auction sales, and research facilities with other provisions of this chapter, as so amended, and the regulations thereunder, shall commence upon the expiration of 90 days after April 22, 1976: Provided, however, That compliance by all persons with subsections (b), (c), and (d) of section 2143 and with section 2156 of this title, as so amended, shall commence upon the expiration of said ninety-day period. In all other respects, said amendments shall become effective upon April 22, 1976.

§ 2155. ANNUAL REPORT TO THE PRESIDENT OF THE SENATE AND THE SPEAKER OF THE HOUSE OF REPRESENTATIVES

Not later than March of each year, the Secretary shall submit to the President of the Senate and the Speaker of the House of Representatives a comprehensive and detailed written report with respect to—

1. the identification of all research facilities, exhibitors, and other persons and establishments licensed by the Secretary under section 2133 and section 2142 of this title;

2. the nature and place of all investigations and inspections conducted by the Secretary under section 2146 of this title, and all reports received by the Secretary under section 2143 of this title;

3. recommendations for legislation to improve the administration of this chapter or any provisions thereof;

4. recommendations and conclusions concerning the aircraft environment as it relates to the carriage of live animals in air transportation; and

5. the information and recommendations described in section 1830 of Title 15.

This report as well as any supporting documents, data, or findings shall not be released to any other persons, non-Federal agencies, or organizations unless and until it has been made public by an appropriate committee of the Senate or the House of Representatives.

§ 2156. ANIMAL FIGHTING VENTURE PROHIBITION

a. Sponsoring or exhibiting animal in any fighting venture

It shall be unlawful for any person to knowingly sponsor or exhibit an animal in any animal fighting venture to which any animal was moved in interstate or foreign commerce.

b. Buying, selling, delivering, or transporting animals for participation in animal fighting venture

It shall be unlawful for any person to knowingly sell, buy, transport, or deliver to another person or receive from another person for purposes of transportation, in interstate or foreign commerce, any dog or other animal for purposes of having the dog or other animal participate in an animal fighting venture.

c. Use of Postal Service or other interstate instrumentality for promoting or furthering animal fighting venture

It shall be unlawful for any person to knowingly use the mail service of the United States Postal Service or any interstate instrumentality for purposes of promoting or in any other manner furthering an animal fighting venture except as performed outside the limits of the States of the United States.

d. Violation of State law

Notwithstanding the provisions of subsections (a), (b), or (c) of this section, the activities prohibited by such subsections shall be unlawful with respect to fighting ventures involving live birds only if the fight is to take place in a State where it would be in violation of the laws thereof.

e. Penalties

Any person who violates subsection (a), (b), or (c) of this section shall be fined not more than $5,000 or imprisoned for not more than 1 year, or both, for each such violation.

f. Investigation of violations by Secretary; assistance by other Federal agencies; issuance of search warrant; forfeiture; costs recoverable in forfeiture or civil action

The Secretary or any other person authorized by him shall make such investigations as the Secretary deems necessary to determine whether any person has violated or is violating any provision of this section, and the Secretary may obtain the assistance of the Federal Bureau of Investigation, the Department of the Treasury, or other law enforcement agencies of the United States, and State and local governmental agencies, in the conduct of such investigations, under cooperative agreements with such agencies. A warrant to search for and seize any animal which there is probable cause to believe was involved in any violation of this section may be issued by any judge of the United States or of a State court of record or by a United States magistrate within the district wherein the animal sought is located. Any United States marshal or any person authorized under this section to conduct investigations may apply for and execute any such warrant, and any animal seized under such a warrant shall be held by the United States marshal or other authorized person pending disposition thereof by the court in accordance with this subsection. Necessary care including veterinary treatment shall be provided while the animals are so held in custody. Any animal involved in any violation of this section shall be liable to be proceeded against and forfeited to the United States at any time on complaint filed in any United States district court or other court of the United States for any jurisdiction in which the animal is found and upon a judgment of forfeiture shall be disposed of by sale for lawful purposes or by other humane means, as the court may direct. Costs incurred by the United States for care of animals seized and forfeited under this section shall be recoverable from the owner of the animals if he appears in such forfeiture proceeding or in a separate civil action brought in the jurisdiction in which the owner is found, resides, or transacts business.

g. Definitions

For purposes of this section—

1. the term "animal fighting venture" means any event which involves a fight between at least two animals and is conducted for purposes of sport, wagering, or entertainment except that the term "animal fighting venture" shall not be deemed to include any activity the primary purpose of which involves the use of one or more animals in hunting another animal or animals, such as waterfowl, bird, raccoon, or fox hunting;

2. the term "interstate or foreign commerce" means—

A. any movement between any place in a State to any place in another State or between places in the same State through another State; or

B. any movement from a foreign country into any State;

3. the term "interstate instrumentality" means telegraph, telephone, radio, or television operating in interstate or foreign commerce;

4. the term "State" means any State of the United States, the District of Columbia, the Commonwealth of Puerto Rico, and any territory or possession of the United States;

5. the term "animal" means any live bird, or any live dog or other mammal, except man; and

6. the conduct by any person of any activity prohibited by this section shall not render such person subject to the other sections of this chapter as a dealer, exhibitor, or otherwise.

h. Conflict with State law

The provisions of this chapter shall not supersede or otherwise invalidate any such State, local, or municipal legislation or ordinance relating to animal fighting ventures except in case of a direct and irreconcilable conflict between any requirements thereunder and this chapter or any rule, regulation, or standard hereunder.

§ 2157. RELEASE OF TRADE SECRETS

a. Release of confidential information prohibited

It shall be unlawful for any member of an Institutional Animal Committee to release any confidential information of the research facility including any information that concerns or relates to—

1. the trade secrets, processes, operations, style of work, or apparatus; or

2. the identity, confidential statistical data, amount or source of any income, profits, losses, or expenditures, of the research facility.

b.Wrongful use of confidential information prohibited

It shall be unlawful for any member of such Committee—

1. to use or attempt to use to his advantages; or

2. to revel to any other person, any information which is entitled to protection as confidential information under subsection (a) of this section.

c. Penalties

A violation of subsection (a) or (b) of this section is punishable by—

1. removal from such Committee; and

2. A. a fine of not more than $1,000 and imprisonment of not more than one year; or

2.B. if such violation is willful, a fine of not more than $10,000 and imprisonment of not more than three years.

d. Recovery of damages by injured person; costs; attorney's fee

Any person, including any research facility, injured in its business or property by reason of a violation of this section may recover all actual and consequential damages sustained by such person and the cost of the suit including a reasonable attorney's fee.

e. Other rights and remedies

Nothing in this section shall be construed to affect any other rights of a person injured in its business or property by reason of a violation of this section. Subsection (d) of this section shall not be construed to the exercise of any such rights arising out of or relating to a violation of subsections (a) and (b) of this section.

§ 2158. PROTECTION OF PETS

a. Holding period

1. Requirement

In the case of each dog or cat acquired by an entity described in paragraph (2), such entity shall hold and care for such dog or cat for a period of not less than five days to enable such dog or cat to be recovered by its original owner or adopted by other individuals before such entity sells such dog or cat to a dealer.

2. Entities described

An entity subject to paragraph (1) is—

A. each State, county, or city owned and operated pound or shelter;

B. each private entity established for the purpose of caring for animals, such as a humane society, or other organization that is under contract with a State, county, or city that operates as a pound or shelter and that releases animals on a voluntary basis; and

C. each research facility licensed by the Department of Agriculture.

b. Certification

1. In general

A dealer may not sell, provide, or make available to any individual or entity a random source dog or cat unless such dealer provides the recipient with a valid certification that meets the requirements of paragraph (2) and indicates compliance with subsection (a) of this section.

2. Requirements

A valid certification shall contain—

A. the name, address, and Department of Agriculture license or registration number (if such number exists) of the dealer;

B. the name, address, Department of Agriculture license or registration number (if such number exists), and the signature of the recipient of the dog or cat;

C. a description of the dog or cat being provided that shall include—

i. the species and breed or type of such;

ii. the sex of such;

iii. the date of birth (if known) of such;

iv. the color and any distinctive marking of such; and

v. any other information that the Secretary by regulation shall determine to be appropriate;

D. the name and address of the person, pound, or shelter from which the dog or cat was purchased or otherwise acquired by the dealer, and an assurance that such person, pound, or shelter was notified that such dog or cat may be used for research or educational purposes;

E. the date of the purchase or acquisition referred to in subparagraph (D);

F. a statement by the pound or shelter (if the dealer acquired the dog or cat from such) that it satisfied the requirements of subsection (a) of this section; and

G. any other information that the Secretary of Agriculture by regulation shall determine appropriate.

3. Records

The original certification required under paragraph (1) shall accompany the shipment of a dog or cat to be sold, provided, or otherwise made available by the dealer, and shall be kept and maintained by the research facility for a period of at least one year for enforcement purposes. The dealer shall retain one copy of the certification provided under this paragraph for a period of at least one year for enforcement

4. Transfers

In instances where one research facility transfers animals to another research facility a copy of the certificate must accompany such transfer.

5. Modification

Certification requirements may be modified to reflect technological advances in identification techniques, such as microchip technology, if the Secretary determines that adequate information such as described in this section, will be collected, transferred, and maintained through technology.

c. Enforcement

1. In general

Dealers who fail to act according to the requirements of this section or who include false information in the certification required under subsection (b) of this section, shall be subject to the penalties provided for under section 2149 of this title.

2. Subsequent violations

Any dealer who violates this section more than one time shall be subject to a fine of $5,000 per dog or cat acquired or sold in violation of this section.

3. Permanent revocations

Any dealer who violates this section three or more times shall have such dealers license permanently revoked.

d. Regulation

Not later than 180 days after November 28, 1990, the Secretary shall promulgate regulations to carry out this section.

§ 2159. AUTHORITY TO APPLY FOR INJUNCTIONS

a. Request

Whenever the Secretary has reason to believe that any dealer, carrier, exhibitor, or intermediate handler is dealing in stolen animals, or is placing the health of any animal in serious danger in violation of this chapter or the regulations or standards promulgated thereunder, the Secretary shall notify the Attorney General, who may apply to the United district court in which such dealer, carrier, exhibitor, or intermediate handler resides or conducts business for a temporary restraining order or injunction to prevent any such person from operating in violation of this chapter or the regulations and standards prescribed under this chapter.

b. Issuance

The court shall, upon a proper showing, issue a temporary restraining order or injunction under subsection (a) of this section without bond. Such injunction or order shall remain in effect until a complaint pursuant to section 2149 of this title is issued and dismissed by the Secretary or until an order to cease and desist made thereon by the Secretary has become final and effective or is set aside on appellate review. Attorneys of the Department of Agriculture may, with the approval of the Attorney General, appear in the United States district court representing the Secretary in any action brought under this section.

APPENDIX 4:
COMPLAINT—KISSINGER v. BOARD OF TRUSTEES OF OHIO STATE UNIVERSITY COLLEGE OF VETERINARY MEDICINE

IN THE UNITED STATES DISTRICT COURT FOR THE SOUTHERN DISTRICT OF OHIO EASTERN DIVISION

JENNIFER KISSINGER,	:
	:
Plaintiff,	:
v.	: CIVIL ACTION
	:
THE BOARD OF TRUSTEES OF OHIO STATE	:
UNIVERSITY-COLLEGE OF VETERINARY	:
MEDICINE, RONALD WRIGHT, WILLIAM	:
MUIR, JAMES BLAKESLEE, LAWRENCE	:
HEIDER, RICHARD BEDNARSKI,	: DKT NO. C2-90-887
STEPHEN J. BIRCHARD, in their	:
official capacities, and	:
MILTON WYMAN, in his official	:
capacity and individually,	:
	:
Defendants.	:
	:

COMPLAINT

Plaintiff, Jennifer Kissinger, residing at 422 East 20th Ave., Apt. 3, Columbus, Ohio, 43201, by way of Complaint against the Defendants named herein says:

INTRODUCTION

1. This action is brought to enjoin Defendants from penalizing Plaintiff, a veterinary student who refuses on sincerely held religious and moral grounds to use and kill healthy animals as part of her laboratory requirements, where alternatives acceptable to the student are available. Declaratory relief is also sought. In failing to respect Plaintiff's sincerely held religious and moral beliefs, Defendants are in violation of the protections granted her under the free exercise clause of the first amendment of the United States Constitution, and the analogous provision of the Ohio State Constitution. Defendants are also in violation of the free speech and free association protection granted her under the first amendment of the United States Constitution and the analogous provisions of the Ohio State Constitution. Defendants have further violated the due process guarantee afforded Plaintiff under the United States Constitution, and the equal protection guarantees afforded by the United States Constitution and analogous provisions of the Ohio State Constitution.

Additionally, Defendants have breached their contractual obligation to Plaintiff, and induced her to rely detrimentally on misleading assertions. Finally, Defendant Wyman has exhibited a reckless, wanton, and malicious disregard for Plaintiff's religious and moral beliefs and have caused emotional harm to Plaintiff.

JURISDICTION

2. This action arises under the first amendment of the Constitution of the United States; the analogous provision of the Ohio State Constitution; and the Civil Rights Act, namely 42 U.S.C. 1983. Jurisdiction is conferred on this Court by 28 U.S.C. 1331 and 28 U.S.C. 1343. Declaratory relief is sought under 28 U.S.C. 2201 and 2202. Pendant claims under state law are also alleged.

3. No adequate administrative remedies are available that can provide the relief requested by Plaintiff.

PARTIES

4. Plaintiff, Jennifer Kissinger, is a third year veterinary student at Ohio State University—College of Veterinary Medicine ("OSU-CVM") and resides at 422 East 20th Ave., Apt. 3, Columbus, Ohio, 43201.

5. Defendant Milton Wyman is named as a Defendant in this action, both as an individual and in his official capacity. To the best of Plaintiff's knowledge and belief, Defendant Wyman is an Associate Dean, Office of Student Affairs, and Dean of Students, at OSU-CVM. In his capacity as student advocate, Defendant Wyman is obligated to be available to all veterinary students for consultation regarding their professional program and personal problems. It is his designated responsibility to ensure that productive and meaningful lines of communications are maintained between students, faculty and administration and that students' problems are addressed in a meaningful manner.

6. Defendant Ronald Wright is named as a Defendant in this action, in his official capacity. To the best of Plaintiff's knowledge and belief, Defendant Wright is the Dean of OSU-CVM.

7. Defendant William Muir is named as a Defendant in this action, in his official capacity. To the best of Plaintiff's knowledge and belief, Defendant Muir is a Professor and Chairman of the Department of Veterinary Clinical Sciences at OSU-CVM.

8. Defendant James Blakeslee is named as a Defendant in this action, in his official capacity. To the best of Plaintiff's knowledge and belief, Defendant Blakeslee is the Chair of the Veterinary Anatomy Department at OSU-CVM.

9. Defendant Lawrence Heider is named as a Defendant in this action, in his official capacity. To the best of Plaintiff's knowledge and belief, Defendant Heider is the Chair of Preventative Medicine at OSU-CVM.

10. Defendant Richard Bednarski is named as a Defendant in this action, in his official capacity. To the best of Plaintiff's knowledge and belief, Defendant Bednarski is an Associate Professor and Head of the Anesthesiology Department of Veterinary Clinical Sciences at OSU-CVM.

11. Defendant Stephen J. Birchard is named as a Defendant in this action, in his official capacity. To the best of Plaintiff's knowledge and belief, Defendant Birchard is an Associate Professor, Acting Team Leader of the Operative Practice (VM 620), and Head of the Small Animal Surgery Section, Department of Veterinary Clinical Sciences at OSU-CVM.

12. The Board of Trustees of the Ohio State University-School of Veterinary Medicine are a duly appointed Board of Trustees of a state educational in-

stitution, and as such are state actors for purposes of the United States Constitution. OSU-CVM has delegated its authority regarding curricular control and standards for passing and failing students to its faculty, and at all times relevant herein, the faculty's actions are pursuant to this delegated authority and are under color of state law.

VENUE

13. Venue is properly laid in this Court since all of the events leading to this cause of action occurred in Columbus, Ohio. As the claim arose here, 28 U.S.C. 1391(a) permits that venue be laid in this District.

STATEMENT OF FACTS

14. Plaintiff is a third year veterinary student at OSU-CVM and is currently enrolled in the College's Operative Practice and Techniques Course 620/621 (hereinafter "course 620/21").

15. To the best of Plaintiff's knowledge and belief, course 620/21 is a required course designed to teach students to administer technical and surgical skills.

16. To the best of Plaintiff's knowledge and belief, course 620/21 is a prerequisite to other required courses.

17. Plaintiff has sincerely held religious and moral objections to the killing of healthy animals and the performance of surgical techniques on healthy animals solely for educational purposes when accepted alternatives exist. Her religious and moral beliefs relate to an ultimate concern and influence Plaintiff's life in a profound way, affecting, among other things, her diet, her choice of clothing, and her views about the use of animals in experiments and education.

18. Alternative curricula have been set up at several veterinary medical colleges across the United States, and abroad. These alternative curricula offer a range of options to students who conscientiously object to the killing of healthy animals and the performance of surgical techniques on healthy animals solely for educational purposes. Students who have learned by these alternative means have graduated and competed successfully for employment in the veterinary medical field.

19. OSU-CVM has already indicated that it accepts as pedagogically sound alternatives that are offered at other veterinary schools.

20. In or about January of 1990, Plaintiff notified the faculty of OSU-CVM of her objections to the course 620/21 curriculum and requested information regarding the availability of an alternative.

21. In or about the week of April 16, 1990, Plaintiff met with Dr. Smeak who informed her of a student participation spay/neuter clinic scheduled to be functional in the fall, when she would need to have an alternative, and suggested that, as an alternative, she learn the required surgery skills with an outside veterinarian, Dr. Deborah McMichael, with whom Plaintiff had previously worked.

22. In or about the week of April 16, 1990, Plaintiff met with Defendant Wyman, at which time Defendant Wyman said that he and most of the faculty disagreed with Plaintiff's position. He stated his fear that if an alternative were available for Plaintiff, other students might also want an alternative. He told Plaintiff that she could fulfill her surgery requirements at OSU-CVM by taking the alternative program offered at Tufts University Veterinary School, and then returning to OSU-CVM for her senior year.

23. On or about April 30, 1990, Dr. Smeak informed Plaintiff that the idea of working with a private veterinarian as an alternative would not be approved by OSU-CVM.

24. On or about May 1, 1990, Defendant Wyman told Plaintiff that she probably would not have been admitted as a student at OSU-CVM if she had expressed her religious and moral views when she applied for admission.

25. On or about May 1, 1990, Plaintiff met with Defendant Birchard, at which time he informed Plaintiff that the faculty would discuss a proposal for an alternative in a meeting on May 8, 1990. Plaintiff asked to attend to present her views, but was told *not* to attend, since her opinions were of no importance. Upon information and belief, this meeting was held sometime in early May, but no final decision regarding an alternative was made at that time.

26. On or about June 14, 1990, Plaintiff met with Defendant Blakeslee, who asked about Plaintiff's involvement with the animal rights movement and stated a fear that those who believed in animal rights were infiltrating the campus and that the Plaintiff should not "make waves." Defendant Blakeslee told Plaintiff that it would be in her best interest to fulfill the OSU-CVM surgery requirement by taking the equivalent course at Tufts, since Tufts already had in place an alternative.

27. On or about June 15, 1990, Plaintiff met with Defendant Heider, who stated that his major objection to providing an alternative is that it would drain the school's resources, and take prime faculty members and administrators away from their duties.

28. On or about June 18, 1990, in a meeting with Dr. Smeak, Plaintiff was informed that although the surgery department had approved an alternative for Plaintiff, the faculty had met and rejected the implementation of an alternative and that the faculty was directed not to speak with Plaintiff.

29. In addition, on or about June 18, 1990, Defendant Muir told Plaintiff in an afternoon meeting that the faculty had rejected an alternatives proposal for three reasons: (1) an alternative would cost money; (2) it would occupy faculty members' time and detract from their other duties; and (3) an alternative entailing work on client-owned animals would interfere with the education of seniors who would otherwise have handled those cases.

30. After continuing to meet with faculty and members of the administration for the purpose of finding an acceptable alternative, Defendant Wyman called Plaintiff in the morning of June 26, 1990 and informed her that she could present her concerns in a faculty meeting later that afternoon. After making a presentation and answering questions from the faculty, Plaintiff was asked to leave so that the faculty could deliberate over the alternatives issue.

31. In a letter from Defendant Wyman to Plaintiff, dated June 27, 1990, Defendant Wyman stated that Defendant Wright had formed an ad hoc college-wide committee to develop an alternative program for the use of animals in OSU-CVM teaching programs. Defendant Wyman stated that the development of the alternative might extend beyond fall quarter, necessitating possible modification in Plaintiff's educational timetable, and making it appear as if an alternative would be in place in a relatively timely fashion. Plaintiff indicated that this would be acceptable and acted in reliance on Defendant Wyman's representation.

32. In or about the week of July 2, 1990, Defendant Wyman stated that the committee was working on an alternative at that time, so that it would not be "unreasonable" to think that the committee might have the alternative developed by winter quarter, again making it appear as if an alternative would be in place in a relatively timely fashion. Again, Plaintiff indicated that this would be acceptable and acted in reliance on Defendant Wyman's representation.

33. As a result of Defendant Wyman's June 27 letter and the subsequent meeting, Plaintiff reasonably believed that the faculty and administration were sensitive to her position and would accommodate her religious and moral convictions within a reasonable time.

34. During July 1990, Plaintiff met with Dr. David Wilkie, who is the chair of the OSU-CVM ad hoc committee on alternatives. Dr. Wilkie stated that he was enthusiastic about developing an alternative, and discussed vari-

ous specific types of alternatives with Plaintiff. As a result, Plaintiff reasonably believed that the faculty and administration were sensitive to her position and would accommodate her religious and moral convictions within a reasonable time.

35. In or about the end of August, 1990, Defendant Wyman indicated to Plaintiff for the first time that the committee might not ever institute an alternative. As a result, Plaintiff canceled her plans for a September internship with a veterinarian practicing in Maryland so that she could devote her time to trying to obtain an alternative.

36. By letter dated September 13, 1990, Defendants' Counsel, Gary E. Brown and James E. Meeks, stated that it was the judgment of the faculty of the College that it is impossible to properly train a veterinarian without using some live, acquired animals, that there is simply no way that Plaintiff can complete, now or in the foreseeable future, the 620/21 course sequence without performing the procedures that violate Plaintiff's sincerely held religious and moral beliefs, and that if she is unwilling to do these procedures she will fail the course. The letter further states that failure to perform the surgery will result in preclusion from ever earning a degree at OSU-CVM. The letter then states that if Plaintiff's beliefs are so strong on this issue, she should consider a different career path.

37. On September 19, 1990, Plaintiff began her fall quarter. Since that time, she has sought and received reading and other assignments by instructors in course 620/21. She has completed each assignment given to her and in every possible way has attempted to learn the information and skills necessary to her chosen profession.

38. On or about September 20, 1990, Ms. Betty Hudson, of the Provost's office, told Plaintiff that it would take at least four to five years to establish an alternative.

39. In a letter, dated September 21, 1990, Plaintiff was told by Defendant Birchard, that failure to participate in the Operative Practice Laboratories without a valid excuse will result in a failing grade at the end of Fall Quarter.

40. In a letter from Defendant Bednarski, Head of Anesthesiology, dated September 26, 1990, Plaintiff was informed that it is the position of the anesthesia faculty that there currently exists no acceptable alternative to participation in the Operative Practice course, and that Plaintiff would receive a failing grade for all anesthesia laboratories.

41. In a letter from Defendant Muir, dated September 27, 1990, Plaintiff was informed that she has been issued a failing grade for the September 20, 1990 laboratory, in which she refused to participate for religious reasons.

42. On October 3, 1990, Defendant Wyman requested a meeting with Plaintiff. At this meeting, Defendant Wyman explained that he simply requested the meeting since procedure dictated that he meet with any "failing" student. Having fulfilled the protocol requirements for "failing" students, Defendant Wyman had nothing further to say and the meeting was concluded.

43. On or about November 7, 1990, certain OSU-CVM students circulated a letter that criticized Plaintiff, and that had been edited upon the advice of Defendant Wyman to exclude reference to Plaintiff's religious beliefs, further demonstrating Defendant Wyman's utter disregard for Plaintiff's free exercise of her religion.

44. On November 7, 1990, Defendant Wyman held a meeting of Plaintiff's class, ostensibly to discuss curricular concerns. At that meeting, Defendant Wyman ridiculed Plaintiff's religious and moral beliefs, misrepresented Plaintiff's position about her request for an alternative, and did nothing to stop other students in the room from ridiculing Plaintiff's religious and moral beliefs.

45. On November 16, 1990, Plaintiff participated in a radio interview on WTVN in Columbus, Ohio. The host of the interview was Mr. James Bleikamp. Also interviewed during the same program were two of Plaintiff's fellow students, Mr. John Manolukas and Mr. George Belbey. During the interview, Mr. Manolukas admitted that he had received information about Plaintiff's request for an educational alternative from Defendant Wyman. Plaintiff maintains that the information provided by Defendant Wyman to Mr. Manolukas was viewed as confidential by Plaintiff and, in any event, was not represented accurately.

46. To the best of Plaintiff's knowledge and belief, at least one other student at OSU-CVM has continued to be enrolled in the veterinary school, as a senior, without having passed a junior level course.

47. To the best of Plaintiff's knowledge and belief, other students at OSU-CVM were allowed to perform many techniques on client-owned animals without having any prior experience in live acquired animal surgery and/or techniques.

48. To the best of Plaintiff's knowledge and belief, at least one other student has been provided with alternatives in senior-level mandatory courses at OSU-CVM.

49. Plaintiff has been and remains ready, willing, and able to perform alternative work in order to satisfy the requirements of course 620/21. She has proposed, as an alternative, that she participate in every aspect of course 620/21 that does not involve live animal use, that she practice surgical and technical skills on cadavers of animals that were not killed solely

for educational purposes, that she perform surgery on client-owned or other non-experimental animals who require the procedures under the supervision of a veterinarian (and to receive an "incomplete" until such arrangements are made), that she extend her surgical rotations during her fourth year, and that she take all surgical electives offered to fourth-year students which utilize client-owned or other non-experimental animals, to ensure adequate experience in live animal surgery.

50. Plaintiff has suffered and is suffering the following harm: (1) Plaintiff has received and will continue to receive zero credit towards her third year surgery lab requirements as a result of her religious and moral beliefs; (2) Plaintiff is facing imminent failure of required course 620/21; (3) Plaintiff is facing imminent expulsion from school by mid-December 1990; and (4) Defendants' discriminatory actions have threatened Plaintiff's career and wasted valuable time and resources.

COUNT ONE

51. Plaintiff repeats each and every allegation contained in paragraphs 1 through 49, as set forth herein in their entirety and makes the same a part hereof by reference thereto.

52. Defendants' refusal to provide Plaintiff an alternative, despite Plaintiff's sincerely held religious and moral beliefs, deny Plaintiff the right to free exercise of religion under the first amendment of the Constitution of the United States, as applied to the State of Ohio by the fourteenth amendment to the Constitution of the United States. In addition, Defendants' actions and policies undertaken pursuant to the laws, customs, usages, and practices of the State of Ohio are, therefore, unconstitutional and unlawful pursuant to 42 U.S.C. 1983.

COUNT TWO

53. Plaintiff repeats each and every allegation contained in paragraphs 1 through 51, as set forth herein in their entirety and makes the same a part hereof by reference thereto.

54. Defendants' refusal to provide Plaintiff an alternative, despite Plaintiff's sincerely held religious and moral beliefs, violate Article I, section 7 of the Ohio State Constitution, which guarantees inalienable rights including the free exercise of religion.

COUNT THREE

55. Plaintiff repeats and realleges the allegations of paragraphs 1 through

53, as set forth herein in their entirety and makes the same a part hereof by reference thereto.

56. Defendants' actions, including, but not limited to, inquiring into Plaintiff's animal rights beliefs, instructing Plaintiff not to "make waves" regarding Plaintiff's concerns, and instructing faculty not to speak with Plaintiff, deny Plaintiff the right to free speech under the first amendment to the Constitution of the United States as applied to the State of Ohio by the fourteenth amendment to the Constitution of the United States. In addition, Defendants' actions and policies undertaken pursuant to the laws, customs, usages, and practices of the state of Ohio are, therefore, unconstitutional and unlawful pursuant to 42 U.S.C. 1983.

COUNT FOUR

57. Plaintiff repeats and realleges the allegations of paragraphs 1 through 55, as set forth herein in their entirety and makes the same a part hereof by reference thereto.

58. Defendants' actions, including, but not limited to, inquiring into Plaintiff's animal rights beliefs, instructing Plaintiff not to "make waves" regarding Plaintiff's concerns, and instructing faculty not to speak with Plaintiff, deny Plaintiff the right to free speech under Article I, section 11 of the Constitution of the State of Ohio.

COUNT FIVE

59. Plaintiff repeats each and every allegation contained in paragraphs 1 through 57, as set forth herein in their entirety and makes the same a part hereof by reference thereto.

60. Defendants' actions, including, but not limited to, inquiring into Plaintiff's animal rights beliefs, instructing Plaintiff not to "make waves" regarding Plaintiff's concerns, and instructing faculty not to speak with Plaintiff, deny Plaintiff the right to free association under the first amendment to the Constitution of the United States as applied to the State of Ohio by the fourteenth amendment to the Constitution of the United States. In addition, Defendants' actions and policies undertaken pursuant to the laws, customs, usages, and practices of the state of Ohio are, therefore, unconstitutional and unlawful pursuant to 42 U.S.C. 1983.

COUNT SIX

61. Plaintiff repeats and realleges the allegations of paragraphs 1 through 59, as set forth herein in their entirety and makes the same a part hereof by reference thereto.

62. Defendants' actions, including, but not limited to, inquiring into Plaintiff's animal rights beliefs, instructing Plaintiff not to "make waves" regarding Plaintiff's concerns, and instructing faculty not to speak with Plaintiff, deny Plaintiff the right to free association under Article I, section 3 of the Constitution of the State of Ohio.

COUNT SEVEN

63. Plaintiff repeats each and every allegation contained in paragraphs 1 through 61, as set forth herein in their entirety and makes the same a part hereof by reference thereto.

64. Defendants' denial to Plaintiff of an educational alternative to the surgery course 620/21 requirements despite her religious and moral beliefs, and Defendants' consequent violation of Plaintiff's fundamental rights, violate the due process clause of the fourteenth amendment to the United States Constitution. In addition, Defendants' actions and policies undertaken pursuant to the laws, customs, usages, and practices of the state of Ohio are, therefore, unconstitutional and unlawful pursuant to 42 U.S.C. 1983.

COUNT EIGHT

65. Plaintiff repeats each and every allegation contained in paragraphs 1 through 63, as set forth herein in their entirety and makes the same a part hereof by reference thereto.

66. The actions of the Defendants, individually and collectively, violate the fourteenth amendment to the United States Constitution, in that they have deprived, and are continuing to deprive, Plaintiff of her property interest in her education, of her liberty interests in her reputation, standing, and future educational and career opportunities, all without procedural due process. Defendants' refusal to accommodate Plaintiff's religious and moral beliefs, and refusal to undertake reasonable alternative studies and actions penalizing her were based on unlawful, irrelevant, unfounded and arbitrary and capricious criteria.

67. This deprivation of Plaintiff's property and liberty interests occurred as a result of Defendants' failure to consider the religious and moral nature

of Plaintiff's beliefs and objections to vivisection and the possibility and value of alternative assignments. In addition, Defendants' actions and policies undertaken pursuant to the laws, customs, usages, and practices of the State of Ohio are, therefore, unconstitutional and unlawful pursuant to 42 U.S.C. 1983.

COUNT NINE

68. Plaintiff repeats each and every allegation contained in paragraphs 1 through 65, as set forth herein in their entirety and makes the same a part hereof by reference thereto.

69. Defendants' refusal to provide Plaintiff an alternative, despite her religious and moral beliefs, and discriminatory actions towards Plaintiff based on her religious and moral beliefs, and in light of Defendants' differential treatment of other students constitutes an impermissible burden on her first amendment rights, and as such, creates a state classification of discrimination against students with her religious and moral beliefs. Such classification violates Plaintiff's equal protection rights under the fourteenth amendment of the Constitution of the United States.

Defendants' actions and policies undertaken pursuant to the laws, customs, usages, and practices of the State of Ohio are, therefore, unconstitutional and unlawful pursuant to 42 U.S.C. 1983.

COUNT TEN

70. Plaintiff repeats each and every allegation contained in paragraphs 1 through 68, as set forth herein in their entirety and makes the same a part hereof by reference thereto.

71. Defendants' refusal to provide Plaintiff an alternative, despite her religious and moral beliefs, and Defendants' discriminatory actions towards Plaintiff based on her religious and moral beliefs, constitutes an impermissible burden on her first amendment rights, and as such, creates a state classification of discrimination against students with her religious and moral beliefs. Such classification violates Plaintiff's equal protection rights under Article II, Section 26 of the Ohio Constitution.

COUNT ELEVEN

72. Plaintiff repeats each and every allegation contained in paragraphs 1 through 70, as set forth herein in their entirety and makes the same a part hereof by reference thereto.

73. Defendants' denial to Plaintiff of an educational alternative to the course 620/21 curriculum because of her religious and moral beliefs, violates the contract between Plaintiff and Defendants, in which Plaintiff has paid money in exchange for and education that is nondiscriminatory and respectful of a student's religious and moral principles. By making decisions about Plaintiff's education that were not based on Plaintiff's best interest or any legitimate interests that Defendants may have, and by instead making decisions based on animus against Plaintiff because of her sincerely held religious and moral beliefs, Defendants have violated their contract with Plaintiff.

COUNT TWELVE

74. Plaintiff repeats each and every allegation contained in paragraphs 1 through 72, as set forth herein in their entirety and makes the same a part hereof by reference thereto.

75. Defendants' assurances in the early summer that an alternative would be made available within a reasonable period of time and would likely be in place before the end of Plaintiff's third year, reasonably induced Plaintiff to rely on those promises to her detriment, thus making Defendants liable to Plaintiff under a promissory estoppel theory.

COUNT THIRTEEN

76. Plaintiff repeats each and every allegation contained in paragraphs 1 through 74, as set forth herein in their entirety and makes the same a part hereof by reference thereto.

77. Defendant Wyman's blatant failure to fulfill his designated responsibility to act as a student advocate on behalf of Plaintiff, and his failure to ensure that productive and meaningful lines of communication are maintained between students, faculty and administration, and that students' problems are addressed in a meaningful manner, constitutes a violation of Defendant's contractual obligations to Plaintiff.

COUNT FOURTEEN

78. Plaintiff repeats each and every allegation contained in paragraphs 1 through 76, as set forth herein in their entirety and makes the same a part hereof by reference hereto.

79. Defendant Wyman's conduct, including, but not limited to, his harassment of Plaintiff, through public ridicule of her deeply held religious and moral beliefs, and his disclosure to other students of information about

Plaintiff made confidential under federal law, has been motivated by an intent to retaliate against Plaintiff for the free expression of her deeply held religious and moral beliefs, by an animus toward Plaintiff's religious and moral beliefs, and for the purpose of chilling her expression of such beliefs, and has caused, and continues to cause, Plaintiff emotional harm, embarrassment, and ridicule.

COUNT FIFTEEN

80. Plaintiff repeats each and every allegation contained in paragraphs 1 through 78, as set forth herein in their entirety and makes the same a part hereof by reference hereto.

81. Defendant Wyman's conduct, including, but not limited to, his disclosure of information about Plaintiff's educational status without express permission from Plaintiff violates 20 U.S.C. 1232g, and is actionable under 42 U.S.C. 1983.

WHEREFORE, Plaintiff requests this Court to:

(1) declare that the actions of the Defendants denied Plaintiff the right to free exercise of religion under the first amendment of the United States Constitution and Article I, section 11 of the Ohio Constitution, and are, therefore, unconstitutional and void;

(2) declare that the actions of the Defendants denied Plaintiff the right to free speech under the first amendment of the Constitution of the United States, and Article I, Section 11 of the Ohio State Constitution;

(3) declare that the actions of the Defendants denied Plaintiff the right to free association under the first amendment of the Constitution of the United States, and Article I, Section 3 of the Ohio State Constitution;

(4) declare that the actions of the Defendants denied Plaintiff the right to due process under the fourteenth amendment of the Constitution of the United States;

(5) declare that the actions of Defendants denied Plaintiff the right to equal protection under the fourteenth amendment of the Constitution of the United States and Article 2, Section 26 of the Ohio State Constitution;

(6) declare that the Defendants violated their contractual relationship with Plaintiff to provide a nondiscriminatory education which is respectful of her religious and moral principles, and breached their promise to provide Plaintiff with an alternative within a reasonable period of time, knowing Plaintiff would rely upon this promise, and which promise Plaintiff did reasonably rely upon to her detriment;

(7) declare that Defendant Wyman`s actions have caused, and are continuing to cause, Plaintiff emotional harm, embarrassment, and ridicule;

(8) direct Defendants to provide Plaintiff an alternative to using, harming, and killing healthy animals and to provide full credit to Plaintiff for the course 620/21 curriculum upon her completion of that alternative;

(9) enjoin temporarily and permanently, the Defendants from failing Plaintiff as a result of her refusal to complete course 620/21 or to participate in the actions to which Plaintiff objects on sincerely held religious and moral grounds;

(10) enjoin temporarily and permanently, the Defendants from imposing on Plaintiff any penalty of any kind as a result of her refusal to complete course 620/21 or to participate in the actions to which Plaintiff objects on sincerely held religious and moral grounds;

(11) direct Defendants to rectify and remove, or otherwise refrain from including, penalties or comments from Plaintiff's academic record resulting from her religious and moral objection to the current 620/21 surgery lab requirements;

(12) award Plaintiff compensatory and punitive damages;

(13) award Plaintiff attorneys fees and costs; and

(14) direct other relief as this Court deems just and equitable.

Respectfully submitted,

Kathleen B. Schulte (0031448)
SPATER, GITTES, SCHULTE & KOLMAN
723 Oak Street
Columbus, Ohio 43205
(614) 221-1160
Trial Attorney for Plaintiff

Of Counsel:

Gary L. Francione
Professor of Law
Rutgers Law School
15 Washington Street
Newark, New Jersey 07102

(201) 648-5989

JURY DEMAND

Pursuant to Federal Rules of Civil Procedure 38(b) and 39, Plaintiff hereby demands a trial by jury as to all issues triable by jury.

Source: Rutgers University School of Law Animal Rights Law Project.

APPENDIX 5:
STATE HUNTER HARASSMENT STATUTES

STATE	STATUTE
ALASKA	Alaska Statutes Sec. 16.05.790
ARIZONA	Ariz. Rev. Stat. Ann. § 17-316
ARKANSAS	Ark. Code Ann. § 5-71-228
CALIFORNIA	Ca. Fish & Game Code § 2009
COLORADO	Colo. Rev. Stat. § 33-6-115.5
CONNECTICUT	Conn. Gen. Stat. § 53a-183a
FLORIDA	28 Fla. Stat. ch. § 372.705
GEORGIA	Ga. Code Ann. § 27-3-151
IDAHO	Idaho Code § 36-1510
ILLINOIS	Ill. Rev. Stat. ch. 720 § 125/2
INDIANA	Ind. Code § 14-22-34-5; § 14-22-37-2
IOWA	Iowa Code. § 481A.125
KANSAS	Kan. Stat. Ann. § 32-1014
KENTUCKY	Ky. Rev. State. Ann. § 150.710
MAINE	Me. Rev. Stat. Ann. tit. 12 § 7541
MARYLAND	Md. Code Ann. Nat. Res.§ 10-422
MASSACHUSETTS	Mass. Gen. L. ch. 131, § 5c
MINNESOTA	Minn. Stat. § 97A.037
MISSISSIPPI	Miss. Code Ann. § 49-7-147
MISSOURI	Mo. Rev. Stat. § 578.152
MONTANA	Mont. Code. Ann. § 87-3-141
NEW HAMPSHIRE	N.H. Rev. Stat. Ann. § 207:57

STATE	STATUTE
NEW JERSEY	N.J.S.A. § 23:7A-1; § 23:7A-2
NEW MEXICO	N.M. Stat. Ann. § 17-2-7.1
NEW YORK	N.Y. Envir. Conserv. § 11-0110
NEVADA	Nev. Rev. Stat. § 503.015
NORTH CAROLINA	N.C. Gen. Stat. § 113-295
NORTH DAKOTA	N.D. Cent. Code § 20.1-01-31
OHIO	Ohio Rev. Code Ann. § 1533.03
OKLAHOMA	Ok. Stat. tit. 29, § 5-212
OREGON	Or. Rev. Stat. § 496.994
PENNSYLVANIA	34 Pa. Cons. Stat. § 2302
RHODE ISLAND	R. I. Gen. Laws § 20-13-16
SOUTH CAROLINA	S.C. Code Ann. § 50-1-137
SOUTH DAKOTA	S.D. Codified Laws Ann. § 41-1-8
TENNESSEE	Tenn. Code Ann. § 70-4-301; §70-4-302
TEXAS	Tx. Parks & Wild. § 62.0125
UTAH	Utah Code Ann. § 23-20-29
VERMONT	Vt. Stat. Ann. tit. 10, § 4708
VIRGINIA	Va. Code Ann. § 29.1-521.1
WASHINGTON	Wash. Rev. Code § 77.16.340

APPENDIX 6:
SAMPLE HUNTER HARASSMENT
STATUTE—STATE OF MASSACHUSETTS

MASSACHUSETTS GENERAL LAW

PART I. ADMINISTRATION OF THE GOVERNMENT

TITLE XIX. AGRICULTURE AND CONSERVATION

CHAPTER 131. INLAND FISHERIES AND GAME AND OTHER NATURAL RESOURCES

§ 5C. INTERFERENCE WITH HUNTING, FISHING OR TRAPPING PROHIBITED; PENALTY.

No person shall obstruct, interfere with or otherwise prevent the lawful taking of fish or wildlife by another at the locale where such activity is taking place. It shall be a violation of this section for a person to intentionally

(1) drive or disturb wildlife or fish for the purpose of interrupting a lawful taking;

(2) block, follow, impede or otherwise harass another who is engaged in the lawful taking of fish or wildlife;

(3) use natural or artificial visual, aural, olfactory or physical stimulus to effect wildlife in order to hinder or prevent such taking;

(4) erect barriers with the intent to deny ingress or egress to areas where the lawful taking of wildlife may occur;

(5) interject himself into the line of fire;

(6) effect the condition or placement of personal or public property intended for use in the taking of wildlife; or

(7) enter or remain upon public lands, or upon private lands without the permission of the owner or his agent, with intent to violate this section. The superior court shall have jurisdiction to issue an injunction to enjoin any such conduct or conspiracy in violation of the provisions of this section. A person who sustains damage as a result of any act which is in violation of this section may bring a civil action for punitive damages. Environmental protection officers and other law enforcement officers with arrest powers shall be authorized to enforce the provisions of this section.

This section shall not apply to the owners of the lands or waters or tenants or other persons acting under the authority of such owners of the lands or waters.

APPENDIX 7:
WILD AND FREE-ROAMING HORSES AND BURROS ACT

UNITED STATES CODE

TITLE 16. CONSERVATION

CHAPTER 30. WILD HORSES, AND BURROS: PROTECTION, MANAGEMENT, AND CONTROL

§ 1331. CONGRESSIONAL FINDINGS AND DECLARATION OF POLICY

Congress finds and declares that wild free-roaming horses and burros are living symbols of the historic and pioneer spirit of the West; that they contribute to the diversity of life forms within the Nation and enrich the lives of the American people; and that these horses and burros are fast disappearing from the American scene. It is the policy of Congress that wild free-roaming horses and burros shall be protected from capture, branding, harassment, or death; and to accomplish this they are to be considered in the area where presently found, as an integral part of the natural system of the public lands.

§ 1332. DEFINITIONS

As used in this Act [16 USCS §§ 1331 et seq.]—

(a) "Secretary" means the Secretary of the Interior when used in connection with public lands administered by him through the Bureau of Land Management and the Secretary of Agriculture in connection with public lands administered by him through the Forest Service;

(b) "wild free-roaming horses and burros" means all unbranded and unclaimed horses and burros on public lands of the United States;

(c) "range" means the amount of land necessary to sustain an existing herd or herds of wild free-roaming horses and burros, which does not exceed their known territorial limits, and which is devoted principally but not necessarily exclusively to their welfare in keeping with the multiple-use management concept for the public lands;

(d) "herd" means one or more stallions and his mares; [and]

(e) "public lands" means any lands administered by the Secretary of the Interior through the Bureau of Land Management or by the Secretary of Agriculture through the Forest Service. [; and]

(f) "excess animals" means wild free-roaming horses or burros (1) which have been removed from an area by the Secretary pursuant to applicable law or, (2) which must be removed from an area in order to preserve and maintain a thriving natural ecological balance and multiple-use relationship in that area.

§ 1333. POWERS AND DUTIES OF SECRETARY

(a) Jurisdiction; management; ranges; ecological balance objectives; scientific recommendations; forage allocation adjustments. All wild free-roaming horses and burros are hereby declared to be under the jurisdiction of the Secretary for the purpose of management and protection in accordance with the provisions of this Act [16 USCS §§ 1331 et seq.]. The Secretary is authorized and directed to protect and manage wild free-roaming horses and burros as components of the public lands, and he may designate and maintain specific ranges on public lands as sanctuaries for their protection and preservation, where the Secretary after consultation with the wildlife agency of the State wherein any such range is proposed and with the Advisory Board established in section 7 of this Act [16 USCS § 1337] deems such action desirable. The Secretary shall manage wild free-roaming horses and burros in a manner that is designed to achieve and maintain a thriving natural ecological balance on the public lands. He shall consider the recommendations of qualified scientists in the field of biology and ecology, some of whom shall be independent of both Federal and State agencies and may include members of the Advisory Board established in section 7 of this Act [16 USCS § 1337]. All management activities shall be at the minimal feasible level and shall be carried out in consultation with the wildlife agency of the State wherein such lands are located in order to protect the natural ecological balance of all wildlife species which inhabit such lands, particularly endangered wildlife species. Any adjustments in forage allocations on any such lands shall take into consideration the needs of other wildlife species which inhabit such lands.

(b) Inventory and determinations; consultation; overpopulation; research study: submittal to Congress.

(1) The Secretary shall maintain a current inventory of wild free-roaming horses and burros on given areas of the public lands. The purpose of such inventory shall be to: make determinations as to whether and where an overpopulation exists and whether action should be taken to remove excess animals; determine appropriate management levels of wild free-roaming horses and burros on these areas of the public lands; and determine whether appropriate management levels should be achieved by the removal or destruction of excess animals, or other options (such as sterilization, or natural controls on population levels). In making such determinations the Secretary shall consult with the United States Fish and Wildlife Service, wildlife agencies of the State or States wherein wild free-roaming horses and burros are located, such individuals independent of Federal and State government as have been recommended by the National Academy of Sciences, and such other individuals whom he determines have scientific expertise and special knowledge of wild horse and burro protection, wildlife management and animal husbandry as related to rangeland management.

(2) Where the Secretary determines on the basis of (i) the current inventory of lands within his jurisdiction; (ii) information contained in any land use planning completed pursuant to section 202 of the Federal Land Policy and Management Act of 1976 [43 USCS § 1712]; (iii) information contained in court ordered environmental impact statements as defined in section 2 [3] of the Public Range Lands Improvement Act of 1978 [43 USCS § 1902]; and (iv) such additional information as becomes available to him from time to time, including that information developed in the research study mandated by this section, or in the absence of the information contained in (i—iv) above on the basis of all information currently available to him, that an overpopulation exists on a given area of the public lands and that action is necessary to remove excess animals, he shall immediately remove excess animals from the range so as to achieve appropriate management levels. Such action shall be taken, in the following order and priority, until all excess animals have been removed so as to restore a thriving natural ecological balance to the range, and protect the range from the deterioration associated with overpopulation:

(A) The Secretary shall order old, sick, or lame animals to be destroyed in the most humane manner possible;

(B) The Secretary shall cause such number of additional excess wild free-roaming horses and burros to be humanely captured and removed for private maintenance and care for which he determines an adoption demand exists by qualified individuals, and for which he determines he can assure humane treatment and care (including proper transportation, feeding, and handling): Provided, That, not more than four animals may be adopted per year by any individual unless the Secretary determines in writing that such individual is capable of humanely caring for more than four animals, including the transportation of such animals by the adopting party; and

(C) The Secretary shall cause additional excess wild free-roaming horses and burros for which an adoption demand by qualified individuals does not exist to be destroyed in the most humane and cost efficient manner possible.

(3) For the purpose of furthering knowledge of wild horse and burro population dynamics and their interrelationship with wildlife, forage and water resources, and assisting him in making his determination as to what constitutes excess animals, the Secretary shall contract for a research study of such animals with such individuals independent of Federal and State government as may be recommended by the National Academy of Sciences for having scientific expertise and special knowledge of wild horse and burro protection, wildlife management and animal husbandry as related to rangeland management. The terms and outline of such research study shall be determined by a research design panel to be appointed by the President of the National Academy of Sciences. Such study shall be completed and submitted by the Secretary to the Senate and House of Representatives on or before January 1, 1983.

(c) Title of transferee to limited number of excess animals adopted for requisite period. Where excess animals have been transferred to a qualified individual for adoption and private maintenance pursuant to this Act [16 USCS §§ 1331 et seq.] and the Secretary determines that such individual has provided humane conditions, treatment and care for such animal or animals for a period of one year, the Secretary is authorized upon application by the transferee to grant title to not more than four animals to the transferee at the end of the one-year period.

(d) Loss of status as wild free-roaming horses and burros; exclusion from coverage. Wild free-roaming horses and burros or their remains shall lose their status as wild free-roaming horses or burros and shall no longer be considered as falling within the purview of this Act [16 USCS §§ 1331 et seq.]—

(1) upon passage of title pursuant to subsection (c) except for the limitation of subsection (c)(1) of this section; or

(2) if they have been transferred for private maintenance or adoption pursuant to this Act [16 USCS §§ 1331 et seq.] and die of natural causes before passage of title; or

(3) upon destruction by the Secretary or his designee pursuant to subsection (b) of this section; or

(4) if they die of natural causes on the public lands or on private lands where maintained thereon pursuant to section 4 [16 USCS § 1334] and disposal is authorized by the Secretary or his designee; or

(5) upon destruction or death for purposes of or incident to the program authorized in section 3 of this Act [this section]; Provided, That no wild free-roaming horse or burro or its remains may be sold or transferred for consideration for processing into commercial products.

§ 1334. PRIVATE MAINTENANCE; NUMERICAL APPROXIMATION; STRAYS ON PRIVATE LANDS; REMOVAL: DESTRUCTION BY AGENTS

If wild free-roaming horses or burros stray from public lands onto privately owned land, the owners of such land may inform the nearest Federal marshal or agent of the Secretary, who shall arrange to have the animals removed. In no event shall such wild free-roaming horses and burros be destroyed except by the agents of the Secretary. Nothing in this section shall be construed to prohibit a private landowner from maintaining wild free-roaming horses or burros on his private lands, or lands leased from the Government, if he does so in a manner that protects them from harassment, and if the animals were not willfully removed or enticed from the public lands. Any individuals who maintain such wild free-roaming horses or burros on their private lands or lands leased from the Government shall notify the appropriate agent of the Secretary and supply him with a reasonable approximation of the number of animals so maintained.

§ 1337. JOINT ADVISORY BOARD; APPOINTMENT; MEMBERSHIP; FUNCTIONS; QUALIFICATIONS; REIMBURSEMENT LIMITATIONS

The Secretary of the Interior and the Secretary of Agriculture are authorized and directed to appoint a joint advisory board of not more than nine members to advise them on any matter relating to wild free-roaming horses and burros and their management and protection. They shall select as advisers persons who are not employees of the Federal or State Governments and whom they deem to have special knowledge about protection of horses and burros, management of wildlife, animal husbandry, or natural resources management. Members of the board shall not receive reimbursement except for travel and other expenditures necessary in connection with their services.

§ 1338. CRIMINAL PROVISIONS

(a) Violations; penalties; trial. Any person who—

(1) willfully removes or attempts to remove a wild free-roaming horse or burro from the public lands, without authority from the Secretary, or

(2) converts a wild free-roaming horse or burro to private use, without authority from the Secretary, or

(3) maliciously causes the death or harassment of any wild free-roaming horse or burro, or

(4) processes or permits to be processed into commercial products the remains of a wild free-roaming horse or burro, or

(5) sells, directly or indirectly, a wild free-roaming horse or burro maintained on private or leased land pursuant to section 4 of this Act [16 USCS § 1334], or the remains thereof, or

(6) willfully violates a regulation issued pursuant to this Act [16 USCS §§ 1331 et seq.],

shall be subject to a fine of not more than $ 2,000, or imprisonment for not more than one year, or both. Any person so charged with such violation by the Secretary may be tried and sentenced by any United States commissioner or magistrate designated for that purpose by the court by which he was appointed, in the same manner and subject to the same conditions as provided for in section 3401, title 18, United States Code [18 USCS § 3401].

(b) Arrest; appearance for examination or trial; warrants: issuance and execution. Any employee designated by the Secretary of the Interior or the Secretary of Agriculture shall have power, without warrant, to arrest any person committing in the presence of such employee a violation of this Act [16 USCS §§ 1331 et seq.] or any regulation made pursuant thereto, and to take such person immediately for examination or trial before an officer or court of competent jurisdiction, and shall have power to execute any warrant or other process issued by an officer or court of competent jurisdiction to enforce the provisions of this Act [16 USCS §§ 1331 et seq.] or regulations made pursuant thereto. Any judge of a court established under the laws of the United States, or any United States magistrate may, within his respective jurisdiction, upon proper oath or affirmation showing probable cause, issue warrants in all such cases.

§ 1339. LIMITATIONS OF AUTHORITY

Nothing in this Act [16 USCS §§ 1331 et seq.] shall be construed to authorize the Secretary to relocate wild free-roaming horses or burros to areas of the public lands where they do not presently exist.

§ 1340. JOINT REPORT TO CONGRESS; CONSULTATION AND COORDINATION OF IMPLEMENTATION, ENFORCEMENT, AND DEPARTMENTAL ACTIVITIES; STUDIES

After the expiration of thirty calendar months following the date of enactment of this Act [enacted Dec. 15, 1971], and every twenty-four calendar months thereafter, the Secretaries of the Interior and Agriculture will submit to Congress a joint report on the administration of this Act [16 USCS §§ 1331 et seq.], including a summary of enforcement and/or other actions taken thereunder, costs, and such recommendations for legislative or other actions as he might deem appropriate.

The Secretary of the Interior and the Secretary of Agriculture shall consult with respect to the implementation and enforcement of this Act [16 USCS §§ 1331 et seq.] and to the maximum feasible extent coordinate the activities of their respective departments and in the implementation and enforcement of this Act [16 USCS §§ 1331 et seq.]. The Secretaries are authorized and directed to undertake those studies of the habits of wild free-roaming horses and burros that they may deem necessary in order to carry out the provisions of this Act [16 USCS §§ 1331 et seq.].

APPENDIX 8:
ENDANGERED SPECIES—CATEGORIZED BY STATE

SPECIES (COMMON NAME)	SPECIES (SCIENTIFIC NAME)
ALABAMA	
Acornshell, southern	Epioblasma othcaloogensis
Bat, Indiana	Myotis sodalis
Bat, gray	Myotis grisescens
Cavefish, Alabama	Speoplatyrhinus poulsoni
Chub, spotfin	Hybopsis monacha
Clubshell, black	Pleurobema curtum
Clubshell, ovate	Pleurobema perovatum
Clubshell, southern	Pleurobema decisum
Combshell, southern	Epioblasma penita
Combshell, upland	Epioblasma metastriata
Darter, boulder	Etheostoma wapiti
Darter, goldline	Percina aurolineata
Darter, slackwater	Etheostoma boschungi
Darter, snail	Percina tanasi
Darter, watercress	Etheostoma nuchale
Eagle, bald	Haliaeetus leucocephalus
Falcon, American peregrine	Falco peregrinus anatum
Fanshell	Cyprogenia stegaria
Heelsplitter, inflated	Potamilus inflatus
Kidneyshell, triangular	Ptychobranchus greeni

SPECIES (COMMON NAME)	SPECIES (SCIENTIFIC NAME)
ALABAMA Cont'd	
Lampmussel, Alabama	Lampsilis virescens
Manatee, West Indian	Trichechus manatus
Moccasinshell, Alabama	Medionidus acutissimus
Moccasinshell, Coosa	Medionidus parvulus
Mouse, Alabama beach	Peromyscus polionotus ammobates
Mouse, Perdido Key beach	Peromyscus polionotus trissyllepsis
Mucket, orange-nacre	Lampsilis perovalis
Mussel, ring pink	Obovaria retusa
Pearlymussel, Cumberland monkeyface	Quadrula intermedia
Pearlymussel, cracking	Hemistena lata
Pearlymussel, dromedary	Dromus dromas
Pearlymussel, little-wing	Pegias fabula
Pearlymussel, orange-foot pimple back	Plethobasus cooperianus
Pearlymussel, pale lilliput	Toxolasma cylindrellus
Pearlymussel, pink mucket	Lampsilis abrupta
Pearlymussel, purple cat's paw	Epioblasma obliquata obliquata
Pearlymussel	turgid-blossom, Epioblasma turgidula
Pearlymussel, white wartyback	Plethobasus cicatricosus
Pearlymussel, yellow-blossom	Epioblasma florentina
Pigtoe, dark	Pleurobema furvum
Pigtoe, fine-rayed	Fusconaia cuneolus
Pigtoe, flat	Pleurobema marshalli
Pigtoe, heavy	Pleurobema taitianum
Pigtoe, rough	Pleurobema plenum
Pigtoe, shiny	Fusconaia cor edgariana
Pigtoe, southern	Pleurobema georgianum
Plover, piping	Charadrius melodus
Pocketbook, fine-lined	Lampsilis altilis
Riversnail, Anthony's	Athearnia anthonyi
Salamander, Red Hills	Phaeognathus hubrichti
Sculpin, pygmy	Cottus pygmaeus

SPECIES (COMMON NAME)	SPECIES (SCIENTIFIC NAME)

ALABAMA Cont'd

Shiner, Cahaba	Notropis cahabae
Shiner, Palezone	Notropis
Shiner, blue	Cyprinella caerulea
Shrimp, Alabama cave	Palaemonias alabamae
Snail, tulotoma	Tulotoma magnifica
Snake, eastern indigo	Drymarchon corais couperi
Stirrupshell	Quadrula stapes
Stork, wood	Mycteria americana
Sturgeon, Gulf	Acipenser oxyrhynchus desotoi
Tortoise, gopher	Gopherus polyphemus
Turtle	Pseudemys alabamensis
Turtle, Kemp's	Lepidochelys kempii
Turtle, flattened musk	Sternotherus depressus
Turtle, green sea	Chelonia mydas
Turtle, hawksbill sea	Eretmochelys imbricata
Turtle, leatherback sea	Dermochelys coriacea
Turtle, loggerhead sea	Caretta caretta
Woodpecker, red-cockaded	Picoides borealis

ALASKA

Curlew, Eskimo	Numenius borealis
Eider, spectacled	Somateria fischeri
Falcon, American peregrine	Falco peregrinus anatum
Goose, Aleutian Canada	Branta canadensis leucopareia

ARIZONA

Ambersnail, Kanab	Oxyloma haydeni kanabensis
Bat, lesser	Leptonycteris curasoae yerbabuenae
Bobwhite, masked	Colinus virginianus ridgwayi
Catfish	Yaqui, Ictalurus pricei
Chub, Sonora	Gila ditaenia
Chub, Virgin River	Gila robusta semidnuda
Chub, Yaqui	Gila purpurea

SPECIES (COMMON NAME)	SPECIES (SCIENTIFIC NAME)
ARIZONA Cont'd	
Chub, bonytail	Gila elegans
Chub, humpback	Gila cypha
Eagle, bald	Haliaeetus leucocephalus
Falcon, American peregrine	Falco peregrinus anatum
Flycatcher, Southwestern willow	Empidonax traillii extimus
Jaguarundi	Felis yagouaroundi tolteca
Minnow	loach, Tiaroga) cobitis
Ocelot	Felis pardalis
Owl, Mexican spotted	Strix occidentalis lucida
Pronghorn, Sonoran	Antilocapra americana sonoriensis
Pupfish, desert	Cyprinodon macularius
Rail, Yuma clapper	Rallus longirostris yumanensis
Shiner, beautiful	Notropis formosa
Spikedace	Meda fulgida
Spinedace, Little Colorado	Lepidomeda vittata
Squawfish, Colorado	Ptychocheilus lucius
Squirrel, Mount Graham red	Tamiasciurus hudsonicus grahamensis
Sucker, razorback	Xyrauchen texanus
Topminnow	Poeciliopsis occidentalis
Tortoise, desert	Gopherus agassizii
Trout, Apache	Oncorhynchus apache
Trout, Gila	Oncorhynchus Salmo gilae
Vole	Microtus mexicanus hualpaiensis
Woundfin	Plagopterus argentissimus

ARKANSAS

Bat, Indiana	Myotis sodalis
Bat, Ozark big-eared	Plecotus townsendii ingens
Bat, gray	Myotis grisescens
Beetle, American burying	Nicrophorus americanus
Cavefish, Ozark	Amblyopsis rosae
Crayfish, cave [no common name	Cambarus aculabrum

SPECIES (COMMON NAME)	SPECIES (SCIENTIFIC NAME)

ARKANSAS Cont'd

Crayfish, cave	Cambarus zophonastes
Darter, leopard	Percina pantherina
Eagle, bald	Haliaeetus leucocephalus
Falcon, American peregrine	Falco peregrinus anatum
Fatmucket, Arkansas	Lampsilis powelli
Pearlymussel, Curtis'	Dysnomia florentina curtisi
Pearlymussel, pink mucket	Lampsilis abrupta
Pocketbook, fat	Potamilus Proptera capax
Pocketbook, speckled	Lampsilis streckeri
Rock-pocketbook, Ouachita	Arkansia wheeleri
Shagreen, Magazine Mountain	Mesodon magazinensis
Sturgeon	pallid, Scaphirhynchus albus
Tern, least	Sterna antillarum
Woodpecker, red-cockaded	Picoides borealis

CALIFORNIA

Beetle, delta green ground	Elaphrus viridis
Beetle, valley elderberry longhorn	Desmocerus californicus dimorphus
Butterfly, El Segundo blue	Euphilotes battoides allyni
Butterfly, Lange's metalmark	Apodemia mormo langei
Butterfly, Myrtle's silverspot	Speyeria zerene myrtleae
Butterfly, Oregon silverspot	Speyeria zerene hippolyta
Butterfly, Palos Verdes blue	Glaucopsyche lygdamus palosverdesensis
Butterfly, San Bruno elfin	Callophrys mossii bayensis
Butterfly, Smith's blue	Euphilotes enoptes smithi
Butterfly, bay checkerspot	Euphydryas editha bayensis
Butterfly, lotis blue	Lycaeides argyrognomon lotis
Butterfly, mission blue	Icaricia icarioides missionensis
Chub, Mohave tui	Gila bicolor mohavensis
Chub, Owens tui	Gila bicolor snyderi
Chub, bonytail	Gila elegans
Condor, California	Gymnogyps californianus

SPECIES (COMMON NAME)	SPECIES (SCIENTIFIC NAME)
CALIFORNIA Cont'd	
Crayfish, Shasta	Pacifastacus fortis
Eagle, bald	Haliaeetus leucocephalus
Fairy shrimp, Conservancy	Branchinecta conservatio
Fairy shrimp, longhorn	Branchinecta longiantenna
Fairy shrimp, riverside	Streptocephalus woottoni
Fairy shrimp, vernal pool	Branchinecta lynchi
Falcon, American peregrine	Falco peregrinus anatum
Fly, Delhi Sands flower-loving	Rhaphiomidas terminatus abdominalis
Flycatcher, Southwestern willow	Empidonax traillii extimus
Fox, San Joaquin kit	Vulpes macrotis mutica
Frog, California red-legged	Rana aurora draytonii
Gnatcatcher, coastal California	Polioptila californica californica
Goby, tidewater	Eucyclogobius newberryi
Goose, Aleutian Canada	Branta canadensis leucopareia
Kangaroo rat, Fresno	Dipodomys nitratoides exilis
Kangaroo rat, Morro Bay	Dipodomys heermanni morroensis
Kangaroo rat, Stephens	Dipodomys stephensi
Kangaroo rat, Tipton	Dipodomys nitratoides nitratoides
Kangaroo rat, giant	Dipodomys ingens
Lizard, Coachella Valley fringe-toed	Uma inornata
Lizard, Island night	Xantusia riversiana
Lizard, blunt-nosed leopard	Gambelia silus
Moth, Kern primrose sphinx	Euproserpinus euterpe
Mountain beaver, Point Arena	Aplodontia rufa nigra
Mouse, Pacific pocket	Perognathus longimembris pacificus
Mouse, salt marsh harvest	Reithrodontomys raviventris
Murrelet, marbled	Brachyramphus marmoratus marmoratus
Otter, southern sea	Enhydra lutris nereis
Owl, northern spotted	Strix occidentalis caurina
Pelican, brown	Pelecanus occidentalis
Plover, western snowy	Charadrius alexandrinus nivosus

SPECIES (COMMON NAME)	SPECIES (SCIENTIFIC NAME)
CALIFORNIA Cont'd	
Pupfish, Owens	Cyprinodon radiosus
Pupfish, desert	Cyprinodon macularius
Rail, California clapper	Rallus longirostris obsoletus
Rail, Yuma clapper	Rallus longirostris yumanensis
Rail, light-footed clapper	Rallus longirostris levipes
Salamander, Santa Cruz long-toed	Ambystoma macrodactylum croceum
Salamander, desert slender	Batrachoseps aridus
Shrike, San Clemente loggerhead	Lanius ludovicianus mearnsi
Shrimp, California freshwater	Syncaris pacifica
Smelt, delta	Hypomesus transpacificus
Snail, Morro shoulderband	Helminthoglypta walkeriana
Snake, San Francisco garter	Thamnophis sirtalis tetrataenia
Snake, giant garter	Thamnophis gigas
Sparrow, San Clemente sage	Amphispiza belli clementeae
Squawfish, Colorado	Ptychocheilus lucius
Stickleback, unarmored threespine	Gasterosteus aculeatus williamsoni
Sucker, Lost River	Deltistes luxatus
Sucker, Modoc	Catostomus microps
Sucker, razorback	Xyrauchen texanus
Sucker, shortnose	Chasmistes brevirostris
Tadpole shrimp, vernal pool	Lepidurus packardi
Tern, California least	Sterna antillarum browni
Toad, arroyo southwestern	Bufo microscaphus californicus
Tortoise, desert	Gopherus agassizii
Towhee, Inyo California	Pipilo crissalis eremophilus
Trout, Lahontan cutthroat	Oncorhynchus clarki henshawi
Trout, Little Kern golden	Oncorhynchus aguabonita whitei
Trout, Paiute cutthroat	Oncorhynchus clarki seleniris
Turtle, green sea	Chelonia mydas
Turtle, leatherback sea	Dermochelys coriacea
Turtle, loggerhead sea	Caretta caretta

SPECIES (COMMON NAME)	SPECIES (SCIENTIFIC NAME)

CALIFORNIA Cont'd

Turtle, olive	Lepidochelys olivacea
Vireo, least Bell's	Vireo bellii pusillus
Vole, Amargosa	Microtus californicus scirpensis

COLORADO

Bear, grizzly	Ursus arctos
Butterfly, Uncompahgre fritillary	Boloria acrocnema
Chub, bonytail	Gila elegans
Chub, humpback	Gila cypha
Crane, whooping	Grus americana
Eagle, bald	Haliaeetus leucocephalus
Falcon, American peregrine	Falco peregrinus anatum
Ferret, black-footed	Mustela nigripes
Flycatcher, Southwestern willow	Empidonax traillii extimus
Owl, Mexican spotted	Strix occidentalis lucida
Plover, piping	Charadrius melodus
Skipper, Pawnee montane	Hesperia leonardus
Squawfish, Colorado	Ptychocheilus lucius
Sucker, razorback	Xyrauchen texanus
Tern, least	Sterna antillarum
Trout, greenback cutthroat	Oncorhynchus clarki stomias
Wolf, gray	Canis lupus

CONNECTICUT

Beetle, Puritan tiger	Cicindela puritana
Beetle, northeastern beach tiger	Cicindela dorsalis dorsalis
Eagle, bald	Haliaeetus leucocephalus
Falcon, American peregrine	Falco peregrinus anatum
Mussel, dwarf wedge	Alasmidonta heterodon
Plover, piping	Charadrius melodus
Tern, roseate	Sterna dougallii dougallii
Turtle, Kemp's	Lepidochelys kempii
Turtle, green sea	Chelonia mydas

SPECIES (COMMON NAME)	SPECIES (SCIENTIFIC NAME)
CONNECTICUT Cont'd	
Turtle, hawksbill sea	Eretmochelys imbricata
Turtle, leatherback sea	Dermochelys coriacea
Turtle, loggerhead sea	Caretta caretta

DELAWARE

Eagle, bald	Haliaeetus leucocephalus
Falcon, American peregrine	Falco peregrinus anatum
Plover, piping	Charadrius melodus
Squirrel, Delmarva Peninsula fox	Sciurus niger cinereus
Turtle, Kemp's (Atlantic) ridley sea	Lepidochelys kempii
Turtle, green sea	Chelonia mydas
Turtle, hawksbill sea	Eretmochelys imbricata
Turtle, leatherback sea	Dermochelys coriacea
Turtle, loggerhead sea	Caretta caretta

DISTRICT OF COLUMBIA

Amphipod, Hay's Spring	Stygobromus hayi
Eagle, bald	Haliaeetus leucocephalus
Falcon, American peregrine	Falco peregrinus anatum

FLORIDA

Bat, gray	Myotis grisescens
Butterfly, Schaus swallowtail	Heraclides aristodemus ponceanus
Caracara, Audubon's crested	Polyborus plancus audubonii
Crocodile, American	Crocodylus acutus
Darter, Okaloosa	Etheostoma okaloosae
Deer, key	Odocoileus virginianus clavium
Eagle, bald	Haliaeetus leucocephalus
Falcon, American peregrine	Falco peregrinus anatum
Jay, Florida scrub Aphelocoma coerulescens coerulescens	
Kite, Everglade snail	Rostrhamus sociabilis plumbeus
Manatee, West Indian	Trichechus manatus
Mouse, Anastasia Island beach	Peromyscus polionotus phasma
Mouse, Choctawahatchee beach	Peromyscus polionotus allophrys

SPECIES (COMMON NAME)	SPECIES (SCIENTIFIC NAME)

FLORIDA Cont'd

Mouse, Key Largo cotton	Peromyscus gossypinus allapaticola
Mouse, Perdido Key beach	Peromyscus polionotus trissyllepsis
Mouse, southeastern beach	Peromyscus polionotus niveiventris
Panther, Florida	Felis concolor coryi
Plover, piping	Charadrius melodus
Rabbit, Lower Keys	Sylvilagus palustris hefneri
Rice rat	Oryzomys palustris natator
Shrimp, Squirrel Chimney Cave	Palaemonetes cummingi
Skink, bluetail	Eumeces egregius lividus
Skink, sand	Neoseps reynoldsi
Snail, Stock Island tree	Orthalicus reses
Snake, Atlantic salt marsh	Nerodia clarkii taeniata
Snake, eastern indigo	Drymarchon corais couperi
Sparrow, Cape Sable seaside	Ammodramus maritimus mirabilis
Sparrow, Florida grasshopper	Ammodramus savannarum floridanus
Stork, wood	Mycteria americana
Sturgeon, Gulf	Acipenser oxyrhynchus desotoi
Tern, roseate	Sterna dougallii dougallii
Turtle, Kemp's	Lepidochelys kempii
Turtle, green sea	Chelonia mydas
Turtle, hawksbill sea	Eretmochelys imbricata
Turtle, leatherback sea	Dermochelys coriacea
Turtle, loggerhead sea	Caretta caretta
Vole, Florida salt marsh	Microtus pennsylvanicus dukecampbelli
Woodpecker, red-cockaded	Picoides borealis
Woodrat, Key Largo	Neotoma floridana smalli

GEORGIA

Acornshell, southern	Epioblasma othcaloogensis
Bat, Indiana	Myotis sodalis
Bat, gray	Myotis grisescens
Clubshell, ovate	Pleurobema perovatum

SPECIES (COMMON NAME)	SPECIES (SCIENTIFIC NAME)
GEORGIA Cont'd	
Clubshell, southern	Pleurobema decisum
Combshell, upland	Epioblasma metastriata
Darter, Cherokee	Etheostoma
Darter, Etowah	Etheostoma etowahae
Darter, amber	Percina antesella
Darter, goldline	Percina aurolineata
Darter, snail	Percina tanasi
Eagle, bald	Haliaeetus leucocephalus
Falcon, American peregrine	Falco peregrinus anatum
Kidneyshell, triangular	Ptychobranchus greeni
Logperch, Conasauga	Percina jenkinsi
Manatee, West Indian	Trichechus manatus
Moccasinshell, Alabama	Medionidus acutissimus
Moccasinshell, Coosa	Medionidus parvulus
Pigtoe, southern	Pleurobema georgianum
Plover, piping	Charadrius melodus
Pocketbook, fine-lined	Lampsilis altilis
Shiner, blue	Cyprinella caerulea
Snake, eastern indigo	Drymarchon corais couperi
Stork, wood	Mycteria americana
Turtle, Kemp's	Lepidochelys kempii
Turtle, green sea	Chelonia mydas
Turtle, hawksbill sea	Eretmochelys imbricata
Turtle, leatherback sea	Dermochelys coriacea
Turtle, loggerhead sea	Caretta caretta
Woodpecker, red-cockaded	Picoides borealis

HAWAII

Bat, Hawaiian hoary	Lasiurus cinereus semotus
Coot, Hawaiian	Fulica americana alai
Creeper, Hawaii	Oreomystis mana
Creeper, Molokai	Paroreomyza flammeA

SPECIES (COMMON NAME)	SPECIES (SCIENTIFIC NAME)
HAWAII Cont'd	
Creeper, Oahu	Paroreomyza maculata
Crow, Hawaiian	Corvus hawaiiensis
Duck, Hawaiian	Anas wyvilliana
Duck, Laysan	Anas laysanensis
Finch, Laysan (honeycreeper	Telespyza cantans
Finch, Nihoa	Telespyza ultima
Goose, Hawaiian	Nesochen sandvicensis
Hawk, Hawaiian	Buteo solitarius
Honeycreeper, crested	Palmeria dolei
Millerbird, Nihoa	Acrocephalus familiaris kingi
Moorhen, Hawaiian common	Gallinula chloropus sandvicensis
Nukupu`u	Hemignathus lucidus
Palila	Loxioides bailleui
Parrotbill, Maui	Pseudonestor xanthophrys
Petrel, Hawaiian dark-rumped	Pterodroma phaeopygia sandwichensis
Po`ouli	Melamprosops phaeosoma
Shearwater, Newell's Townsend's	Puffinus auricularis newell
Snails, Oahu tree	Achatinella
Stilt, Hawaiian	Himantopus mexicanus knudseni
Thrush, Molokai	Myadestes lanaiensis rutha
Thrush, large Kauai	Myadestes myadestinus
Thrush, small Kauai	Myadestes palmeri
Turtle, green sea	Chelonia mydas
Turtle, hawksbill sea	Eretmochelys imbricata
Turtle, leatherback sea	Dermochelys coriacea
Turtle, loggerhead sea	Caretta caretta
Turtle, olive	Lepidochelys olivacea
`Akepa, Hawaii	Loxops coccineus coccineus
`Akepa, Maui	Loxops coccineus ochraceus
`Akialoa, Kauai	Hemignathus procerus
`Akiapola`au	Hemignathus munroi

SPECIES (COMMON NAME)	SPECIES (SCIENTIFIC NAME)

HAWAII Cont'd

| `O`o, Kauai | Moho braccatus |
| `O`u | Psittirostra psittacea |

IDAHO

Bear, grizzly	Ursus arctos
Caribou, woodland	Rangifer tarandus caribou
Crane, whooping	Grus americana
Eagle, bald	Haliaeetus leucocephalus
Falcon, American peregrine	Falco peregrinus anatum
Limpet, Banbury Springs	Lanx
Snail, Bliss Rapids	Taylorconcha serpenticola
Snail, Snake River physa	Physa natricina
Snail, Utah valvata	Valvata utahensis
Springsnail, Bruneau Hot	Pyrgulopsis bruneauensis
Springsnail, Idaho	Fontelicella idahoensis
Sturgeon, white	Acipenser transmontanus
Wolf, gray	Canis lupus

ILLINOIS

Bat, Indiana	Myotis sodalis
Bat, gray	Myotis grisescens
Butterfly, Karner blue	Lycaeides melissa samuelis
Dragonfly, Hine's emerald	Somatochlora hineana
Eagle, bald	Haliaeetus leucocephalus
Falcon, American peregrine	Falco peregrinus anatum
Fanshell	Cyprogenia stegaria
Pearlymussel, Higgins' eye	Lampsilis higginsi
Pearlymussel, orange-foot pimple back	Plethobasus cooperianus
Pearlymussel, pink mucket	Lampsilis abrupta
Pocketbook, fat	Potamilus capax
Snail, Iowa Pleistocene	Discus macclintocki
Sturgeon, pallid	Scaphirhynchus albus
Tern, least	Sterna antillarum

SPECIES (COMMON NAME)	SPECIES (SCIENTIFIC NAME)
INDIANA	
Bat, Indiana	Myotis sodalis
Bat, gray	Myotis grisescens
Butterfly, Karner blue	Lycaeides melissa samuelis
Butterfly, Mitchell's satyr	Neonympha mitchellii mitchellii
Clubshell	Pleurobema clava
Eagle, bald	Haliaeetus leucocephalus
Falcon, American peregrine	Falco peregrinus anatum
Fanshell	Cyprogenia stegaria
Mussel, ring pink	Obovaria retusa
Pearlymussel, cracking	Hemistena lata
Pearlymussel, orange-foot pimple back	Plethobasus cooperianus
Pearlymussel, pink mucket	Lampsilis abrupta
Pearlymussel, tubercled-blossom	Epioblasma torulosa torulosa
Pearlymussel, white cat's paw	Epioblasma obliquata perobliqua
Pearlymussel, white wartyback	Plethobasus cicatricosus
Pigtoe, rough	Pleurobema plenum
Plover, piping	Charadrius melodus
Pocketbook, fat	Potamilus capax
Riffleshell, northern	Epioblasma torulosa rangiana
Tern, least	Sterna antillarum
IOWA	
Bat, Indiana	Myotis sodalis
Eagle, bald	Haliaeetus leucocephalus
Falcon, American peregrine	Falco peregrinus anatum
Pearlymussel, Higgins' eye	Lampsilis higginsi
Plover, piping	Charadrius melodus
Snail, Iowa Pleistocen	Discus macclintocki
Sturgeon, pallid	Scaphirhynchus albus
Tern, least	Sterna antillarum
KANSAS	
Bat, Indiana	Myotis sodalis

SPECIES (COMMON NAME)	SPECIES (SCIENTIFIC NAME)

KANSAS Cont'd

Bat, gray	Myotis grisescens
Crane, whooping	Grus american
Curlew, Eskimo	Numenius borealis
Eagle, bald	Haliaeetus leucocephalus
Falcon, American peregrine	Falco peregrinus anatum
Ferret, black-footed	Mustela nigripes
Madtom, Neosho	Noturus placidus
Plover, piping	Charadrius melodus
Sturgeon, pallid	Scaphirhynchus albus
Tern, least	Sterna antillarum
Vireo, black-capped	Vireo atricapillus

KENTUCKY

Bat, Indiana	Myotis sodalis
Bat, Virginia big-eared	Plecotus townsendii virginianus
Bat, gray	Myotis grisescens
Clubshell	Pleurobema clava
Dace, blackside	Phoxinus cumberlandensis
Darter, relict	Etheostoma chienense
Eagle, bald	Haliaeetus leucocephalus
Falcon, American peregrine	Falco peregrinus anatum
Fanshell	Cyprogenia stegaria
Mussel, ring pink	Obovaria retusa
Mussel, winged mapleleaf	Quadrula fragosa
Pearlymussel, Cumberland bean	Villosa trabalis
Pearlymussel, cracking	Hemistena lata
Pearlymussel, dromedary	Dromus dromas
Pearlymussel, little-wing	Pegias fabula
Pearlymussel, orange-foot pimple back	Plethobasus cooperianus
Pearlymussel, pink mucket	Lampsilis abrupta
Pearlymussel, purple cat's paw	Epioblasma obliquata obliquata
Pearlymussel, tubercled-blossom	Epioblasma torulosa torulosa

SPECIES (COMMON NAME)	SPECIES (SCIENTIFIC NAME)
KENTUCKY Cont'd	
Pearlymussel, white wartyback	Plethobasus cicatricosus
Pigtoe, rough	Pleurobema plenum
Plover, piping	Charadrius melodus
Pocketbook, fat	Potamilus capax
Riffleshell, northern	Epioblasma torulosa rangiana
Riffleshell, tan	Epioblasma walkeri
Shiner, Palezone	Notropis
Shrimp, Kentucky cave	Palaemonias ganteri
Sturgeon, pallid	Scaphirhynchus albus
Tern, least	Sterna antillarum
Woodpecker, red-cockaded	Picoides borealis
LOUISIANA	
Bear, Louisiana black	Ursus americanus luteolus
Eagle, bald	Haliaeetus leucocephalus
Falcon, American peregrin	Falco peregrinus anatum
Heelsplitter, inflated	Potamilus inflatus
Manatee, West Indian	Trichechus manatus
Pearlshell, Louisiana	Margaritifera hembeli
Pearlymussel, pink mucket	Lampsilis abrupta
Pelican, brown	Pelecanus occidentalis
Plover, piping	Charadrius melodus
Sturgeon, Gulf	Acipenser oxyrhynchus desotoi
Sturgeon, pallid	Scaphirhynchus albus
Tern, least	Sterna antillarum
Tortoise, gopher	Gopherus polyphemus
Turtle, Kemp's	Lepidochelys kempii
Turtle, green sea	Chelonia mydas
Turtle, hawksbill sea	Eretmochelys imbricata
Turtle, leatherback sea	Dermochelys coriacea
Turtle, loggerhead sea	Caretta caretta
Turtle, ringed map	Graptemys oculifera

SPECIES (COMMON NAME)	SPECIES (SCIENTIFIC NAME)
LOUISIANA Cont'd	
Vireo, black-capped	Vireo atricapillus
Woodpecker, red-cockaded	Picoides borealis
MAINE	
Eagle, bald	Haliaeetus leucocephalus
Falcon, American peregrine	Falco peregrinus anatum
Plover, piping	Charadrius melodus
Tern, roseate	Sterna dougallii dougallii
Turtle, leatherback sea	Dermochelys coriacea
MARYLAND	
Bat, Indiana	Myotis sodalis
Beetle, Puritan tiger	Cicindela puritana
Beetle, northeastern beach tiger	Cicindela dorsalis dorsalis
Darter, Maryland	Etheostoma sellare
Eagle, bald	Haliaeetus leucocephalus
Falcon, American peregrine	Falco peregrinus anatum
Mussel, dwarf wedge	Alasmidonta heterodon
Plover	piping (Charadrius melodus)
Squirrel	Delmarva Peninsula fox (Sciurus niger cinereus)
Turtle	Kemp's (Atlantic) ridley sea (Lepidochelys kempii)
Turtle	green sea (Chelonia mydas)
Turtle	hawksbill sea (Eretmochelys imbricata)
Turtle	leatherback sea (Dermochelys coriacea)
Turtle	loggerhead sea (Caretta caretta)
MASSACHUSETTS	
Beetle, American burying	Nicrophorus americanus
Beetle, Puritan tiger	Cicindela puritana
Beetle, northeastern beach tiger	Cicindela dorsalis dorsalis
Eagle, bald	Haliaeetus leucocephalus
Falcon, American peregrine	Falco peregrinus anatum
Mussel, dwarf wedge	Alasmidonta heterodon

SPECIES (COMMON NAME)	SPECIES (SCIENTIFIC NAME)

MASSACHUSETTS Cont'd

Plover, piping	Charadrius melodus
Tern, roseate	Sterna dougallii dougallii
Turtle, Kemp's	Lepidochelys kempii
Turtle, Plymouth redbelly	Pseudemys rubriventris bangsi
Turtle, hawksbill sea	Eretmochelys imbricata
Turtle, leatherback sea	Dermochelys coriacea
Turtle, loggerhead sea	Caretta caretta

MICHIGAN

Bat, Indiana	Myotis sodalis
Beetle, American burying	Nicrophorus americanus
Beetle, Hungerford's crawling water	Brychius hungerfordi
Butterfly, Karner blue	Lycaeides melissa samuelis
Butterfly, Mitchell's satyr	Neonympha mitchellii mitchellii
Clubshell	Pleurobema clava
Eagle, bald	
Falcon, American peregrine	Falco peregrinus anatum
Plover, piping	Charadrius melodus
Riffleshell, northern	Epioblasma torulosa rangiana
Warbler, Kirtland's	Dendroica kirtlandii
Wolf, gray	Canis lupus

MINNESOTA

Butterfly, Karner blue	Lycaeides melissa samuelis
Eagle, bald	Haliaeetus leucocephalus
Falcon, American peregrine	Falco peregrinus anatum
Mussel, winged mapleleaf	Quadrula fragosa
Pearlymussel, Higgins' eye	Lampsilis higginsi
Plover, piping	Charadrius melodus
Wolf, gray	Canis lupus

MISSISSIPPI

Bat, Indiana	Myotis sodalis
Bear, Louisiana black	Ursus americanus luteolus

SPECIES (COMMON NAME)	SPECIES (SCIENTIFIC NAME)
MISSISSIPPI Cont'd	
Clubshell, black	Pleurobema curtum
Clubshell, ovate	Pleurobema perovatum
Clubshell, southern	Pleurobema decisum
Combshell, southern	Epioblasma penita
Crane, Mississippi sandhill	Grus canadensis pulla
Darter, bayou	Etheostoma rubrum
Eagle, bald	Haliaeetus leucocephalus
Falcon, American peregrine	Falco peregrinus anatum
Heelsplitter, inflated	Potamilus inflatus
Manatee, West Indian	Trichechus manatus
Moccasinshell, Alabama	Medionidus acutissimus
Mucket, orange-nacre	Lampsilis perovalis
Pelican, brown	Pelecanus occidentalis
Pigtoe, flat	Pleurobema marshalli
Pigtoe, heavy	Pleurobema taitianum
Plover, piping	Charadrius melodus
Pocketbook, fat	Potamilus capax
Snake, eastern indigo	Drymarchon corais couperi
Stirrupshell	Quadrula stapes
Sturgeon, Gulf	Acipenser oxyrhynchus desotoi
Sturgeon, pallid	Scaphirhynchus albus
Tern, least	Sterna antillarum
Tortoise, gopher	Gopherus polyphemus
Turtle, Kemp's	Lepidochelys kempii
Turtle, green sea	Chelonia mydas
Turtle, hawksbill sea	Eretmochelys imbricata
Turtle, leatherback sea	Dermochelys coriacea
Turtle, loggerhead sea	Caretta caretta
Turtle, ringed map	Graptemys oculifera
Turtle, yellow-blotched map	Graptemys flavimaculata
Woodpecker, red-cockaded	Picoides borealis

SPECIES (COMMON NAME)	SPECIES (SCIENTIFIC NAME)
MISSOURI	
Bat, Indiana	Myotis sodalis
Bat, Ozark big-eared	Plecotus townsendii ingens
Bat, gray	Myotis grisescens
Cavefish, Ozark	Amblyopsis rosae
Darter, Niangua	Etheostoma nianguae
Eagle, bald	Haliaeetus leucocephalus
Falcon, American peregrine	Falco peregrinus anatum
Madtom, Neosho	Noturus placidus
Pearlymussel, Curtis	Epioblasma florentina curtisi
Pearlymussel, Higgins' eye	Lampsilis higginsi
Pearlymussel, pink mucket	Lampsilis abrupta
Plover, piping	Charadrius melodus
Pocketbook, fat	Potamilus capax
Sturgeon, pallid	Scaphirhynchus albus
Tern, least	Sterna antillarum
MONTANA	
Bear, grizzly	Ursus arctos
Crane, whooping	Grus americana
Curlew, Eskimo	Numenius borealis
Eagle, bald	Haliaeetus leucocephalus
Falcon, American peregrine	Falco peregrinus anatum
Ferret, black-footed	Mustela nigripes
Plover, piping	Charadrius melodus
Sturgeon, pallid	Scaphirhynchus albus
Sturgeon, white	Acipenser transmontanus
Tern, least	Sterna antillarum
Wolf, gray	Canis lupus
NEBRASKA	
Beetle, American burying	Nicrophorus americanus
Crane, whooping	Grus americana
Curlew, Eskimo	Numenius borealis

SPECIES (COMMON NAME)	SPECIES (SCIENTIFIC NAME)
NEBRASKA Cont'd	
Eagle, bald	Haliaeetus leucocephalus
Falcon, American peregrine	Falco peregrinus anatum
Ferret	black-footed, Mustela nigripes
Plover, piping	Charadrius melodus
Sturgeon, pallid	Scaphirhynchus albus
Tern, least	terna antillarum

NEVADA

Chub, Pahranagat roundtail	Gila robusta jordani
Chub, Virgin River	Gila robusta semidnuda
Chub, bonytail	Gila elegans
Cui-ui	Chasmistes cujus
Dace, Ash Meadows speckled	Rhinichthys osculus nevadensis
Dace, Clover Valley speckled	Rhinichthys osculus oligoporus
Dace, Independence Valley speckled	Rhinichthys osculus lethoporus
Dace, Moapa	Moapa coriacea
Dace, desert	Eremichthys acros
Eagle, bald	Haliaeetus leucocephalus
Falcon, American peregrine	Falco peregrinus anatum
Naucorid, Ash Meadows	Ambrysus amargosus
Poolfish, Pahrump	Empetrichthys latos
Pupfish, Ash Meadows Amargosa	Cyprinodon nevadensis mionectes
Pupfish, Devils Hole	Cyprinodon diabolis
Pupfish,Warm Springs	Cyprinodon nevadensis pectoralis
Spinedace, Big Spring	Lepidomeda mollispinis pratensis
Spinedace, White River	Lepidomeda albivallis
Springfish, Hiko White River	Crenichthys baileyi grandis
Springfish, Railroad Valley	Crenichthys nevadae
Springfish, White River	Crenichthys baileyi baileyi
Sucker, razorback	Xyrauchen texanus
Tortoise, desert	Gopherus agassizii
Trout, Lahontan cutthroat	Oncorhynchus clarki henshawi

SPECIES (COMMON NAME)	SPECIES (SCIENTIFIC NAME)

NEVADA Cont'd

| Woundfin | Plagopterus argentissimus |

NEW HAMPSHIRE

Beetle, Puritan tiger	Cicindela puritana
Butterfly, Karner blue	Lycaeides melissa samuelis
Eagle, bald	Haliaeetus leucocephalus
Falcon, American peregrine	Falco peregrinus anatum
Mussel, dwarf wedge	Alasmidonta heterodon
Turtle, leatherback sea	Dermochelys coriace

NEW JERSEY

Bat, Indiana	Myotis sodalis
Beetle, northeastern beach tiger	Cicindela dorsalis dorsalis
Eagle, bald	Haliaeetus leucocephalus
Falcon, American peregrine	Falco peregrinus anatum
Plover, piping	Charadrius melodus
Tern, roseate	Sterna dougallii dougallii
Turtle, Kemp's	Lepidochelys kempii
Turtle, hawksbill sea	Eretmochelys imbricata
Turtle, leatherback sea	Dermochelys coriacea
Turtle, loggerhead sea	Caretta caretta

NEW MEXICO

Bat, Mexican long-nosed	Leptonycteris nivalis
Bat, lesser long-nosed	Leptonycteris curasoae yerbabuenae
Chub, Chihuahua	Gila nigrescens
Crane, whooping	Grus americana
Eagle, bald	Haliaeetus leucocephalus
Falcon, American peregrine	Falco peregrinus anatum
Flycatcher, Southwestern willow	Empidonax traillii extimus
Gambusia, Pecos	Gambusia nobilis
Isopod, Socorro	Thermosphaeroma thermophilus
Minnow, Rio Grande silvery	Hybognathus amarus
Minnow, loach	Rhinichthys cobitis

SPECIES (COMMON NAME)	SPECIES (SCIENTIFIC NAME)

NEW MEXICO Cont'd

Owl, Mexican spotted	Strix occidentalis lucid
Rattlesnake, New Mexican ridge-nosed	Crotalus willardi obscurus
Shiner, Pecos bluntnose	Notropis simus pecosensis
Shiner, beautiful	Cyprinella formosa
Spikedace	Meda fulgida
Springsnail, Alamosa	Tryonia alamosae
Springsnail, Socorro	Pyrgulopsis neomexicana
Sucker, razorback	Xyrauchen texanus
Tern, least	Sterna antillarum
Topminnow, Gila	Poeciliopsis occidentalis
Trout, Gila	Oncorhynchus gilae
Woundfin	Plagopterus argentissimus

NEW YORK

Butterfly, Karner blue	Lycaeides melissa samuelis
Eagle, bald	Haliaeetus leucocephalus
Falcon, American peregrine	Falco peregrinus anatum
Mussel, dwarf wedge	Alasmidonta heterodon
Plover, piping	Charadrius melodus
Snail, Chittenango ovate amber	Succinea chittenangoensis
Tern, roseate	Sterna dougallii dougallii
Turtle, Kemp's	Lepidochelys kempii
Turtle, green sea	Chelonia mydas
Turtle, hawksbill sea	Eretmochelys imbricata
Turtle, leatherback sea	Dermochelys coriacea
Turtle, loggerhead sea	Caretta caretta

NORTH CAROLINA

Bat, Indiana	Myotis sodalis
Bat, Virginia big-eared	Plecotus townsendii virginianus
Butterfly, Saint Francis' satyr	Neonympha mitchellii francisci
Chub, spotfin	Cyprinella monacha
Eagle, bald	Haliaeetus leucocephalus

SPECIES (COMMON NAME)	SPECIES (SCIENTIFIC NAME)

NORTH CAROLINA Cont'd

Elktoe, Appalachian	Alasmidonta raveneliana
Falcon, American peregrine	Falco peregrinus anatum
Heelsplitter, Carolina	Lasmigona decorata
Manatee, West Indian	Trichechus manatus
Mussel, dwarf wedge	Alasmidonta heterodon
Pearlymussel, little-wing	Pegias fabula
Plover, piping	Charadrius melodus
Shiner, Cape Fear	Notropis mekistocholas
Shrew, Dismal Swamp southeastern	Sorex longirostris fisheri
Silverside, Waccamaw	Menidia extensa
Snail, noonday	Mesodon clarki nantahala
Spider, spruce-fir moss	Microhexura montivaga
Spinymussel, Tar River	Elliptio steinstansana
Squirrel, Carolina northern flying	Glaucomys sabrinus coloratus
Tern, roseate	Sterna dougallii dougallii
Turtle, Kemp's	Lepidochelys kempii
Turtle, green sea	Chelonia mydas
Turtle, hawksbill sea	Eretmochelys imbricata
Turtle, leatherback sea	Dermochelys coriacea
Turtle, loggerhead sea	Caretta caretta
Wolf, red	Canis rufus
Woodpecker, red-cockaded	Picoides borealis

NORTH DAKOTA

Crane, whooping	Grus americana
Curlew, Eskimo	Numenius borealis
Eagle, bald	Haliaeetus leucocephalus
Falcon, American peregrine	Falco peregrinus anatum
Ferret, black-footed	Mustela nigripe
Plover, piping	Charadrius melodus
Sturgeon, pallid	Scaphirhynchus albus
Tern, least	Sterna antillarum

SPECIES (COMMON NAME)	SPECIES (SCIENTIFIC NAME)

NORTH DAKOTA Cont'd

Wolf, gray	Canis lupus

OHIO

Bat, Indiana	Myotis sodalis
Beetle, American burying	Nicrophorus americanus
Butterfly, Karner blue	Lycaeides melissa samuelis
Butterfly, Mitchell's satyr	Neonympha mitchellii mitchellii
Clubshell	Pleurobema clava
Dragonfly, Hine's emerald	Somatochlora hineana
Eagle, bald	Haliaeetus leucocephalus
Falcon, American peregrine	Falco peregrinus anatum
Fanshell	Cyprogenia stegaria
Madtom, Scioto	Noturus trautmani
Pearlymussel, pink mucket	Lampsilis abrupta
Pearlymussel, purple cat's paw	Epioblasma obliquata obliquata
Pearlymussel, white cat's paw	Epioblasma obliquata perobliqua
Plover, piping	Charadrius melodus
Riffleshell, northern	Epioblasma torulosa rangiana

OKLAHOMA

Bat, Indiana	Myotis sodalis
Bat, Ozark big-eared	Plecotus townsendii ingens
Bat, gray	Myotis grisescens
Beetle, American burying	Nicrophorus americanus
Cavefish, Ozark	Amblyopsis rosae
Crane, whooping	Grus americana
Curlew, Eskimo	Numenius borealis
Darter, leopard	Percina pantherina
Eagle, bald	Haliaeetus leucocephalus
Falcon, American peregrine	Falco peregrinus anatum
Madtom, Neosho	Noturus placidus
Plover, piping	Charadrius melodus
Rock-pocketbook, Ouachita	Arkansia wheeleri

SPECIES (COMMON NAME)	SPECIES (SCIENTIFIC NAME)
OKLAHOMA Cont'd	
Tern, least	Sterna antillarum
Vireo, black-capped	Vireo atricapillus
Woodpecker, red-cockaded	Picoides borealis

OREGON

Butterfly, Oregon silverspot	Speyeria zerene hippolyta
Chub, Borax Lake	Gila boraxobius
Chub, Hutton tui	Gila bicolor
Chub, Oregon	Oregonichthys crameri
Dace, Foskett speckled	Rhinichthys osculus
Deer, Columbian white-tailed	Odocoileus virginianus leucurus
Eagle, bald	Haliaeetus leucocephalus
Falcon, American peregrine	Falco peregrinus anatum
Goose, Aleutian Canada	Branta canadensis leucopareia
Murrelet, marbled	Brachyramphus marmoratus marmoratus
Owl, northern spotted	Strix occidentalis caurina
Pelican, brown	Pelecanus occidentalis
Plover, western snowy	Charadrius alexandrinus nivosus
Sucker, Lost River	Deltistes luxatus
Sucker, Warner	Catostomus warnerensis
Sucker, shortnose	Chasmistes brevirostris
Trout, Lahontan cutthroat	Oncorhynchu clarki henshawi
Turtle, green sea	Chelonia mydas
Turtle, leatherback sea	Dermochelys coriacea
Turtle, loggerhead sea	Caretta caretta
Turtle, olive	Lepidochelys olivacea

PENNSYLVANIA

Bat, Indiana	Myotis sodalis
Clubshell	Pleurobema clava
Eagle, bald	Haliaeetus leucocephalus
Falcon, American peregrine	Falco peregrinus anatum
Mussel, dwarf wedge	Alasmidonta heterodon

SPECIES (COMMON NAME)	SPECIES (SCIENTIFIC NAME)

PENNSYLVANIA Cont'd

Mussel, ring pink	Obovaria retusa
Pearlymussel, cracking	Hemistena lata
Pearlymussel, orange-foot pimple back	Plethobasus cooperianus
Pearlymussel, pink mucket	Lampsilis abrupta
Pigtoe, rough	Pleurobema plenum
Plover, piping	Charadrius melodus
Riffleshell, northern	Epioblasma torulosa rangiana

RHODE ISLAND

Beetle, American burying	Nicrophorus americanus
Beetle, northeastern beach tiger	Cicindela dorsalis dorsalis
Eagle, bald	Haliaeetus leucocephalus
Falcon, American peregrine	Falco peregrinus anatum
Plover, piping	Charadrius melodus
Tern, roseate	Sterna dougallii dougallii
Turtle, Kemp's	Lepidochelys kempii
Turtle, hawksbill sea	Eretmochelys imbricata
Turtle, leatherback sea	Dermochelys coriacea
Turtle, loggerhead sea	Caretta caretta

SOUTH CAROLINA

Bat, Indiana	Myotis sodalis
Eagle, bald	Haliaeetus leucocephalus
Falcon, American peregrine	Falco peregrinus anatum
Heelsplitter, Carolina	Lasmigona decorata
Manatee, West Indian	Trichechus manatus
Plover, piping	Charadrius melodus
Snake, eastern indigo	Drymarchon corais couperi
Stork, wood	Mycteria americana
Tern, roseate	Sterna dougallii dougallii
Turtle, Kemp's	Lepidochelys kempii
Turtle, green sea	Chelonia mydas
Turtle, hawksbill sea	Eretmochelys imbricata

SPECIES (COMMON NAME)	SPECIES (SCIENTIFIC NAME)

SOUTH CAROLINA

Turtle, leatherback sea	Dermochelys coriacea
Turtle, loggerhead sea	Caretta caretta
Woodpecker, red-cockaded	Picoides borealis

SOUTH DAKOTA

Beetle, American burying	Nicrophorus americanus
Crane, whooping	Grus americana
Curlew, Eskimo	Numenius borealis
Eagle, bald	Haliaeetus leucocephalus
Falcon, American peregrine	Falco peregrinus anatum
Ferret, black-footed	Mustela nigripes
Plover, piping	Charadrius melodus
Sturgeon, pallid	Scaphirhynchus albus
Tern, least	Sterna antillarum
Wolf, gray	Canis lupus

TENNESSEE

Acornshell, southern	Epioblasma othcaloogensis
Bat, Indiana	Myotis sodalis
Bat, gray	Myotis grisescens
Chub, slender	Erimystax cahni
Chub, spotfin	Cyprinella monacha
Clubshell, ovate	Pleurobema perovatum
Clubshell, southern	Pleurobema decisum
Combshell, upland	Epioblasma metastriata
Crayfish, Nashville	Orconectes shoupi
Dace, blackside	Phoxinus cumberlandensis
Darter, amber	Percina antesella
Darter, bluemask	Etheostoma
Darter, boulder	Etheostoma wapiti
Darter, duskytail	Etheostoma
Darter, slackwater	Etheostoma boschungi
Darter, snail	Percina tanasi

SPECIES (COMMON NAME)	SPECIES (SCIENTIFIC NAME)
TENNESSEE Cont'd	
Eagle, bald	Haliaeetus leucocephalus
Elktoe, Appalachian	Alasmidonta raveneliana
Falcon, American peregrine	Falco peregrinus anatum
Fanshell	Cyprogenia stegaria
Kidneyshell, triangular	Ptychobranchus greeni
Lampmussel, Alabama	Lampsilis virescens
Logperch, Conasauga	Percina jenkinsi
Madtom, Smoky	Noturus baileyi
Madtom, pygmy	Noturus stanauli
Madtom, yellowfin	Noturus flavipinnis
Marstonia (snail)	Pyrgulopsis ogmoraphe
Moccasinshell, Alabama	Medionidus acutissimus
Moccasinshell, Coosa	Medionidus parvulus
Mussel, ring pink	Obovaria retusa
Mussel, winged mapleleaf	Quadrula fragosa
Pearlymussel, Appalachian monkeyface	Quadrula sparsa
Pearlymussel, Cumberland bean	Villosa trabalis
Pearlymussel, Cumberland monkeyface	Quadrula intermedia
Pearlymussel, birdwing	Conradilla caelata
Pearlymussel, cracking	Hemistena lata
Pearlymussel, dromedary	Dromus dromas
Pearlymussel, green-blossom	Epioblasma torulosa gubernaculum
Pearlymussel, little-wing	Pegias fabula
Pearlymussel, orange-foot pimple back	Plethobasus cooperianus
Pearlymussel, pale lillipu	Toxolasma cylindrellus
Pearlymussel, pink mucket	Lampsilis abrupta
Pearlymussel, purple cat's paw	Epioblasma obliquata obliquata
Pearlymussel, tubercled-blossom	Epioblasma torulosa torulosa
Pearlymussel, turgid-blossom	Epioblasma turgidula
Pearlymussel, white wartyback	Plethobasus cicatricosus
Pearlymussel, yellow-blossom	Epioblasma florentina

SPECIES (COMMON NAME)	SPECIES (SCIENTIFIC NAME)
TENNESSEE Cont'd	
Pigtoe, Cumberland	Pigtoe, Cumberland
Pigtoe	fine-rayed (Fusconaia cuneolus)
Pigtoe, rough	Pleurobema plenum
Pigtoe, shiny	Fusconaia cor
Pigtoe, southern	Pleurobema georgianum
Pocketbook, fine-lined	Lampsilis altilis
Riffleshell, tan	Epioblasma walkeri
Riversnail, Anthony's	Athearnia anthonyi
Shiner, blue	Cyprinella caerulea
Snail, painted snake coiled forest	Anguispira picta
Spider, spruce-fir moss	Microhexura montivaga
Squirrel, Carolina northern flying	Glaucomys sabrinus coloratus
Sturgeon, pallid	Scaphirhynchus albus
Tern, least	Sterna antillarum
Wolf, red	Canis rufus
Woodpecker, red-cockaded	Picoides borealis

TEXAS

Bat, Mexican long-nosed	Leptonycteris nivalis
Bear, Louisiana black	Ursus americanus luteolus
Beetle, Coffin Cave mold	Batrisodes texanus
Beetle, Kretschmarr Cave mold	Texamaurops reddelli
Beetle, Tooth Cave ground	Rhadine persephone
Crane, whooping	Grus americana
Curlew, Eskimo	Numenius borealis
Darter, fountain	Etheostoma fonticola
Eagle, bald	Haliaeetus leucocephalus
Falcon, American peregrine	Falco peregrinus anatum
Falcon, northern aplomado	Falco femoralis septentrionalis
Flycatcher, Southwestern willow	Empidonax traillii extimus
Gambusia, Big Bend	Gambusia gaige
Gambusia, Clear Creek	Gambusia heterochir

SPECIES (COMMON NAME)	SPECIES (SCIENTIFIC NAME)

TEXAS Cont'd

Gambusia, Pecos	Gambusia nobilis
Gambusia, San Marcos	Gambusia georgei
Harvestman, Bee Creek Cave	Texella reddelli
Harvestman, Bone Cave	Texella reyesi
Jaguarundi	Felis yagouaroundi cacomitli
Manatee, West Indian	Trichechus manatus
Minnow, Rio Grande silvery	Hybognathus amarus
Ocelot	Felis pardalis
Owl, Mexican spotted	trix occidentalis lucida
Pelican, brown	Pelecanus occidentalis
Plover, piping	Charadrius melodus
Prairie-chicken, Attwater's greater	Tympanuchus cupido attwateri
Pseudoscorpion, Tooth Cave	Tartarocreagris texana
Pupfish, Comanche Springs	Cyprinodon elegans
Pupfish, Leon Springs	Cyprinodon bovinus
Salamander, San Marcos	Eurycea nana
Salamander, Texas blind	Typhlomolge rathbuni
Snake, Concho water	Nerodia paucimaculata
Spider, Tooth Cave	Neoleptoneta myopica
Tern, least	Sterna antillarum
Toad, Houston	Bufo houstonensis
Turtle, Kemp's	Lepidochelys kempii
Turtle, green sea	Chelonia mydas
Turtle, hawksbill sea	Eretmochelys imbricata
Turtle, leatherback sea	Dermochelys coriacea
Turtle, loggerhead sea	Caretta caretta
Vireo, black-capped	Vireo atricapillus
Warbler, golden-cheeked	Dendroica chrysoparia
Woodpecker, red-cockaded	Picoides borealis

UTAH

Ambersnail, Kanab	Oxyloma haydeni kanabensis

SPECIES (COMMON NAME)	SPECIES (SCIENTIFIC NAME)

UTAH Cont'd

Chub, Virgin River	Gila robusta semidnuda
Chub, bonytai	Gila elegans
Chub, humpback	Gila cypha
Crane, whooping	Grus americana
Eagle, bald	Haliaeetus leucocephalus
Falcon, American peregrine	Falco peregrinus anatum
Ferret, black-footed	Mustela nigripes
Flycatcher, Southwestern willow	Empidonax traillii extimus
Owl, Mexican spotted	Strix occidentalis lucid
Prairie dog, Utah	Cynomys parvidens
Snail, Utah valvata	Valvata utahensis
Squawfish, Colorado	Ptychocheilus lucius
Sucker, June	Chasmistes liorus
Sucker, razorback	Xyrauchen texanus
Tortoise, desert	Gopherus agassizii
Trout, Lahontan cutthroat	Oncorhynchus clarki henshawi
Woundfin	Plagopterus argentissimus

VERMONT

Bat, Indiana	Myotis sodalis
Beetle, Puritan tiger	Cicindela puritana
Eagle, bald	Haliaeetus leucocephalus
Falcon, American peregrine	Falco peregrinus anatum
Mussel, dwarf wedge	Alasmidonta heterodon

VIRGINIA

Bat, Indiana	Myotis sodalis
Bat, Virginia big-eared	Plecotus townsendii virginianus
Bat, gray	Myotis grisescens
Beetle, northeastern beach tiger	Cicindela dorsalis dorsalis
Chub, slender	Erimystax cahni
Chub, spotfin	Cyprinella monacha
Darter, duskytail	Etheostoma

SPECIES (COMMON NAME)	SPECIES (SCIENTIFIC NAME)
VIRGINIA Cont'd	
Eagle, bald	Haliaeetus leucocephalus
Falcon, American peregrine	Falco peregrinus anatum
Falcon, American peregrine	Falco peregrinus anatum
Fanshell	Cyprogenia stegaria
Isopod, Lee County cave	Lirceus usdagalun
Isopod, Madison Cave	Antrolana lira
Logperch, Roanoke	Percina rex
Madtom, yellowfin	Noturus flavipinnis
Mussel, dwarf wedge	Alasmidonta heterodon
Pearlymussel, Appalachian monkeyface	Quadrula sparsa
Pearlymussel, Cumberland monkeyface	Quadrula intermedia
Pearlymussel, birdwing	Conradilla caelata
Pearlymussel, cracking	Hemistena lata

APPENDIX 9:
THE ENDANGERED SPECIES ACT

§ 1531. CONGRESSIONAL FINDINGS AND DECLARATION OF PURPOSES AND POLICY [ESA SECTION 2]

(a) Findings

The Congress finds and declares that—

(1) various species of fish, wildlife, and plants in the United States have been rendered extinct as a consequence of economic growth and development untempered by adequate concern and conservation;

(2) other species of fish, wildlife, and plants have been so depleted in numbers that they are in danger of or threatened with extinction;

(3) these species of fish, wildlife, and plants are of aesthetic, ecological, educational, historical, recreational, and scientific value to the Nation and its people;

(4) the United States has pledged itself as a sovereign state in the international community to conserve to the extent practicable the various species of fish or wildlife and plants facing extinction, pursuant to—

(A) migratory bird treaties with Canada and Mexico;

(B) the Migratory and Endangered Bird Treaty with Japan;

(C) the Convention on Nature Protection and Wildlife Preservation in the Western Hemisphere;

(D) the International Convention for the Northwest Atlantic Fisheries;

(E) the International Convention for the High Seas Fisheries of the North Pacific Ocean;

(F) the Convention on International Trade in Endangered Species of Wild Fauna and Flora; and

(G) other international agreements; and

(5) encouraging the States and other interested parties, through Federal financial assistance and a system of incentives, to develop and maintain conservation programs which meet national and international standards is a key to meeting the Nation's international commitments and to better safeguarding, for the benefit of all citizens, the Nation's heritage in fish, wildlife, and plants.

(b) Purposes

The purposes of this chapter are to provide a means whereby the ecosystems upon which endangered species and threatened species depend may be conserved, to provide a program for the conservation of such endangered species and threatened species, and to take such steps as may be appropriate to achieve the purposes of the treaties and conventions set forth in subsection (a) of this section.

(c) Policy

(1) It is further declared to be the policy of Congress that all Federal departments and agencies shall seek to conserve endangered species and threatened species and shall utilize their authorities in furtherance of the purposes of this chapter.

(2) It is further declared to be the policy of Congress that Federal agencies shall cooperate with State and local agencies to resolve water resource issues in concert with conservation of endangered species.

§ 1532. DEFINITIONS [ESA SECTION 3]

For the purposes of this chapter—

(1) The term "alternative courses of action" means all alternatives and thus is not limited to original project objectives and agency jurisdiction.

(2) The term "commercial activity" means all activities of industry and trade, including, but not limited to, the buying or selling of commodities and activities conducted for the purpose of facilitating such buying and selling: Provided, however, That it does not include exhibition of commodities by museums or similar cultural or historical organizations.

(3) The terms "conserve", "conserving", and "conservation" mean to use and the use of all methods and procedures which are necessary to bring any endangered species or threatened species to the point at which the measures provided pursuant to this chapter are no longer necessary. Such methods and procedures include, but are not limited to, all activities associated with scientific resources management such as research, census, law enforcement, habitat acquisition and maintenance, propagation, live trapping, and transplantation, and, in the extraordinary case where popula-

tion pressures within a given ecosystem cannot be otherwise relieved, may include regulated taking.

(4) The term "Convention" means the Convention on International Trade in Endangered Species of Wild Fauna and Flora, signed on March 3, 1973, and the appendices thereto.

(5)(A) The term "critical habitat" for a threatened or endangered species means—

(i) the specific areas within the geographical area occupied by the species, at the time it is listed in accordance with the provisions of section 1533 of this title, on which are found those physical or biological features (I) essential to the conservation of the species and (II) which may require special management considerations or protection; and

(ii) specific areas outside the geographical area occupied by the species at the time it is listed in accordance with the provisions of section 1533 of this title, upon a determination by the Secretary that such areas are essential for the conservation of the species.

(5)(B) Critical habitat may be established for those species now listed as threatened or endangered species for which no critical habitat has heretofore been established as set forth in subparagraph (A) of this paragraph.

(5)(C) Except in those circumstances determined by the Secretary, critical habitat shall not include the entire geographical area which can be occupied by the threatened or endangered species.

(6) The term "endangered species" means any species which is in danger of extinction throughout all or a significant portion of its range other than a species of the Class Insecta determined by the Secretary to constitute a pest whose protection under the provisions of this chapter would present an overwhelming and overriding risk to man.

(7) The term "Federal agency" means any department, agency, or instrumentality of the United States.

(8) The term "fish or wildlife" means any member of the animal kingdom, including without limitation any mammal, fish, bird (including any migratory, nonmigratory, or endangered bird for which protection is also afforded by treaty or other international agreement), amphibian, reptile, mollusk, crustacean, arthropod or other invertebrate, and includes any part, product, egg, or offspring thereof, or the dead body or parts thereof.

(9) The term "foreign commerce" includes, among other things, any transaction—

(A) between persons within one foreign country;

(B) between persons in two or more foreign countries;

(C) between a person within the United States and a person in a foreign country; or

(D) between persons within the United States, where the fish and wild-life in question are moving in any country or countries outside the United States.

(10) The term "import" means to land on, bring into, or introduce into, or attempt to land on, bring into, or introduce into, any place subject to the jurisdiction of the United States, whether or not such landing, bringing, or introduction constitutes an importation within the meaning of the customs laws of the United States.

(11) Repealed. Pub.L. 97-304, Section 4(b), Oct. 13, 1982, 96 Stat. 1420.

(12) The term "permit or license applicant" means, when used with respect to an action of a Federal agency for which exemption is sought under section 1536 of this title, any person whose application to such agency for a permit or license has been denied primarily because of the application of section 1536(a) of this title to such agency action.

(13) The term "person" means an individual, corporation, partnership, trust, association, or any other private entity; or any officer, employee, agent, department, or instrumentality of the Federal Government, of any State, municipality, or political subdivision of a State, or of any foreign government; any State, municipality, or political subdivision of a State; or any other entity subject to the jurisdiction of the United States.

(14) The term "plant" means any member of the plant kingdom, including seeds, roots and other parts thereof.

(15) The term "Secretary" means, except as otherwise herein provided, the Secretary of the Interior or the Secretary of Commerce as program responsibilities are vested pursuant to the provisions of Reorganization Plan Numbered 4 of 1970; except that with respect to the enforcement of the provisions of this chapter and the Convention which pertain to the importation or exportation of terrestrial plants, the term also means the Secretary of Agriculture.

(16) The term "species" includes any subspecies of fish or wildlife or plants, and any distinct population segment of any species of vertebrate fish or wildlife which interbreeds when mature.

(17) The term "State" means any of the several States, the District of Columbia, the Commonwealth of Puerto Rico, American Samoa, the Virgin Islands, Guam, and the Trust Territory of the Pacific Islands.

(18) The term "State agency" means any State agency, department, board, commission, or other governmental entity which is responsible for the management and conservation of fish, plant, or wildlife resources within a State.

(19) The term "take" means to harass, harm, pursue, hunt, shoot, wound, kill, trap, capture, or collect, or to attempt to engage in any such conduct.

(20) The term "threatened species" means any species which is likely to become an endangered species within the foreseeable future throughout all or a significant portion of its range.

(21) The term "United States", when used in a geographical context, includes all States.

§ 1533. DETERMINATION OF ENDANGERED SPECIES AND THREATENED SPECIES [ESA SECTION 4]

(a) Generally

(1) The Secretary shall by regulation promulgated in accordance with subsection (b) of this section determine whether any species is an endangered species or a threatened species because of any of the following factors:

(A) the present or threatened destruction, modification, or curtailment of its habitat or range;

(B) overutilization for commercial, recreational, scientific, or educational purposes;

(C) disease or predation;

(D) the inadequacy of existing regulatory mechanisms; or

(E) other natural or manmade factors affecting its continued existence.

(2) With respect to any species over which program responsibilities have been vested in the Secretary of Commerce pursuant to Reorganization Plan Numbered 4 of 1970—

(A) in any case in which the Secretary of Commerce determines that such species should—

(i) be listed as an endangered species or a threatened species, or

(ii) be changed in status from a threatened species to an endangered species, he shall so inform the Secretary of the Interior, who shall list such species in accordance with this section;

(B) in any case in which the Secretary of Commerce determines that such species should—

(i) be removed from any list published pursuant to subsection (c) of this section, or

(ii) be changed in status from an endangered species to a threatened species, he shall recommend such action to the Secretary of the Interior, and the Secretary of the Interior, if he concurs in the recommendation, shall implement such action; and

(C) the Secretary of the Interior may not list or remove from any list any such species, and may not change the status of any such species which are listed, without a prior favorable determination made pursuant to this section by the Secretary of Commerce.

(3) The Secretary, by regulation promulgated in accordance with subsection (b) of this section and to the maximum extent prudent and determinable—

(A) shall, concurrently with making a determination under paragraph (1) that a species is an endangered species or a threatened species, designate any habitat of such species which is then considered to be critical habitat; and

(B) may, from time-to-time thereafter as appropriate, revise such designation.

(b) Basis for determinations

(1)(A) The Secretary shall make determinations required by subsection (a)(1) of this section solely on the basis of the best scientific and commercial data available to him after conducting a review of the status of the species and after taking into account those efforts, if any, being made by any State or foreign nation, or any political subdivision of a State or foreign nation, to protect such species, whether by predator control, protection of habitat and food supply, or other conservation practices, within any area under its jurisdiction, or on the high seas.

(1)(B) In carrying out this section, the Secretary shall give consideration to species which have been—

(i) designated as requiring protection from unrestricted commerce by any foreign nation, or pursuant to any international agreement; or

(ii) identified as in danger of extinction, or likely to become so within the foreseeable future, by any State agency or by any agency of a foreign nation that is responsible for the conservation of fish or wildlife or plants.

(2) The Secretary shall designate critical habitat, and make revisions thereto, under subsection (a) (3) of this section on the basis of the best scientific data available and after taking into consideration the economic impact, and any other relevant impact, of specifying any particular area as critical habitat. The Secretary may exclude any area from critical habitat if he determines that the benefits of such exclusion outweigh the benefits of specifying such area as part of the critical habitat, unless he determines, based on the best scientific and commercial data available, that the failure to designate such area as critical habitat will result in the extinction of the species concerned.

(3)(A) To the maximum extent practicable, within 90 days after receiving the petition of an interested person under section 553(e) of Title 5 to add a species to, or to remove a species from, either of the lists published under subsection (c) of this section, the Secretary shall make a finding as to whether the petition presents substantial scientific or commercial information indicating that the petitioned action may be warranted. If such a petition is found to present such information, the Secretary shall promptly commence a review of the status of the species concerned. The Secretary shall promptly publish each finding made under this subparagraph in the Federal Register.

(3)(B) Within 12 months after receiving a petition that is found under subparagraph (A) to present substantial information indicating that the petitioned action may be warranted, the Secretary shall make one of the following findings:

(i) The petitioned action is not warranted, in which case the Secretary shall promptly publish such finding in the Federal Register.

(ii) The petitioned action is warranted, in which case the Secretary shall promptly publish in the Federal Register a general notice and the complete text of a proposed regulation to implement such action in accordance with paragraph (5).

(iii) The petitioned action is warranted, but that—

(I) the immediate proposal and timely promulgation of a final regulation implementing the petitioned action in accordance with paragraphs (5) and (6) is precluded by pending proposals to determine whether any species is an endangered species or a threatened species, and

(II) expeditious progress is being made to add qualified species to either of the lists published under subsection (c) of this section and to remove from such lists species for which the protections of this chapter are no longer necessary, in which case the Secretary shall promptly publish such finding in the Federal Register, together with a description and evaluation of the reasons and data on which the finding is based.

(3)(C)(i) A petition with respect to which a finding is made under subparagraph (B)(iii) shall be treated as a petition that is resubmitted to the Secretary under subparagraph (A) on the date of such finding and that presents substantial scientific or commercial information that the petitioned action may be warranted.

(3)(C)(ii) Any negative finding described in subparagraph (A) and any finding described in subparagraph (B) (i) or (iii) shall be subject to judicial review.

(3)(C)(iii) The Secretary shall implement a system to monitor effectively the status of all species with respect to which a finding is made under subparagraph (B)(iii) and shall make prompt use of the authority under paragraph 7 to prevent a significant risk to the well being of any such species.

(3)(D)(i) To the maximum extent practicable, within 90 days after receiving the petition of an interested person under section 553(e) of Title 5, to revise a critical habitat designation, the Secretary shall make a finding as to whether the petition presents substantial scientific information indicating that the revision may be warranted. The Secretary shall promptly publish such finding in the Federal Register.

(3)(D)(ii) Within 12 months after receiving a petition that is found under clause (i) to present substantial information indicating that the requested revision may be warranted, the Secretary shall determine how he intends to proceed with the requested revision, and shall promptly publish notice of such intention in the Federal Register.

(4) Except as provided in paragraphs (5) and (6) of this subsection, the provisions of section 553 of Title 5 (relating to rulemaking procedures), shall apply to any regulation promulgated to carry out the purposes of this chapter.

(5) With respect to any regulation proposed by the Secretary to implement a determination, designation, or revision referred to in subsection (a) (1) or (3) of this section, the Secretary shall—

(A) not less than 90 days before the effective date of the regulation—

(i) publish a general notice and the complete text of the proposed regulation in the Federal Register, and

(ii) give actual notice of the proposed regulation (including the complete text of the regulation) to the State agency in each State in which the species is believed to occur, and to each county or equivalent jurisdiction in which the species is believed to occur, and invite the comment of such agency, and each such jurisdiction, thereon;

(B) insofar as practical, and in cooperation with the Secretary of State, give notice of the proposed regulation to each foreign nation in which the species is believed to occur or whose citizens harvest the species on the high seas, and invite the comment of such nation thereon;

(C) give notice of the proposed regulation to such professional scientific organizations as he deems appropriate;

(D) publish a summary of the proposed regulation in a newspaper of general circulation in each area of the United States in which the species is believed to occur; and

(E) promptly hold one public hearing on the proposed regulation if any person files a request for such a hearing within 45 days after the date of publication of general notice.

(6)(A) Within the one-year period beginning on the date on which general notice is published in accordance with paragraph (5) (A) (i) regarding a proposed regulation, the Secretary shall publish in the Federal Register—

(i) if a determination as to whether a species is an endangered species or a threatened species, or a revision of critical habitat, is involved, either—

(I) a final regulation to implement such determination,

(II) a final regulation to implement such revision or a finding that such revision should not be made,

(III) notice that such one-year period is being extended under subparagraph (B) (i), or

(IV) notice that the proposed regulation is being withdrawn under subparagraph (B) (ii), together with the finding on which such withdrawal is based; or

(ii) subject to subparagraph (C), if a designation of critical habitat is involved, either—

(I) a final regulation to implement such designation, or

(II) notice that such one-year period is being extended under such subparagraph.

(6)(B)(i) If the Secretary finds with respect to a proposed regulation referred to in subparagraph (A) (i) that there is substantial disagreement regarding the sufficiency or accuracy of the available data relevant to the determination or revision concerned, the Secretary may extend the one-year period specified in subparagraph (A) for not more than six months for purposes of soliciting additional data.

(6)(B)(ii) If a proposed regulation referred to in subparagraph (A) (i) is not promulgated as a final regulation within such one-year period (or longer period if extension under clause (i) applies) because the Secretary finds that there is not sufficient evidence to justify the action proposed by the regulation, the Secretary shall immediately withdraw the regulation. The finding on which a withdrawal is based shall be subject to judicial review. The Secretary may not propose a regulation that has previously been withdrawn under this clause unless he determines that sufficient new information is available to warrant such proposal.

(6)(B)(iii) If the one-year period specified in subparagraph (A) is extended under clause (i) with respect to a proposed regulation, then before the close of such extended period the Secretary shall publish in the Federal Register either a final regulation to implement the determination or revision concerned, a finding that the revision should not be made, or a notice of withdrawal of the regulation under clause (ii), together with the finding on which the withdrawal is based.

(6)(C) A final regulation designating critical habitat of an endangered species or a threatened species shall be published concurrently with the final regulation implementing the determination that such species is endangered or threatened, unless the Secretary deems that—

(i) it is essential to the conservation of such species that the regulation implementing such determination be promptly published; or

(ii) critical habitat of such species is not then determinable, in which case the Secretary, with respect to the proposed regulation to designate such habitat, may extend the one-year period specified in subparagraph (A) by not more than one additional year, but not later than the close of such additional year the Secretary must publish a final regulation, based on such data as may be available at that time, designating, to the maximum extent prudent, such habitat.

(7) Neither paragraph (4), (5), or (6) of this subsection nor section 553 of Title 5 shall apply to any regulation issued by the Secretary in regard to any emergency posing a significant risk to the well-being of any species of fish or wildlife or plants, but only if—

(A) at the time of publication of the regulation in the Federal Register the Secretary publishes therein detailed reasons why such regulation is necessary; and

(B) in the case such regulation applies to resident species of fish or wildlife, or plants, the Secretary gives actual notice of such regulation to the State agency in each State in which such species is believed to occur. Such regulation shall, at the discretion of the Secretary, take effect immediately upon the publication of the regulation in the Federal Register. Any regulation promulgated under the authority of this paragraph shall cease to have force and effect at the close of the 240-day period following the date of publication unless, during such 240-day period, the rulemaking procedures which would apply to such regulation without regard to this paragraph are complied with. If at any time after issuing an emergency regulation the Secretary determines, on the basis of the best appropriate data available to him, that substantial evidence does not exist to warrant such regulation, he shall withdraw it.

(8) The publication in the Federal Register of any proposed or final regulation which is necessary or appropriate to carry out the purposes of this chapter shall include a summary by the Secretary of the data on which such regulation is based and shall show the relationship of such data to such regulation; and if such regulation designates or revises critical habitat, such summary shall, to the maximum extent practicable, also include a brief description and evaluation of those activities (whether public or private) which, in the opinion of the Secretary, if undertaken may adversely modify such habitat, or may be affected by such designation.

(c) Lists

(1) The Secretary of the Interior shall publish in the Federal Register a list of all species determined by him or the Secretary of Commerce to be endangered species and a list of all species determined by him or the Secretary of Commerce to be threatened species. Each list shall refer to the species contained therein by scientific and common name or names, if any, specify with respect to each such species over what portion of its range it is endangered or threatened, and specify any critical habitat within such range. The Secretary shall from time to time revise each list published under the authority of this subsection to reflect recent determinations, designations, and revisions made in accordance with subsections (a) and (b) of this section.

(2) The Secretary shall—

(A) conduct, at least once every five years, a review of all species included in a list which is published pursuant to paragraph (1) and which is in effect at the time of such review; and (B) determine on the basis of such review whether any such species should—

(i) be removed from such list;

(ii) be changed in status from an endangered species to a threatened species; or

(iii) be changed in status from a threatened species to an endangered species.

Each determination under subparagraph (B) shall be made in accordance with the provisions of subsections (a) and (b) of this section.

(d) Protective regulations

Whenever any species is listed as a threatened species pursuant to subsection (c) of this section, the Secretary shall issue such regulations as he deems necessary and advisable to provide for the conservation of such species. The Secretary may by regulation prohibit with respect to any threatened species any act prohibited under section 1538(a)(1) of this title, in the case of fish or wildlife, or section 1538(a)(2) of this title, in the case of plants, with respect to endangered species; except that with respect to the taking of resident species of fish or wildlife, such regulations shall apply in any State which has entered into a cooperative agreement pursuant to section 1535(c) of this title only to the extent that such regulations have also been adopted by such State.

(e) Similarity of appearance cases

The Secretary may, by regulation of commerce or taking, and to the extent he deems advisable, treat any species as an endangered species or threatened species even though it is not listed pursuant to this section if he finds that—

(A) such species so closely resembles in appearance, at the point in question, a species which has been listed pursuant to such section that enforcement personnel would have substantial difficulty in attempting to differentiate between the listed and unlisted species;

(B) the effect of this substantial difficulty is an additional threat to an endangered or threatened species; and

(C) such treatment of an unlisted species will substantially facilitate the enforcement and further the policy of this chapter.

(f) Recovery plans

(1) The Secretary shall develop and implement plans (hereinafter in this subsection referred to as "recovery plans") for the conservation and survival of endangered species and threatened species listed pursuant to this section, unless he finds that such a plan will not promote the conservation of the species. The Secretary, in developing and implementing recovery plans, shall, to the maximum extent practicable—

(A) give priority to those endangered species or threatened species, without regard to taxonomic classification, that are most likely to benefit from such plans, particularly those species that are, or may be, in conflict with construction or other development projects or other forms of economic activity;

(B) incorporate in each plan—

(i) a description of such site-specific management actions as may be necessary to achieve the plan's goal for the conservation and survival of the species;

(ii) objective, measurable criteria which, when met, would result in a determination, in accordance with the provisions of this section, that the species be removed from the list; and

(iii) estimates of the time required and the cost to carry out those measures needed to achieve the plan's goal and to achieve intermediate steps toward that goal.

(2) The Secretary, in developing and implementing recovery plans, may procure the services of appropriate public and private agencies and institutions, and other qualified persons. Recovery teams appointed pursuant to this subsection shall not be subject to the Federal Advisory Committee Act.

(3) The Secretary shall report every two years to the Committee on Environment and Public Works of the Senate and the Committee on Merchant Marine and Fisheries of the House of Representatives on the status of efforts to develop and implement recovery plans for all species listed pursuant to this section and on the status of all species for which such plans have been developed.

(4) The Secretary shall, prior to final approval of a new or revised recovery plan, provide public notice and an opportunity for public review and comment on such plan. The Secretary shall consider all information presented during the public comment period prior to approval of the plan.

(5) Each Federal agency shall, prior to implementation of a new or revised recovery plan, consider all information presented during the public comment period under paragraph (4).

(g) Monitoring

(1) The Secretary shall implement a system in cooperation with the States to monitor effectively for not less than five years the status of all species which have recovered to the point at which the measures provided pursuant to this chapter are no longer necessary and which, in accordance with the provisions of this section, have been removed from either of the lists published under subsection (c) of this section.

(2) The Secretary shall make prompt use of the authority under paragraph 7 of subsection (b) of this section to prevent a significant risk to the well being of any such recovered species.

(h) Agency guidelines; publication in Federal Register; scope; proposals and amendments: notice and opportunity for comments

The Secretary shall establish, and publish in the Federal Register, agency guidelines to insure that the purposes of this section are achieved efficiently and effectively. Such guidelines shall include, but are not limited to—

(1) procedures for recording the receipt and the disposition of petitions submitted under subsection (b)(3) of this section;

(2) criteria for making the findings required under such subsection with respect to petitions;

(3) a ranking system to assist in the identification of species that should receive priority review under subsection (a)(1) of this section; and

(4) a system for developing and implementing, on a priority basis, recovery plans under subsection (f) of this section.

The Secretary shall provide to the public notice of, and opportunity to submit written comments on, any guideline (including any amendment thereto) proposed to be established under this subsection.

(i) Submission to State agency of justification for regulations inconsistent with State agency's comments or petition

If, in the case of any regulation proposed by the Secretary under the authority of this section, a State agency to which notice thereof was given in accordance with subsection (b)(5)(A)(ii) of this section files comments disagreeing with all or part of the proposed regulation, and the Secretary issues a final regulation which is in conflict with such comments, or if the Secretary fails to adopt a regulation pursuant to an action petitioned by a State agency under subsection (b)(3) of this section, the Secretary shall submit to the State agency a written justification for his failure to adopt regulations consistent with the agency's comments or petition.

§ 1534. LAND ACQUISITION [ESA § 5] [OMITTED]

§ 1535. COOPERATION WITH STATES [ESA § 6]

(a) Generally

In carrying out the program authorized by this chapter, the Secretary shall cooperate to the maximum extent practicable with the States. Such cooperation shall include consultation with the States concerned before acquiring any land or water, or interest therein, for the purpose of conserving any endangered species or threatened species.

§ 1536. INTERAGENCY COOPERATION [ESA §7]

(a) Federal agency actions and consultations

(1) The Secretary shall review other programs administered by him and utilize such programs in furtherance of the purposes of this chapter. All other Federal agencies shall, in consultation with and with the assistance of the Secretary, utilize their authorities in furtherance of the purposes of this chapter by carrying out programs for the conservation of endangered species and threatened species listed pursuant to section 1533 of this title.

(2) Each Federal agency shall, in consultation with and with the assistance of the Secretary, insure that any action authorized, funded, or carried out by such agency (hereinafter in this section referred to as an "agency action") is not likely to jeopardize the continued existence of any endangered species or threatened species or result in the destruction or adverse modification of habitat of such species which is determined by the Secretary, after consultation as appropriate with affected States, to be critical, unless such agency has been granted an exemption for such action by the Committee pursuant to subsection (h) of this section. In fulfilling the requirements of this paragraph each agency shall use the best scientific and commercial data available.

(3) Subject to such guidelines as the Secretary may establish, a Federal agency shall consult with the Secretary on any prospective agency action at the request of, and in cooperation with, the prospective permit or license applicant if the applicant has reason to believe that an endangered species or a threatened species may be present in the area affected by his project and that implementation of such action will likely affect such species.

(4) Each Federal agency shall confer with the Secretary on any agency action which is likely to jeopardize the continued existence of any species proposed to be listed under section 1533 of this title or result in the destruction or adverse modification of critical habitat proposed to be designated for such species. This paragraph does not require a limitation on the commitment of resources as described in subsection (d) of this section.

(b) Opinion of Secretary

(1)(A) Consultation under subsection (a) (2) of this section with respect to any agency action shall be concluded within the 90-day period beginning on the date on which initiated or, subject to subparagraph (B), within such other period of time as is mutually agreeable to the Secretary and the Federal agency.

(1)(B) In the case of an agency action involving a permit or license applicant, the Secretary and the Federal agency may not mutually agree to conclude consultation within a period exceeding 90 days unless the Secretary, before the close of the 90th day referred to in subparagraph (A)—

(i) if the consultation period proposed to be agreed to will end before the 150th day after the date on which consultation was initiated, submits to the applicant a written statement setting forth—

(I) the reasons why a longer period is required,

(II) the information that is required to complete the consultation, and

(III) the estimated date on which consultation will be completed; or

(ii) if the consultation period proposed to be agreed to will end 150 or more days after the date on which consultation was initiated, obtains the consent of the applicant to such period.

The Secretary and the Federal agency may mutually agree to extend a consultation period established under the preceding sentence if the Secretary, before the close of such period, obtains the consent of the applicant to the extension.

(2) Consultation under subsection (a) (3) of this section shall be concluded within such period as is agreeable to the Secretary, the Federal agency, and the applicant concerned.

(3)(A) Promptly after conclusion of consultation under paragraph (2) or (3) of subsection (a) of this section, the Secretary shall provide to the Federal agency and the applicant, if any, a written statement setting forth the Secretary's opinion, and a summary of the information on which the opinion is based, detailing how the agency action affects the species or its critical habitat. If jeopardy or adverse modification is found, the Secretary shall suggest those reasonable and prudent alternatives which he believes would not violate subsection (a) (2) of this section and can be taken by the Federal agency or applicant in implementing the agency action.

(3)(B) Consultation under subsection (a) (3) of this section, and an opinion issued by the Secretary incident to such consultation, regarding an agency action shall be treated respectively as a consultation under subsection (a)

(2) of this section, and as an opinion issued after consultation under such subsection, regarding that action if the Secretary reviews the action before it is commenced by the Federal agency and finds, and notifies such agency, that no significant changes have been made with respect to the action and that no significant change has occurred regarding the information used during the initial consultation.

(4) If after consultation under subsection (a)(2) of this section, the Secretary concludes that—

(A) the agency action will not violate such subsection, or offers reasonable and prudent alternatives which the Secretary believes would not violate such subsection;

(B) the taking of an endangered species or a threatened species incidental to the agency action will not violate such subsection; and

(C) if an endangered species or threatened species of a marine mammal is involved, the taking is authorized pursuant to section 1371(a)(5) of this title; the Secretary shall provide the Federal agency and the applicant concerned, if any, with a written statement that—

(i) specifies the impact of such incidental taking on the species,

(ii) specifies those reasonable and prudent measures that the Secretary considers necessary or appropriate to minimize such impact,

(iii) in the case of marine mammals, specifies those measures that are necessary to comply with section 1371(a)(5) of this title with regard to such taking, and

(iv) sets forth the terms and conditions (including, but not limited to, reporting requirements) that must be complied with by the Federal agency or applicant (if any), or both, to implement the measures specified under clauses (ii) and (iii).

(c) Biological assessment

(1) To facilitate compliance with the requirements of subsection (a) (2) of this section, each Federal agency shall, with respect to any agency action of such agency for which no contract for construction has been entered into and for which no construction has begun on November 10, 1978, request of the Secretary information whether any species which is listed or proposed to be listed may be present in the area of such proposed action. If the Secretary advises, based on the best scientific and commercial data available, that such species may be present, such agency shall conduct a biological assessment for the purpose of identifying any endangered species or threatened species which is likely to be affected by such action. Such assessment shall be completed within 180 days after the date on

which initiated (or within such other period as is mutually agreed to by the Secretary and such agency, except that if a permit or license applicant is involved, the 180-day period may not be extended unless such agency provides the applicant, before the close of such period, with a written statement setting forth the estimated length of the proposed extension and the reasons therefor) and, before any contract for construction is entered into and before construction is begun with respect to such action. Such assessment may be undertaken as part of a Federal agency's compliance with the requirements of section 102 of the National Environmental Policy Act of 1969 (42 U.S.C. 4332).

(2) Any person who may wish to apply for an exemption under subsection (g) of this section for that action may conduct a biological assessment to identify any endangered species or threatened species which is likely to be affected by such action. Any such biological assessment must, however, be conducted in cooperation with the Secretary and under the supervision of the appropriate Federal agency.

(d) Limitation on commitment of resources

After initiation of consultation required under subsection (a) (2) of this section, the Federal agency and the permit or license applicant shall not make any irreversible or irretrievable commitment of resources with respect to the agency action which has the effect of foreclosing the formulation or implementation of any reasonable and prudent alternative measures which would not violate subsection (a) (2) of this section.

(e) Endangered Species Committee

(1) There is established a committee to be known as the Endangered Species Committee (hereinafter in this section referred to as the "Committee").

(2) The Committee shall review any application submitted to it pursuant to this section and determine in accordance with subsection (h) of this section whether or not to grant an exemption from the requirements of subsection (a) (2) of this section for the action set forth in such application.

(3) The Committee shall be composed of seven members as follows:

(A) The Secretary of Agriculture.

(B) The Secretary of the Army.

(C) The Chairman of the Council of Economic Advisors.

(D) The Administrator of the Environmental Protection Agency.

(E) The Secretary of the Interior.

(F) The Administrator of the National Oceanic and Atmospheric Administration.

(G) The President, after consideration of any recommendations received pursuant to subsection (g) (2) (B) of this section shall appoint one individual from each affected State, as determined by the Secretary, to be a member of the Committee for the consideration of the application for exemption for an agency action with respect to which such recommendations are made, not later than 30 days after an application is submitted pursuant to this section.

(4)(A) Members of the Committee shall receive additional pay on account of their service on the Committee.

(4)(B) While away from their homes or regular places of business in the performance of services for the Committee, members of the Committee shall be allowed travel expenses, including per diem in lieu of subsistence, in the same manner as persons employed intermittently in the Government service are allowed expenses under section 5703 of Title 5.

(5)(A) Five members of the Committee or their representatives shall constitute a quorum for the transaction of any function of the Committee, except that, in no case shall any representative be considered in determining the existence of a quorum for the transaction of any function of the Committee if that function involves a vote by the Committee on any matter before the Committee.

(5)(B) The Secretary of the Interior shall be the Chairman of the Committee.

(5)(C) The Committee shall meet at the call of the Chairman or five of its members.

(5)(D) All meetings and records of the Committee shall be open to the public.

(6) Upon request of the Committee, the head of any Federal agency is authorized to detail, on a nonreimbursable basis, any of the personnel of such agency to the Committee to assist it in carrying out its duties under this section.

(7)(A) The Committee may for the purpose of carrying out its duties under this section hold such hearings, sit and act at such times and places, take such testimony, and receive such evidence, as the Committee deems advisable.

(7)(B) When so authorized by the Committee, any member or agent of the Committee may take any action which the Committee is authorized to take by this paragraph.

(7)(C) Subject to the Privacy Act [5 U.S.C.A. Section 552a], the Committee may secure directly from any Federal agency information necessary to enable it to carry out its duties under this section. Upon request of the Chairman of the Committee, the head of such Federal agency shall furnish such information to the Committee.

(7)(D) The Committee may use the United States mails in the same manner and upon the same conditions as a Federal agency.

(7)(E) The Administrator of General Services shall provide to the Committee on a reimbursable basis such administrative support services as the Committee may request.

(8) In carrying out its duties under this section, the Committee may promulgate and amend such rules, regulations, and procedures, and issue and amend such orders as it deems necessary.

(9) For the purpose of obtaining information necessary for the consideration of an application for an exemption under this section the Committee may issue subpoenas for the attendance and testimony of witnesses and the production of relevant papers, books, and documents.

(10) In no case shall any representative, including a representative of a member designated pursuant to paragraph (3) (G) of this subsection, be eligible to cast a vote on behalf of any member.

(f) Promulgation of regulations; form and contents of exemption application

Not later than 90 days after November 10, 1978, the Secretary shall promulgate regulations which set forth the form and manner in which applications for exemption shall be submitted to the Secretary and the information to be contained in such applications. Such regulations shall require that information submitted in an application by the head of any Federal agency with respect to any agency action include, but not be limited to—

(1) a description of the consultation process carried out pursuant to subsection (a) (2) of this section between the head of the Federal agency and the Secretary; and

(2) a statement describing why such action cannot be altered or modified to conform with the requirements of subsection (a) (2) of this section.

(g) Application for exemption; report to Committee

(1) A Federal agency, the Governor of the State in which an agency action will occur, if any, or a permit or license applicant may apply to the Secretary for an exemption for an agency action of such agency if, after consultation under subsection (a) (2) of this section, the Secretary's opinion under subsection (b) of this section indicates that the agency action would violate subsection (a) (2) of this section. An application for an exemption shall be considered initially by the Secretary in the manner provided for in

this subsection, and shall be considered by the Committee for a final determination under subsection (h) of this section after a report is made pursuant to paragraph (5). The applicant for an exemption shall be referred to as the "exemption applicant" in this section.

(2)(A) An exemption applicant shall submit a written application to the Secretary, in a form prescribed under subsection (f) of this section, not later than 90 days after the completion of the consultation process; except that, in the case of any agency action involving a permit or license applicant, such application shall be submitted not later than 90 days after the date on which the Federal agency concerned takes final agency action with respect to the issuance of the permit or license. For purposes of the preceding sentence, the term "final agency action" means

(i) a disposition by an agency with respect to the issuance of a permit or license that is subject to administrative review, whether or not such disposition is subject to judicial review; or

(ii) if administrative review is sought with respect to such disposition, the decision resulting after such review. Such application shall set forth the reasons why the exemption applicant considers that the agency action meets the requirements for an exemption under this subsection.

(2)(B) Upon receipt of an application for exemption for an agency action under paragraph (1), the Secretary shall promptly

(i) notify the Governor of each affected State, if any, as determined by the Secretary, and request the Governors so notified to recommend individuals to be appointed to the Endangered Species Committee for consideration of such application; and

(ii) publish notice of receipt of the application in the Federal Register, including a summary of the information contained in the application and a description of the agency action with respect to which the application for exemption has been filed.

(3) The Secretary shall within 20 days after the receipt of an application for exemption, or within such other period of time as is mutually agreeable to the exemption applicant and the Secretary—

(A) determine that the Federal agency concerned and the exemption applicant have—

(i) carried out the consultation responsibilities described in subsection (a) of this section in good faith and made a reasonable and responsible effort to develop and fairly consider modifications or reasonable and prudent alternatives to the proposed agency action which would not violate subsection (a) (2) of this section;

(ii) conducted any biological assessment required by subsection (c) of this section; and

(iii) to the extent determinable within the time provided herein, refrained from making any irreversible or irretrievable commitment of resources prohibited by subsection (d) of this section; or

(3)(B) deny the application for exemption because the Federal agency concerned or the exemption applicant have not met the requirements set forth in subparagraph (A) (i), (ii), and (iii). The denial of an application under subparagraph (B) shall be considered final agency action for purposes of chapter 7 of Title 5.

(4) If the Secretary determines that the Federal agency concerned and the exemption applicant have met the requirements set forth in paragraph (3) (A) (i), (ii), and (iii) he shall, in consultation with the Members of the Committee, hold a hearing on the application for exemption in accordance with sections 554, 555, and 556 (other than subsection (b) (1) and (2) thereof) of Title 5 and prepare the report to be submitted pursuant to paragraph (5).

(5) Within 140 days after making the determinations under paragraph (3) or within such other period of time as is mutually agreeable to the exemption applicant and the Secretary, the Secretary shall submit to the Committee a report discussing—

(A) the availability of reasonable and prudent alternatives to the agency action, and the nature and extent of the benefits of the agency action and of alternative courses of action consistent with conserving the species or the critical habitat;

(B) a summary of the evidence concerning whether or not the agency action is in the public interest and is of national or regional significance;

(C) appropriate reasonable mitigation and enhancement measures which should be considered by the Committee; and

(D) whether the Federal agency concerned and the exemption applicant refrained from making any irreversible or irretrievable commitment of resources prohibited by subsection (d) of this section.

(6) To the extent practicable within the time required for action under subsection (g) of this section, and except to the extent inconsistent with the requirements of this section, the consideration of any application for an exemption under this section and the conduct of any hearing under this subsection shall be in accordance with sections 554, 555, and 556 (other than subsection (b) (3) of section 556) of Title 5.

(7) Upon request of the Secretary, the head of any Federal agency is authorized to detail, on a nonreimbursable basis, any of the personnel of such agency to the Secretary to assist him in carrying out his duties under this section.

(8) All meetings and records resulting from activities pursuant to this subsection shall be open to the public.

(h) Grant of exemption

(1) The Committee shall make a final determination whether or not to grant an exemption within 30 days after receiving the report of the Secretary pursuant to subsection (g) (5) of this section. The Committee shall grant an exemption from the requirements of subsection (a) (2) of this section for an agency action if, by a vote of not less than five of its members voting in person—

(A) it determines on the record, based on the report of the Secretary, the record of the hearing held under subsection (g) (4) of this section and on such other testimony or evidence as it may receive, that—

(i) there are no reasonable and prudent alternatives to the agency action;

(ii) the benefits of such action clearly outweigh the benefits of alternative courses of action consistent with conserving the species or its critical habitat, and such action is in the public interest;

(iii) the action is of regional or national significance; and

(iv) neither the Federal agency concerned nor the exemption applicant made any irreversible or irretrievable commitment of resources prohibited by subsection (d) of this section; and

(B) it establishes such reasonable mitigation and enhancement measures, including, but not limited to, live propagation, transplantation, and habitat acquisition and improvement, as are necessary and appropriate to minimize the adverse effects of the agency action upon the endangered species, threatened species, or critical habitat concerned. Any final determination by the Committee under this subsection shall be considered final agency action for purposes of chapter 7 of Title 5.

(2)(A) Except as provided in subparagraph (B), an exemption for an agency action granted under paragraph (1) shall constitute a permanent exemption with respect to all endangered or threatened species for the purposes of completing such agency action—

(i) regardless whether the species was identified in the biological assessment; and

(ii) only if a biological assessment has been conducted under subsection (c) of this section with respect to such agency action.

(2)(B) An exemption shall be permanent under subparagraph (A) unless—

(i) the Secretary finds, based on the best scientific and commercial data available, that such exemption would result in the extinction of a species that was not the subject of consultation under subsection (a)(2) of this section or was not identified in any biological assessment conducted under subsection (c) of this section, and

(ii) the Committee determines within 60 days after the date of the Secretary's finding that the exemption should not be permanent.

If the Secretary makes a finding described in clause (i), the Committee shall meet with respect to the matter within 30 days after the date of the finding.

(i) Review by Secretary of State; violation of international treaty or other international obligation of United States

Notwithstanding any other provision of this chapter, the Committee shall be prohibited from considering for exemption any application made to it, if the Secretary of State, after a review of the proposed agency action and its potential implications, and after hearing, certifies, in writing, to the Committee within 60 days of any application made under this section that the granting of any such exemption and the carrying out of such action would be in violation of an international treaty obligation or other international obligation of the United States. The Secretary of State shall, at the time of such certification, publish a copy thereof in the Federal Register.

(j) Exemption for national security reasons

Notwithstanding any other provision of this chapter, the Committee shall grant an exemption for any agency action if the Secretary of Defense finds that such exemption is necessary for reasons of national security.

(k) Exemption decision not considered major Federal action; environmental impact statement

An exemption decision by the Committee under this section shall not be a major Federal action for purposes of the National Environmental Policy Act of 1969 [42 U.S.C.A. Section 4321 et seq.]: Provided, That an environmental impact statement which discusses the impacts upon endangered species or threatened species or their critical habitats shall have been previously prepared with respect to any agency action exempted by such order.

(l) Committee order granting exemption; cost of mitigation and enhancement measures; report by applicant to Council on Environmental Quality

(1) If the Committee determines under subsection (h) of this section that an exemption should be granted with respect to any agency action, the Committee shall issue an order granting the exemption and specifying the mitigation and enhancement measures established pursuant to subsection (h) of this section which shall be carried out and paid for by the exemption applicant in implementing the agency action. All necessary mitigation and enhancement measures shall be authorized prior to the implementing of the agency action and funded concurrently with all other project features.

(2) The applicant receiving such exemption shall include the costs of such mitigation and enhancement measures within the overall costs of continuing the proposed action. Notwithstanding the preceding sentence the costs of such measures shall not be treated as project costs for the purpose of computing benefit-cost or other ratios for the proposed action. Any applicant may request the Secretary to carry out such mitigation and enhancement measures. The costs incurred by the Secretary in carrying out any such measures shall be paid by the applicant receiving the exemption. No later than one year after the granting of an exemption, the exemption applicant shall submit to the Council on Environmental Quality a report describing its compliance with the mitigation and enhancement measures prescribed by this section. Such a report shall be submitted annually until all such mitigation and enhancement measures have been completed. Notice of the public availability of such reports shall be published in the Federal Register by the Council on Environmental Quality.

(m) Notice requirement for citizen suits not applicable

The 60-day notice requirement of section 1540(g) of this title shall not apply with respect to review of any final determination of the Committee under subsection (h) of this section granting an exemption from the requirements of subsection (a) (2) of this section.

(n) Judicial review

Any person, as defined by section 1532(13) of this title, may obtain judicial review, under chapter 7 of Title 5, of any decision of the Endangered Species Committee under subsection (h) of this section in the United States Court of Appeals for

(1) any circuit wherein the agency action concerned will be, or is being, carried out, or (2) in any case in which the agency action will be, or is being, carried out outside of any circuit, the District of Columbia, by filing in such court within 90 days after the date of issuance of the decision, a written petition for review. A copy of such petition shall be transmitted by the clerk of the court to the Committee and the Committee shall file in the court the record in the proceeding, as provided in

section 2112, of Title 28. Attorneys designated by the Endangered Species Committee may appear for, and represent the Committee in any action for review under this subsection.

(o) Exemption as providing exception on taking of endangered species

Notwithstanding sections 1533(d) and 1538(a)(1)(B) and (C) of this title, sections 1371 and 1372 of this title, or any regulation promulgated to implement any such section—

(1) any action for which an exemption is granted under subsection (h) of this section shall not be considered to be a taking of any endangered species or threatened species with respect to any activity which is necessary to carry out such action; and

(2) any taking that is in compliance with the terms and conditions specified in a written statement provided under subsection (b)(4)(iv) of this section shall not be considered to be a prohibited taking of the species concerned.

(p) Exemptions in Presidentially declared disaster areas

In any area which has been declared by the President to be a major disaster area under the Disaster Relief and Emergency Assistance Act [42 U.S.C.A. Section 5121 et seq.], the President is authorized to make the determinations required by subsections (g) and (h) of this section for any project for the repair or replacement of a public facility substantially as it existed prior to the disaster under section 405 or 406 of the Disaster Relief and Emergency Assistance Act [42 U.S.C.A. ss 5171 or 5172], and which the President determines

(1) is necessary to prevent the recurrence of such a natural disaster and to reduce the potential loss of human life, and

(2) to involve an emergency situation which does not allow the ordinary procedures of this section to be followed. Notwithstanding any other provision of this section, the Committee shall accept the determinations of the President under this subsection.

§ 1537. INTERNATIONAL COOPERATION [ESA § 8]

(a) Financial assistance

As a demonstration of the commitment of the United States to the worldwide protection of endangered species and threatened species, the President may, subject to the provisions of section 1306 of Title 31, use foreign currencies accruing to the United States Government under the Agricultural Trade Development and Assistance Act of 1954 [7 U.S.C.A. Section 1691 et seq.] or any other law to provide to any foreign country (with its consent) assistance in the development and management of programs in that country which the Secretary determines to be necessary or useful for the conservation of any endangered species or threatened species listed by the Secretary pursuant to section 1533 of this title. The President shall provide assistance (which includes, but is not limited to, the acquisition, by lease or otherwise, of lands, waters, or interests therein) to foreign countries under this section under such terms and conditions as he deems appropriate. Whenever foreign currencies are available for the provision of assistance under this section, such currencies shall be used in preference to funds appropriated under the authority of section 1542 of this title.

(b) Encouragement of foreign programs

In order to carry out further the provisions of this chapter, the Secretary, through the Secretary of State, shall encourage—

(1) foreign countries to provide for the conservation of fish or wildlife and plants including endangered species and threatened species listed pursuant to section 1533 of this title;

(2) the entering into of bilateral or multilateral agreements with foreign countries to provide for such conservation; and

(3) foreign persons who directly or indirectly take fish or wildlife or plants in foreign countries or on the high seas for importation into the United States for commercial or other purposes to develop and carry out with such assistance as he may provide, conservation practices designed to enhance such fish or wildlife or plants and their habitat.

§ 1537A. CONVENTION IMPLEMENTATION [ESA § 8A]

(a) Management Authority and Scientific Authority

The Secretary of the Interior (hereinafter in this section referred to as the "Secretary") is designated as the Management Authority and the Scientific Authority for purposes of the Convention and the respective functions of each such Authority shall be carried out through the United States Fish and Wildlife Service.

(b) Management Authority functions

The Secretary shall do all things necessary and appropriate to carry out the functions of the Management Authority under the Convention.

(c) Scientific Authority functions; determinations

(1) The Secretary shall do all things necessary and appropriate to carry out the functions of the Scientific Authority under the Convention.

(2) The Secretary shall base the determinations and advice given by him under Article IV of the Convention with respect to wildlife upon the best available biological information derived from professionally accepted wildlife management practices; but is not required to make, or require any State to make, estimates of population size in making such determinations or giving such advice.

(d) Reservations by the United States under Convention

If the United States votes against including any species in Appendix I or II of the Convention and does not enter a reservation pursuant to paragraph (3) of Article XV of the Convention with respect to that species, the Secretary of State, before the 90th day after the last day on which such a reservation could be entered, shall submit to the Committee on Merchant Marine and Fisheries of the House of Representatives, and to the Committee on the Environment and Public Works of the Senate, a written report setting forth the reasons why such a reservation was not entered.

(e) Wildlife Preservation in Western Hemisphere

(1) The Secretary of the Interior (hereinafter in this subsection referred to as the "Secretary"), in cooperation with the Secretary of State, shall act on behalf of, and represent, the United States in all regards as required by the Convention on Nature Protection and Wildlife Preservation in the Western Hemisphere (56 Stat. 1354, T.S. 982, hereinafter in this subsection referred to as the "Western Convention"). In the discharge of these responsibilities, the Secretary and the Secretary of State shall consult with the Secretary of Agriculture, the Secretary of Commerce, and the heads of other agencies with respect to matters relating to or affecting their areas of responsibility.

(2) The Secretary and the Secretary of State shall, in cooperation with the contracting parties to the Western Convention and, to the extent feasible and appropriate, with the participation of State agencies, take such steps as are necessary to implement the Western Convention. Such steps shall include, but not be limited to—

(A) cooperation with contracting parties and international organizations for the purpose of developing personnel resources and programs that will facilitate implementation of the Western Convention;

(B) identification of those species of birds that migrate between the United States and other contracting parties, and the habitats upon which those species depend, and the implementation of cooperative measures to ensure that such species will not become endangered or threatened; and

(C) identification of measures that are necessary and appropriate to implement those provisions of the Western Convention which address the protection of wild plants.

(3) No later than September 30, 1985, the Secretary and the Secretary of State shall submit a report to Congress describing those steps taken in accordance with the requirements of this subsection and identifying the principal remaining actions yet necessary for comprehensive and effective implementation of the Western Convention.

(4) The provisions of this subsection shall not be construed as affecting the authority, jurisdiction, or responsibility of the several States to manage, control, or regulate resident fish or wildlife under State law or regulations.

§ 1538. PROHIBITED ACTS [ESA SECTION 9]

(a) Generally

(1) Except as provided in sections 1535(g)(2) and 1539 of this title, with respect to any endangered species of fish or wildlife listed pursuant to section 1533 of this title it is unlawful for any person subject to the jurisdiction of the United States to—

(A) import any such species into, or export any such species from the United States;

(B) take any such species within the United States or the territorial sea of the United States;

(C) take any such species upon the high seas;

(D) possess, sell, deliver, carry, transport, or ship, by any means whatsoever, any such species taken in violation of subparagraphs (B) and (C);

(E) deliver, receive, carry, transport, or ship in interstate or foreign commerce, by any means whatsoever and in the course of a commercial activity, any such species;

(F) sell or offer for sale in interstate or foreign commerce any such species; or

(G) violate any regulation pertaining to such species or to any threatened species of fish or wildlife listed pursuant to section 1533 of this title and promulgated by the Secretary pursuant to authority provided by this chapter.

(2) Except as provided in sections 1535(g)(2) and 1539 of this title, with respect to any endangered species of plants listed pursuant to section

1533 of this title, it is unlawful for any person subject to the jurisdiction of the United States to—

(A) import any such species into, or export any such species from, the United States;

(B) remove and reduce to possession any such species from areas under Federal jurisdiction; maliciously damage or destroy any such species on any such area; or remove, cut, dig up, or damage or destroy any such species on any other area in knowing violation of any law or regulation of any State or in the course of any violation of a State criminal trespass law;

(C) deliver, receive, carry, transport, or ship in interstate or foreign commerce, by any means whatsoever and in the course of a commercial activity, any such species;

(D) sell or offer for sale in interstate or foreign commerce any such species; or

(E) violate any regulation pertaining to such species or to any threatened species of plants listed pursuant to section 1533 of this title and promulgated by the Secretary pursuant to authority provided by this chapter.

(b) Species held in captivity or controlled environment

(1) The provisions of subsections (a) (1) (A) and (a) (1) (G) of this section shall not apply to any fish or wildlife which was held in captivity or in a controlled environment on (A) December 28, 1973, or (B) the date of the publication in the Federal Register of a final regulation adding such fish or wildlife species to any list published pursuant to subsection (c) of section 1533 of this title: Provided, That such holding and any subsequent holding or use of the fish or wildlife was not in the course of a commercial activity. With respect to any act prohibited by subsections (a) (1) (A) and (a) (1) (G) of this section which occurs after a period of 180 days from (i) December 28, 1973, or (ii) the date of publication in the Federal Register of a final regulation adding such fish or wildlife species to any list published pursuant to subsection (c) of section 1533 of this title, there shall be a rebuttable presumption that the fish or wildlife involved in such act is not entitled to the exemption contained in this subsection.

(2)(A) The provisions of subsection (a) (1) of this section shall not apply to—

(i) any raptor legally held in captivity or in a controlled environment on November 10, 1978; or

(ii) any progeny of any raptor described in clause (i); until such time as any such raptor or progeny is intentionally returned to a wild state.

(2)(B) Any person holding any raptor or progeny described in subparagraph (A) must be able to demonstrate that the raptor or progeny does, in fact, qualify under the provisions of this paragraph, and shall maintain and submit to the Secretary, on request, such inventories, documentation, and records as the Secretary may by regulation require as being reasonably appropriate to carry out the purposes of this paragraph. Such requirements shall not unnecessarily duplicate the requirements of other rules and regulations promulgated by the Secretary.

(c) Violation of Convention

(1) It is unlawful for any person subject to the jurisdiction of the United States to engage in any trade in any specimens contrary to the provisions of the Convention, or to possess any specimens traded contrary to the provisions of the Convention, including the definitions of terms in article I thereof.

(2) Any importation into the United States of fish or wildlife shall, if—

(A) such fish or wildlife is not an endangered species listed pursuant to section 1533 of this title but is listed in Appendix II to the Convention,

(B) the taking and exportation of such fish or wildlife is not contrary to the provisions of the Convention and all other applicable requirements of the Convention have been satisfied,

(C) the applicable requirements of subsections (d), (e), and (f) of this section have been satisfied, and

(D) such importation is not made in the course of a commercial activity, be presumed to be an importation not in violation of any provision of this chapter or any regulation issued pursuant to this chapter.

(d) Imports and exports

(1) In general

It is unlawful for any person, without first having obtained permission from the Secretary, to engage in business—

(A) as an importer or exporter of fish or wildlife (other than shellfish and fishery products which (i) are not listed pursuant to section 1533 of this title as endangered species or threatened species, and (ii) are imported for purposes of human or animal consumption or taken in waters under the jurisdiction of the United States or on the high seas for recreational purposes) or plants; or

(B) as an importer or exporter of any amount of raw or worked African elephant ivory.

(2) Requirements

Any person required to obtain permission under paragraph (1) of this subsection shall—

(A) keep such records as will fully and correctly disclose each importation or exportation of fish, wildlife, plants, or African elephant ivory made by him and the subsequent disposition made by him with respect to such fish, wildlife, plants, or ivory;

(B) at all reasonable times upon notice by a duly authorized representative of the Secretary, afford such representative access to his place of business, an opportunity to examine his inventory of imported fish, wildlife, plants, or African elephant ivory and the records required to be kept under subparagraph (A) of this paragraph, and to copy such records; and

(C) file such reports as the Secretary may require.

(3) Regulations

The Secretary shall prescribe such regulations as are necessary and appropriate to carry out the purposes of this subsection.

(4) Restriction on consideration of value or amount of African elephant ivory imported or exported.

In granting permission under this subsection for importation or exportation of African elephant ivory, the Secretary shall not vary the requirements for obtaining such permission on the basis of the value or amount of ivory imported or exported under such permission.

(e) Reports

It is unlawful for any person importing or exporting fish or wildlife (other than shellfish and fishery products which (1) are not listed pursuant to section 1533 of this title as endangered or threatened species, and (2) are imported for purposes of human or animal consumption or taken in waters under the jurisdiction of the United States or on the high seas for recreational purposes) or plants to fail to file any declaration or report as the Secretary deems necessary to facilitate enforcement of this chapter or to meet the obligations of the Convention.

(f) Designation of ports

(1) It is unlawful for any person subject to the jurisdiction of the United States to import into or export from the United States any fish or wildlife

(other than shellfish and fishery products which (A) are not listed pursuant to section 1533 of this title as endangered species or threatened species, and (B) are imported for purposes of human or animal consumption or taken in waters under the jurisdiction of the United States or on the high seas for recreational purposes) or plants, except at a port or ports designated by the Secretary of the Interior. For the purpose of facilitating enforcement of this chapter and reducing the costs thereof, the Secretary of the Interior, with approval of the Secretary of the Treasury and after notice and opportunity for public hearing, may, by regulation, designate ports and change such designations. The Secretary of the Interior, under such terms and conditions as he may prescribe, may permit the importation or exportation at nondesignated ports in the interest of the health or safety of the fish or wildlife or plants, or for other reasons if, in his discretion, he deems it appropriate and consistent with the purpose of this subsection.

(2) Any port designated by the Secretary of the Interior under the authority of section 668cc-4(d) of this title, shall, if such designation is in effect on December 27, 1973, be deemed to be a port designated by the Secretary under paragraph (1) of this subsection until such time as the Secretary otherwise provides.

(g) Violations

It is unlawful for any person subject to the jurisdiction of the United States to attempt to commit, solicit another to commit, or cause to be committed, any offense defined in this section.

§ 1539. EXCEPTIONS [ESA SECTION 10]

(a) Permits

(1) The Secretary may permit, under such terms and conditions as he shall prescribe—

> (A) any act otherwise prohibited by section 1538 of this title for scientific purposes or to enhance the propagation or survival of the affected species, including, but not limited to, acts necessary for the establishment and maintenance of experimental populations pursuant to subsection (j) of this section; or

> (B) any taking otherwise prohibited by section 1538(a) (1) (B) of this title if such taking is incidental to, and not the purpose of, the carrying out of an otherwise lawful activity.

(2)(A) No permit may be issued by the Secretary authorizing any taking referred to in paragraph (1) (B) unless the applicant therefor submits to the Secretary a conservation plan that specifies—

(i) the impact which will likely result from such taking;

(ii) what steps the applicant will take to minimize and mitigate such impacts, and the funding that will be available to implement such steps;

(iii) what alternative actions to such taking the applicant considered and the reasons why such alternatives are not being utilized; and

(iv) such other measures that the Secretary may require as being necessary or appropriate for purposes of the plan.

(2)(B) If the Secretary finds, after opportunity for public comment, with respect to a permit application and the related conservation plan that—

(i) the taking will be incidental;

(ii) the applicant will, to the maximum extent practicable, minimize and mitigate the impacts of such taking;

(iii) the applicant will ensure that adequate funding for the plan will be provided;

(iv) the taking will not appreciably reduce the likelihood of the survival and recovery of the species in the wild; and

(v) the measures, if any, required under subparagraph (A) (iv) will be met; and he has received such other assurances as he may require that the plan will be implemented, the Secretary shall issue the permit. The permit shall contain such terms and conditions as the Secretary deems necessary or appropriate to carry out the purposes of this paragraph, including, but not limited to, such reporting requirements as the Secretary deems necessary for determining whether such terms and conditions are being complied with.

(2)(C) The Secretary shall revoke a permit issued under this paragraph if he finds that the permittee is not complying with the terms and conditions of the permit.

(b) Hardship exemptions

(1) If any person enters into a contract with respect to a species of fish or wildlife or plant before the date of the publication in the Federal Register of notice of consideration of that species as an endangered species and the subsequent listing of that species as an endangered species pursuant to section 1533 of this title will cause undue economic hardship to such person under the contract, the Secretary, in order to minimize such hardship,

may exempt such person from the application of section 1538(a) of this title to the extent the Secretary deems appropriate if such person applies to him for such exemption and includes with such application such information as the Secretary may require to prove such hardship; except that

(A) no such exemption shall be for a duration of more than one year from the date of publication in the Federal Register of notice of consideration of the species concerned, or shall apply to a quantity of fish or wildlife or plants in excess of that specified by the Secretary;

(B) the one-year period for those species of fish or wildlife listed by the Secretary as endangered prior to December 28, 1973 shall expire in accordance with the terms of section 668cc-3 of this title; and

(C) no such exemption may be granted for the importation or exportation of a specimen listed in Appendix I of the Convention which is to be used in a commercial activity.

(2) As used in this subsection, the term "undue economic hardship" shall include, but not be limited to:

(A) substantial economic loss resulting from inability caused by this chapter to perform contracts with respect to species of fish and wildlife entered into prior to the date of publication in the Federal Register of a notice of consideration of such species as an endangered species;

(B) substantial economic loss to persons who, for the year prior to the notice of consideration of such species as an endangered species, derived a substantial portion of their income from the lawful taking of any listed species, which taking would be made unlawful under this chapter; or

(C) curtailment of subsistence taking made unlawful under this chapter by persons (i) not reasonably able to secure other sources of subsistence; and (ii) dependent to a substantial extent upon hunting and fishing for subsistence; and (iii) who must engage in such curtailed taking for subsistence purposes.

(3) The Secretary may make further requirements for a showing of undue economic hardship as he deems fit. Exceptions granted under this section may be limited by the Secretary in his discretion as to time, area, or other factor of applicability.

(c) Notice and review

The Secretary shall publish notice in the Federal Register of each application for an exemption or permit which is made under this section. Each notice shall invite the submission from interested parties, within thirty days after the date of the notice, of written data, views, or arguments with respect to the application; except that such thirty-day period may be waived by the Secretary in an emergency situation where the health or life of an endangered animal is threatened and no reasonable alternative is available to the applicant, but notice of any such waiver shall be published by the Secretary in the Federal Register within ten days following the issuance of the exemption or permit. Information received by the Secretary as a part of any application shall be available to the public as a matter of public record at every stage of the proceeding.

(d) Permit and exemption policy

The Secretary may grant exceptions under subsections (a) (1) (A) and (b) of this section only if he finds and publishes his finding in the Federal Register that (1) such exceptions were applied for in good faith, (2) if granted and exercised will not operate to the disadvantage of such endangered species, and (3) will be consistent with the purposes and policy set forth in section 1531 of this title.

(e) Alaska natives [omitted]

(f) Pre-Act endangered species parts exemption; application and certification; regulation; validity of sales contract; separability of provisions; renewal of exemption; expiration of renewal certification [omitted]

(g) Burden of proof

In connection with any action alleging a violation of section 1538 of this title, any person claiming the benefit of any exemption or permit under this chapter shall have the burden of proving that the exemption or permit is applicable, has been granted, and was valid and in force at the time of the alleged violation.

(h) Certain antique articles; importation; port designation; application for return of articles [omitted]

(i) Noncommercial transshipments [omitted]

(j) Experimental populations

(1) For purposes of this subsection, the term "experimental population" means any population (including any offspring arising solely therefrom) authorized by the Secretary for release under paragraph (2), but only when, and at such times as, the population is wholly separate geographically from nonexperimental populations of the same species.

(2)(A) The Secretary may authorize the release (and the related transportation) of any population (including eggs, propagules, or individuals) of an endangered species or a threatened species outside the current range of such species if the Secretary determines that such release will further the conservation of such species.

(2)(B) Before authorizing the release of any population under subparagraph (A), the Secretary shall by regulation identify the population and determine, on the basis of the best available information, whether or not such population is essential to the continued existence of an endangered species or a threatened species.

(2)(C) For the purposes of this chapter, each member of an experimental population shall be treated as a threatened species; except that—

(i) solely for purposes of section 1536 of this title (other than subsection (a)(1) thereof), an experimental population determined under subparagraph (B) to be not essential to the continued existence of a species shall be treated, except when it occurs in an area within the National Wildlife Refuge System or the National Park System, as a species proposed to be listed under section 1533 of this title; and

(ii) critical habitat shall not be designated under this chapter for any experimental population determined under subparagraph (B) to be not essential to the continued existence of a species.

(3) The Secretary, with respect to populations of endangered species or threatened species that the Secretary authorized, before October 13, 1982, for release in geographical areas separate from the other populations of such species, shall determine by regulation which of such populations are an experimental population for the purposes of this subsection and whether or not each is essential to the continued existence of an endangered species or a threatened species.

§ 1540. PENALTIES AND ENFORCEMENT [ESA § 11]

(a) Civil penalties

(1) Any person who knowingly violates, and any person engaged in business as an importer or exporter of fish, wildlife, or plants who violates, any provision of this chapter, or any provision of any permit or certificate issued hereunder, or of any regulation issued in order to implement subsection (a)(1)(A), (B), (C), (D), (E), or (F), (a)(2)(A), (B), (C), or (D), (c), (d) (other than regulation relating to recordkeeping or filing of reports), (f) or (g) of section 1538 of this title, may be assessed a civil penalty by the Secretary of not more than $25,000 for each violation. Any person who knowingly violates, and any person engaged in business as an importer or exporter of fish, wildlife, or plants who violates, any provision of any other regulation issued under this chapter may be assessed a civil penalty by the Secretary of not more than $12,000 for each such violation. Any person who otherwise violates provision of this chapter, or any regulation, permit, or certificate hereunder, may be assessed a civil penalty by the Secretary of not more than $500 for each such violation. No penalty may

be assessed under this subsection unless such person is given notice and opportunity for a hearing with respect to such violation. Each violation shall be a separate offense. Any such civil penalty may be remitted or mitigated by the Secretary. Upon any failure to pay a penalty assessed under this subsection, the Secretary may request the Attorney General to institute a civil action in a district court of the United States for any district in which such person is found, resides, or transacts business to collect the penalty and such court shall have jurisdiction to hear and decide any such action. The court shall hear such action on the record made before the Secretary and shall sustain his action if it is supported by substantial evidence on the record considered as a whole.

(2) Hearings held during proceedings for the assessment of civil penalties authorized by paragraph (1) of this subsection shall be conducted in accordance with section 554 of Title 5. The Secretary may issue subpoenas for the attendance and testimony of witnesses and the production of relevant papers, books, and documents, and administer oaths. Witnesses summoned shall be paid the same fees and mileage that are paid to witnesses in the courts of the United States. In case of contumacy or refusal to obey a subpoena served upon any person pursuant to this paragraph, the district court of the United States for any district in which such person is found or resides or transacts business, upon application by the United States and after notice to such person, shall have jurisdiction to issue an order requiring such person to appear and give testimony before the Secretary or to appear and produce documents before the Secretary, or both, and any failure to obey such order of the court may be punished by such court as a contempt thereof.

(3) Notwithstanding any other provision of this chapter, no civil penalty shall be imposed if it can be shown by a preponderance of the evidence that the defendant committed an act based on a good faith belief that he was acting to protect himself or herself, a member of his or her family, or any other individual from bodily harm, from any endangered or threatened species.

(b) Criminal violations

(1) Any person who knowingly violates any provision of this chapter, of any permit or certificate issued hereunder, or of any regulation issued in order to implement subsection (a)(1)(A), (B), (C), (D), (E), or (F); (a)(2)(A), (B), (C), or (D), (c), (d) (other than a regulation relating to recordkeeping, or filing of reports), (f), or (g) of section 1538 of this title shall, upon conviction, be fined not more than $50,000 or imprisoned for not more than one year, or both. Any person who knowingly violates any provision of any other regulation issued under this chapter shall, upon conviction, be

fined not more than $25,000 or imprisoned for not more than six months, or both.

(2) The head of any Federal agency which has issued a lease, license, permit, or other agreement authorizing a person to import or export fish, wildlife, or plants, or to operate a quarantine station for imported wildlife, or authorizing the use of Federal lands, including grazing of domestic livestock, to any person who is convicted of a criminal violation of this chapter or any regulation, permit, or certificate issued hereunder may immediately modify, suspend, or revoke each lease, license, permit, or other agreement. The Secretary shall also suspend for a period of up to one year, or cancel, any Federal hunting or fishing permits or stamps issued to any person who is convicted of a criminal violation of any provision of this chapter or any regulation, permit, or certificate issued hereunder. The United States shall not be liable for the payments of any compensation, reimbursement, or damages in connection with the modification, suspension, or revocation of any leases, licenses, permits, stamps, or other agreements pursuant to this section.

(3) Notwithstanding any other provision of this chapter, it shall be a defense to prosecution under this subsection if the defendant committed the offense based on a good faith belief that he was acting to protect himself or herself, a member of his or her family, or any other individual, from bodily harm from any endangered or threatened species.

(c) District court jurisdiction

The several district courts of the United States, including the courts enumerated in section 460 of Title 28, shall have jurisdiction over any actions arising under this chapter. For the purpose of this chapter, American Samoa shall be included within the judicial district of the District Court of the United States for the District of Hawaii.

(d) Rewards and certain incidental expenses

The Secretary or the Secretary of the Treasury shall pay, from sums received as penalties, fines, or forfeitures of property for any violation of this chapter or any regulation issued hereunder

(1) a reward to any person who furnishes information which leads to an arrest, a criminal conviction, civil penalty assessment, or forfeiture of property for any violation of this chapter or any regulation issued hereunder, and

(2) the reasonable and necessary costs incurred by any person in providing temporary care for any fish, wildlife, or plant pending the disposition of any civil or criminal proceeding alleging a violation of this chapter with respect to that fish, wildlife, or plant. The amount of the

reward, if any, is to be designated by the Secretary or the Secretary of the Treasury, as appropriate. Any officer or employee of the United States or any State or local government who furnishes information or renders service in the performance of his official duties is ineligible for payment under this subsection. Whenever the balance of sums received under this section and section 3375(d) of this title, as penalties or fines, or from forfeitures of property, exceed $500,000, the Secretary of the Treasury shall deposit amount equal to such excess balance in the cooperative endangered species conservation fund established under section 1535(i) of this title.

(e) Enforcement

(1) The provisions of this chapter and any regulations or permits issued pursuant thereto shall be enforced by the Secretary, the Secretary of the Treasury, or the Secretary of the Department in which the Coast Guard is operating, or all such Secretaries. Each such Secretary may utilize by agreement, with or without reimbursement, the personnel, services, and facilities of any other Federal agency or any State agency for purposes of enforcing this chapter.

(2) The judges of the district courts of the United States and the United States magistrates may, within their respective jurisdictions, upon proper oath or affirmation showing probable cause, issue such warrants or other process as may be required for enforcement of this chapter and any regulation issued thereunder.

(3) Any person authorized by the Secretary, the Secretary of the Treasury, or the Secretary of the Department in which the Coast Guard is operating, to enforce this chapter may detain for inspection and inspect any package, crate, or other container, including its contents, and all accompanying documents, upon importation or exportation. Such person may make arrests without a warrant for any violation of this chapter if he has reasonable grounds to believe that the person to be arrested is committing the violation in his presence or view, and may execute and serve any arrest warrant, search warrant, or other warrant or civil or criminal process issued by any officer or court of competent jurisdiction for enforcement of this chapter. Such person so authorized may search and seize, with or without a warrant, as authorized by law. Any fish, wildlife, property, or item so seized shall be held by any person authorized by the Secretary, the Secretary of the Treasury, or the Secretary of the Department in which the Coast Guard is operating pending disposition of civil or criminal proceedings, or the institution of an action in rem for forfeiture of such fish, wildlife, property, or item pursuant to paragraph (4) of this subsection; except that the Secretary may, in lieu of holding such fish, wildlife, property, or item, permit the owner or consignee to post a bond or other surety satisfactory to

the Secretary, but upon forfeiture of any such property to the United States, or the abandonment or waiver of any claim to any such property, it shall be disposed of (other than by sale to the general public) by the Secretary in such a manner, consistent with the purposes of this chapter, as the Secretary shall by regulation prescribe.

(4)(A) All fish or wildlife or plants taken, possessed, sold, purchased, offered for sale or purchase, transported, delivered, received, carried, shipped, exported, or imported contrary to the provisions of this chapter, any regulation made pursuant thereto, or any permit or certificate issued hereunder shall be subject to forfeiture to the United States.

(4)(B) All guns, traps, nets, and other equipment, vessels, vehicles, aircraft, and other means of transportation used to aid the taking, possessing, selling, purchasing, offering for sale or purchase, transporting, delivering, receiving, carrying, shipping, exporting, or importing of any fish or wildlife or plants in violation of this chapter, any regulation made pursuant thereto, or any permit or certificate issued thereunder shall be subject to forfeiture to the United States upon conviction of a criminal violation pursuant to subsection (b)(1) of this section.

(5) All provisions of law relating to the seizure, forfeiture, and condemnation of a vessel for violation of the customs laws, the disposition of such vessel or the proceeds from the sale thereof, and the remission or mitigation of such forfeiture, shall apply to the seizures and forfeitures incurred, or alleged to have been incurred, under the provisions of this chapter, insofar as such provisions of law are applicable and not inconsistent with the provisions of this chapter; except that all powers, rights, and duties conferred or imposed by the customs laws upon any officer or employee of the Treasury Department shall, for the purposes of this chapter, be exercised or performed by the Secretary or by such persons as he may designate.

(6) The Attorney General of the United States may seek to enjoin any person who is alleged to be in violation of any provision of this chapter or regulation issued under authority thereof.

(f) Regulations

The Secretary, the Secretary of the Treasury, and the Secretary of the Department in which the Coast Guard is operating, are authorized to promulgate such regulations as may be appropriate to enforce this chapter, and charge reasonable fees for expenses to the Government connected with permits or certificates authorized by this chapter including processing applications and reasonable inspections, and with the transfer, board, handling, or storage of fish or wildlife or plants and evidentiary items seized and forfeited under this chapter. All such fees collected pursuant to this subsection shall be deposited in the Treasury to the credit of the appropriation which is current and chargeable for the cost of furnishing the services. Appropriated funds may be expended pending reimbursement from parties in interest.

(g) Citizen suits

(1) Except as provided in paragraph (2) of this subsection any person may commence a civil suit on his own behalf—

> (A) to enjoin any person, including the United States and any other governmental instrumentality or agency (to the extent permitted by the eleventh amendment to the Constitution), who is alleged to be in violation of any provision of this chapter or regulation issued under the authority thereof; or

> (B) to compel the Secretary to apply, pursuant to section 1535(g) (2) (B) (ii) of this title, the prohibitions set forth in or authorized pursuant to section 1533(d) or 1538(a) (1) (B) of this title with respect to the taking of any resident endangered species or threatened species within any State; or

> (C) against the Secretary where there is alleged a failure of the Secretary to perform any act or duty under section 1533 of this title which is not discretionary with the Secretary.

The district courts shall have jurisdiction, without regard to the amount in controversy or the citizenship of the parties, to enforce any such provision or regulation, or to order the Secretary to perform such act or duty, as the case may be. In any civil suit commenced under subparagraph (B) the district court shall compel the Secretary to apply the prohibition sought if the court finds that the allegation that an emergency exists is supported by substantial evidence.

(2)(A) No action may be commenced under subparagraph (1)(A) of this section—

> (i) prior to sixty days after written notice of the violation has been given to the Secretary, and to any alleged violator of any such provision or regulation;

> (ii) if the Secretary has commenced action to impose a penalty pursuant to subsection (a) of this section; or

> (iii) if the United States has commenced and is diligently prosecuting a criminal action in a court of the United States or a State to redress a violation of any such provision or regulation.

(2)(B) No action may be commenced under subparagraph (1)(B) of this section—

(i) prior to sixty days after written notice has been given to the Secretary setting forth the reasons why an emergency is thought to exist with respect to an endangered species or a threatened species in the State concerned; or

(ii) if the Secretary has commenced and is diligently prosecuting action under section 1535(g)(2)(B)(ii) of this title to determine whether any such emergency exists.

(2)(C) No action may be commenced under subparagraph (1) (C) of this section prior to sixty days after written notice has been given to the Secretary; except that such action may be brought immediately after such notification in the case of an action under this section respecting an emergency posing a significant risk to the well-being of any species of fish or wildlife or plants.

(3)(A) Any suit under this subsection may be brought in the judicial district in which the violation occurs.

(3)(B) In any such suit under this subsection in which the United States is not a party, the Attorney General, at the request of the Secretary, may intervene on behalf of the United States as a matter of right.

(4) The court, in issuing any final order in any suit brought pursuant to paragraph (1) of this subsection, may award costs of litigation (including reasonable attorney and expert witness fees) to any party, whenever the court determines such award is appropriate.

(5) The injunctive relief provided by this subsection shall not restrict any right which any person (or class of persons) may have under any statute or common law to seek enforcement of any standard or limitation or to seek any other relief (including relief against the Secretary or a State agency).

(h) Coordination with other laws

The Secretary of Agriculture and the Secretary shall provide for appropriate coordination of the administration of this chapter with the administration of the animal quarantine laws (21 U.S.C. 101-105, 111-135b, and 612-614) and section 306 of the Tariff Act of 1930 (19 U.S.C. 1306). Nothing in this chapter or any amendment made by this Act shall be construed as superseding or limiting in any manner the functions of the Secretary of Agriculture under any other law relating to prohibited or restricted importations or possession of animals and other articles and no proceeding or determination under this chapter shall preclude any proceeding or be considered determinative of any issue of fact or law in any proceeding under any Act administered by the Secretary of Agriculture. Nothing in this chapter shall be construed as superseding or limiting in any manner the functions and responsibilities of the Secretary of the Treasury under the Tariff Act of 1930 [19 U.S.C.A. Section 1202 et seq.], including, without limitation, section 527 of that Act (19 U.S.C. 1527), relating to the importation of wildlife taken, killed, possessed, or exported to the United States in violation of the laws or regulations of a foreign country.

APPENDIX 10:
USFWS ENDANGERED SPECIES
PROGRAM OFFICES

REGION	ADDRESS
Headquarters	U.S. Fish and Wildlife Service Division of Endangered Species, Mail Stop 452ARLSQ, 1849 C St., NW, Washington, D.C. 20240
Region One	Division of Endangered Species, Eastside Federal Co.nplex, 911 N.S. 11th Ave, Portland, OR 97232
Region Two	Division of Endangered Species, P.O. Box 1306, Albuquerque, NM 87103
Region Three	Ecological Services Operations, Federal Building, Ft. Snelling, Twin Cities, MN 55111
Region Four	Division of Endangered Species, 1875 Century Blvd., Suite 200, Atlanta, GA 30345
Region Five	Division of Endangered Species, 300 Westgate Center Drive, Hadley, MA 01035
Region Six	Division of Endangered Species, P.O. Box 25486, Denver Federal Center, Denver, CO 80225
Region Seven	Division of Endangered Species, 1011 E. Tudor Rd., Anchorage, AK 990503

Source: U.S. Fish and Wildlife Service, Division of Endangered Species

Glossary

Abandonment—The desertion of an animal due to lack of responsibility.

Adaptation—A change in the structure or function of an animal that produces better adjustment to the environment.

Boycott—To join together in refusing to deal with, so as to punish or coerce.

Captivity—The condition of being captive.

Commercial—Connected with commerce or trade.

Environment—All the conditions, circumstances and influences surrounding an organism or group of organisms and affecting its development.

Euthanasia—Method of causing death painlessly to end suffering.

Experimentation—The process undertaken to discover something not yet known or to demonstrate or test something known.

Exploitation—To make use of or profit from something.

Extinction—The fact or state of being of becoming extinct; dying out, as of a species of animal.

Genus—A category that is used in classifying plants or animals that are similar in structure.

Habitat—The region where a plant or animal naturally grows or lives.

Humane—Kind, tender, merciful, sympathetic, etc.

Inherent—Existing in something as a natural or inseparable quality or right; inborn.

Livestock—Domestic animals kept for use on a farm or raised for sale and profit.

Mammal—Any of a large class of warmblooded vertebrates, generally with hair on the skin, whose offspring are fed with milk secreted by the female mammary glands.

Mandatory—Commanded or required by those in authority.

Monotype—The only type of its group.

Moratorium—Any authorized delay or stopping of some specified activity.

Poisoning—To harm or destroy by means of poison, i.e., a substance causing illness or death when eaten, drunk or absorbed in small quantities.

Scientific—Describes a method in which theories are based on data collected in a systematic way and which are then tested by objective experiments.

Seines—A large fishing net with floats along the top edge and weights along the bottom.

Species—A group of highly similar plants or animals, part of a genus, that can reproduce fertile offspring only among themselves.

Statutory—Fixed by statute.

Sterilization—The act of making an animal incapable of producing others of its kind.

Subspecies—Any natural subdivision of a species that shows small differences in form from other subdivisions of the same species living in different regions.

Taxonomy—The science of classifying things, such as plants and animals into natural, related groups, such as species and genera.

Vegetarian—A person who chooses to eat no meat because of feelings against the killing of animals, or for reasons of health.

Vertebrate—Any of a large group of animals, including all mammals, fishes, birds, reptiles and amphibians, that have a backbone, brain and cranium.

Vivisection—Surgical operations or other experiments done on living animals for scientific purposes, as in studying diseases and trying to find cures for them.

Vivisectionist—A person who practices or favors the practice of vivisection for the good of science.

BIBLIOGRAPHY

Animals and their Legal Rights. Washington, DC: Animal Welfare Institute, 1990.

Black's Law Dictionary, Fifth Edition. St. Paul, MN: West Publishing Company, 1979.

Francione, Gary L., *Animals, Property and the Law*. Philadelphia, PA: Temple University Press, 1995.

Garner, Robert, *Animals, Politics and Morality*. New York, NY: Manchester University Press, 1993.

Ontario Consultants on Religious Tolerance (Date Visited: January 2002)<http://www.religioustolerance.org>.

PETA: People for the Ethical Treatment of Animals (Date Visited: January 2002)<http://www.peta.org>.

Rollin, Bernard E., *Farm Animal Welfare: Social, Bioethical and Research Issues*. Ames, Iowa: Iowa State University Press, 1995.

Rutgers University School of Law Animal Rights Law Project (Date Visited: January 2002)<http://www.animal-law.org>.

Sequoia, Anna, *67 Ways to Save the Animals*. New York, NY: Harper Collins Publishers, 1990.

Sherry, Clifford J., *Animal Rights*. Santa Barbara, CA: ABC-CLIO, Inc., 1994.

U.S. Department of Agriculture (Date Visited: January 2002) <http://www.usda.gov>.

U.S. Fish and Wildlife Service (Date Visited: January 2002) <http://www.fws.gov>.

Webster's New World Dictionary. New York, NY: Simon & Schuster, 1981.